Unbridled
POWER

Unbridled POWER

Inside the Secret Culture of the IRS

Shelley L. Davis

HarperBusiness
A Division of HarperCollinsPublishers

A hardcover edition of this book was published in 1997 by HarperBusiness, a division of HarperCollins Publishers.

HarperCollins books may be purchased for educational, business, or sales promotional use. For information please write: Special Markets Department, HarperCollins Publishers, Inc., 10 East 53rd Street, New York, NY 10022.

First paperback edition published 1998.

Designed by Elina D. Nudelman

The Library of Congress has catalogued the hardcover edition as follows:

Davis, Shelley L.
    Unbridled power : inside the secret culture of the IRS /
Shelley L. Davis. — 1st ed.
       p.   cm.
    Includes index.
    ISBN 0-88730-829-5
    1. United States. Internal Revenue Service—History. 2. Tax administration and procedure—United States—History. I. Title.
    HJ2361.D38   1997
    353.0072'44—dc20   96-46204

ISBN 0-06-097743-4 (pbk.)

98 99 00 01 02 ❖/RRD 10 9 8 7 6 5 4 3 2 1

CONTENTS

To Wallace Peterson and in memory of Eunice Peterson,
loving parents who taught me to believe in myself,
to believe in my country,
and to know that public service means
serving the public

FOREWORD

Let me say this right up front and loud and clear: Shelley Davis has become my personal hero. For any American citizen to stand up to today's IRS takes guts. And when that American has every reason to fear retaliation from an organization that was, until recently, her employer, I call that heroic.

Shelley Davis says she isn't as afraid for herself as she is for the country, unless the IRS is reformed, and reformed fast. But I have to say that I'm afraid for her. Because what Shelley has done is tell the truth about what goes on inside the IRS. And, let me tell you, her story only confirms our worst fears about what goes on behind the impenetrable walls of what she calls the Temple of Doom at 1111 Constitution Avenue. It's a story that the IRS, to put it mildly, didn't want to see told. Talk about incompetence! Talk about corruption! Talk about covering your butt!

The crowning irony, of course, is that telling the truth about the IRS and its history was what Shelley Davis was hired to do in the first place. She had no polemic political ax to grind. This is a person whose only crime was trying to do her job, as best she could. Part of that job involved telling her bosses, "Heads up, guys, but do you know we're breaking the law?"

As she reveals, the IRS routinely destroys its own records. That's against federal law. And the problem with breaking the Federal

Records Act, is, as Shelley says, that without records, there is no history. Without records, there is no accountability.

When Shelley conscientiously reminded her superiors of the law, she was branded a traitor for her trouble. They turned around and investigated her! Shelley Davis ended up being run out of there on a rail for doing the job they hired her to do.

Okay, Shelley herself may not be afraid of the IRS. But I'm afraid when we fear those whom we hire to work for us. Who've managed to garner enough unbridled power to do what they want to us, when they want, however they want. I call Shelley Davis's experience Gulagesque, Kafkaesque, and downright un-American. Shelley's story speaks directly to that pervasive fear so many of us law-abiding Americans feel, deep in our guts, that our own government is, at best, hiding something from us and, at worst, working against those folks it exists to serve.

Shelley Davis found out just that. She found out about the destruction of presidential tax returns and other key records, including files about the Watergate scandal. She discovered the true story of the incredible boondoggle that the IRS calls computerization and modernization. She learned, in short, that as we all suspected, our tax agency indeed does have a lot to hide behind closed doors. A lot to answer for. And a lot to be ashamed of.

The bottom line here is that Shelley Davis's story makes me hopping mad—not to mention that it scares the bejesus out of me. I can bet my bottom dollar that it will make you feel the same way.

Or worse.

—MARY MATALIN

ACKNOWLEDGMENTS

Resigning from a sixteen-year career in public service in protest against wrongdoing and unethical behavior is not an easy thing to do, but I had no choice. Losing my income was a better option than losing my sanity and sense of personal decency, I decided. What I didn't know when I closed my office door for the final time was what lay ahead for me. It turns out writing this book became the first item on my new agenda. I had no idea how challenging writing about my very personal experiences inside the IRS would be.

The bottom line is this book would not have been possible without the help, guidance, and most of all, support from many places. A combination of professional and emotional support has sustained me through the trying first year of my "freedom" from the insanity of a government bureaucracy gone mad.

Of course, there are many friends and former associates who are still working inside the IRS whom I would like to thank personally, but cannot. They know who they are. They include the people who approached me in the halls during my final weeks at the IRS to tell me that I was doing the right thing; that someone had to "do it"— meaning identify and expose the ineptitude and malfeasance running rampant inside the headquarters of the nation's tax collector; that they wished me well. To each and every one of you, I say thanks for the good words. They helped more than you know as I wandered the dreary hallways of 1111 Constitution Avenue for the last time.

Ed Bishop lands at the very top of the list of people I can acknowledge publicly. Ed is my friend, my partner, my soulmate. He stood by me, challenged me, and agreed to live on reduced resources as he watched me sacrifice my career for principle. Because he is so principled himself, Ed understood why I had to do what I did. Thanks, forever and ever.

I owe a debt of gratitude to my mentor and graduate adviser Pete Maslowski, who taught me military history, but also taught me to search for the truth. A great teacher and scholar, Pete is also a great friend who steered me toward this book as I pondered my future. At the other extreme, I owe a similar debt to Kecia McDonald, a brilliant student whom I had the opportunity to mentor during her internship at the IRS. Kecia continues to remind me to always look at the IRS with "outside" lenses and that some Generation Xers are going to make us very, very proud.

Thanks are offered to the family of Don Curtis, who befriended me during their immense grief over the loss of their parents. They, more than anyone inside the IRS, understood the tremendous loss I also felt when I learned of the tragic death of my mentor inside the IRS. The IRS truly lost its soul when it lost Don Curtis.

Prof. John Andrew appeared in my life as the angel of history. Despite what some IRS investigators and bureaucrats seemed to think, I had never heard of Professor Andrew before his now legendary Freedom of Information Act request landed on my desk. It was this innocent and appropriate inquiry into thirty-year-old IRS records that ultimately led to my resignation. I only wish that more researchers would mine for the treasures of the past inside the IRS. The gems are deeply hidden, and many are lost forever, but the search is an honorable and important endeavor as the American people search for truth inside their most powerful federal agency. Thanks, Professor Andrew, for doing your job.

A deep expression of admiration also goes to Stan Welli, a courageous and determined public servant who has struggled for more than a decade to do the right thing against formidable odds inside the IRS. Now retired, Stan awaits a final decision from the Merit Systems Protection Board, through which his case of retaliation for blowing the whistle has wound a tortured and bizarre path. The case of Stan Welli versus his IRS supervisors can be studied as an example of why no one should consider blowing the whistle unless they are prepared to sacrifice endlessly for no reward. Hats off to Stan, a true American hero in my book.

Despite what many inside the IRS headquarters think, I didn't plan to write about my own personal experiences at the tax agency when I quit my job. This book was born of the belief in the strength of my story from my agent, Jimmy Vines, and my HarperBusiness editor, Kirsten Sandberg. It was Pete Maslowski who told me I must write about my experiences and pushed me toward Jimmy Vines. I couldn't have been pushed in a better direction. Thanks, Jimmy, for believing in me. Kirsten Sandberg, a seasoned editor, believed in me and my story from our first brief meeting. I owe her a debt of gratitude. I cannot describe how wonderful it felt to hear that I had done the right thing so soon after living inside the IRS, after fending off false charges and attacks for the previous year.

I was lucky to land in the arms of HarperBusiness as Stage Two of my life began to unfold. Janet Dery was adept at handling a variety of small details to make sure this book would see the light of day. And, most of all, I owe a tremendous hip-hip-hooray to Steve Fenichell, who took my first draft "kitchen sink" manuscript and helped to carve out a coherent book. Working with Steve was a pleasure, even as we rehashed my negative and painful experiences.

And, finally, a few special people deserve mention for the support they have offered me over the past year. To my Nebraska family, which includes Cary, Lisa, Laura, Rebecca, and Andrew and Bonnie Peterson, thanks for believing in me. To Blair Bishop, for being such a great young man and cheering on my fight against the IRS (keep studying, kid). To Leslie, Erika, Elizabeth, Nancy, and Susan—five special women who live around the country, but are always there for me. To Becky Newberry, whose enthusiasm for putting the whistle to my mouth and blowing on it was contagious. To Pete and Steve at the Smithsonian laboratory, who offered shelter from the storm. And to George Guttman, who offered evidence that there is life beyond the walls of the IRS.

And, finally, to the American people, who deserve and must demand an honest and honorable tax collector. Go for it.

PROLOGUE

Look! I am betrayed into the hands of wicked men.

—Mark 14:41

A few minutes after 1:30 P.M. on the date in question—April 15, 1996—I emerged from the Federal Triangle metro station in Washington, directly across the street from IRS headquarters. The building at 1111 Constitution Avenue is a seven-story Neoclassical monument to federal power that sprawls in an ungainly fashion across four square blocks of choice District of Columbia real estate so vast it merits its own zip code.

This being April 15—the only date that ranks up there in infamy in American lore with December 7—the big, bold, bronze Temple of Doom doors fronting on Constitution Avenue were obscured by a gaggle of last-minute filers hoping to snag a few "happy tax forms"—as one ill-advised IRS PR campaign pricelessly called them—in time to meet their midnight deadline.

A bristling battalion of tax protesters fleshed out the milling crowd, performing the annual rite of picketing IRS headquarters, holding up signboards laced with loopy legends, like LOST OUR LEASE ON THE AMERICAN DREAM, INCOME TAX UNCONSTITUTIONAL, and my personal favorite: COMMUNISM, BERLIN WALL, IRS.

1

An NBC News camera crew was shooting tape for that evening's Tax Day special. Because of the long-standing IRS policy of beefing up security around its installations on Tax Day, jolly Dave Junkins, director of support and services, headquarters operations—in charge of building security, that is—was out vigilantly guarding those imposing front steps. From the look of him, he seemed itching for all hell to break loose.

I'd always liked Dave Junkins. I'd known him since my earliest days at the IRS, and we'd always enjoyed pleasant, if inconsequential, dealings. For his part, he couldn't have been friendlier, considering my very public resignation from the IRS just three months before.

"Shelley, how ya doin'? Makin' any money yet?" he ribbed me. Of course, we both knew that I was stone broke, driving a ten-year-old car, having recently forfeited my sweet GM–14 federal salary of $70K for the sake of protecting my professional integrity. But rather than dwell on past injustices, we stuck to banal banter. I'm sure he was a little taken aback to see me, considering that I was pretty much persona non grata around the place I'd practically lived in for seven years. But if he was surprised to see me, he never let on and warmly shook my hand. After a few moments of idle chitchat, I pulled open the brass doors. Inside the vestibule, I ran right smack into the last man in the world I wanted to see: Steve Raisch.

Raisch had been the bane of my Kafkaesque trials at the hands of the IRS. A blond six-footer with the hunky build you'd expect from an IRS internal security special agent, Raisch had perfected the cool-cop stance and epitomized the arrogant federal law enforcement officer who made too many Americans' blood boil. In my experience, Raisch didn't give a hoot about the broad responsibilities of the federal government. Like Junkins, Raisch had been detailed to keep the vestibule free of any potential Unabomber or Oklahoma City mad bomber copycats—this being just four days shy of the anniversary of the Waco and Oklahoma City tragedies.

Determined to keep my cool, I looked evenly at Raisch. He glared back with shock, surprise, and a good dose of contempt. Through his scowl, he seemed to convey that, impressed as he was by my audacity in reentering *his* facility, he still considered me to be a bit of bottom-sucking scum of the earth.

To put his personal animosity into some perspective, I'd put his name in the papers. Front page. I can distinctly recall running into Raisch on a deserted IRS staircase in the days after I went public with my allegations of lawbreaking at the highest reaches of the IRS, just two weeks before my protest resignation. Perhaps not surprisingly, he probably hadn't appreciated the unwelcome publicity. As for strike two against me in his book, I'd gone and gotten him investigated. I believed that Raisch had failed to investigate my claim that there had been a blatant violation of federal law involving destruction of government records. This had been the gist of my beef with the IRS: that it negligently and deliberately destroyed its paper trail, shredded its records, and trashed any chance for accountability, out of some ill-founded and irrational fear of exposure to public scrutiny.

A deep-seated arrogance drove the IRS's behavior in this arena. The IRS did these things because it could get away with them, and because nobody challenged it about this egregious violation of the law that requires government agencies to preserve evidence of what they have done with the public funds they are entrusted to spend. Until I came along.

And here I was, on the day after my fortieth birthday, jobless, salaryless, and, for the time being, futureless. Steve Raisch was still there, still in the loop, still in charge, no doubt still looking forward to a long, lucrative, cushy career as a federal law enforcement officer. Who was the winner and who was the loser? To a cartoon character like Raisch, the answer was obvious. As for me, I wasn't so sure.

"Nice to see you again, Steve." After choking the words out, I bit my tongue.

He peered straight through me before muttering in a self-consciously gravelly, Dirty Harry drawl: "Likewise."

Sweeping past him, I pulled open one heavy bronze door with a defiant tug, waltzed free as a bird up to the front desk, and whipped out my driver's license. Two rent-a-cops, a man and a woman, were minding the station that day. They glanced at my photo ID with bored looks while I borrowed their phone to call my friend Dave Madden, a branch chief in IRS chief counsel's office. Dave had been nice enough and brave enough to call me on my birthday and invite me to his IRS office for lunch. I'd been touched by the gesture:

Despite all my travails at the hands of a cluster of key IRS higher-ups on an official level, on a more purely personal front I still had many close friends who, like Dave—God help them—still earned their living there.

Since I'd already made lunch plans, I invited myself to stop by Dave's office afterward for a friendly chat. That, I swear, was all I had in mind at IRS headquarters that day.

Dave Madden happened to be busy on another line. So he sent his assistant, Lee, to escort me upstairs. I was calmly cooling my heels in the lobby, gazing up at that cavernous coffered ceiling, when I felt the slightest touch at my elbow. Turning around expecting to see some shy old acquaintance, I found myself gazing into the dark, expressionless eyes of an African-American woman of medium height, about my age, and slightly stocky, with shoulder-length hair. I had never seen this person before. Clearly a plainclothes cop. Probably an IRS internal security special agent, by the look of her. Member of Steve Raisch's gang.

"Shelley," she breathed, in that urgent, low-pitched, law enforcement tone of voice, "we have to speak to you." At which point, she began gently but firmly tugging me by the elbow. She started yanking me off to the side of the room, away from the public vestibule, presumably so that we could conduct our little chat in private. I resisted, so that whatever mischief they were planning to commit on my person would occur in public view. The two of us stared at each other as she flipped open her leather-encased security badge to make sure that I knew she was for real.

"IRS INTERNAL SECURITY," the badge read. Though I knew I'd done nothing wrong, I must confess a bit of fear. "Shelley," she said firmly, "we have uncovered evidence that you failed to turn in your IRS identification badge when you left the building last December. You have been banned from the building."

A flash of relief. From the very first tense moment that I initially felt her hand on my elbow, I had envisioned a nightmare scenario in which they would charge me with something a good deal more serious. They had already leveled completely false and unjustified charges against me, launching the ludicrous investigation that had precipitated my resignation.

Practically speaking, they held all the cards. Unlike me, they might have been able to make the charge stick. I had, for example, trusted them implicitly to protect the hundreds of boxes of critical IRS internal documents that I had squirreled away during my less than tranquil tenure as the first (and believe me, the last) official IRS historian. What would have stopped them from trashing that historical stock—which they were dying to do anyway—and then claiming that I'd lost it, stolen it, burned it—who knows? They could have charged me with the destruction of government property, which would have been rich, seeing as how that was the charge I had leveled at them. Or simply claimed that the documents I labored to save had never existed. My word against theirs. We all knew who would win that battle.

At that point, I had a hard time believing they'd stop at anything. But this crazy bit about a lost badge—this was simply too much. If the IRS didn't possess so much power, the scene might even have been funny. By the look and sound of it, it was probably nothing more than a crude put-up job. Some spur-of-the-moment, on-a-whim kind of thing—perhaps even the clumsy improvisation of my old buddy Steve Raisch, thinking fast on his clodhoppers, searching for some legal means to keep me from reentering "his" building.

Fortunately for me—and awkwardly for them—I happened to know just where all my outprocessing paperwork was back home in suburban Virginia, neatly wrapped in its own manila envelope, in a certain locked drawer in my desk. Turning in my IRS ID badge had in fact been my last official act as an IRS employee. I'd saved that little sentimental sendoff for the end of my last day, so that I could finish cleaning out my office, and load my coffeemaker, gym clothes, and seven years' of accumulated knickknacks into my car, without having to go to the trouble of obtaining a visitor's pass every time I wanted to reenter the building.

"You have bad information," I told the strange woman, standing firm, doing my best to raise my voice to an audible level so that the lawfully assembled tax protesters outside, and the miscellaneous filers inside, would all be tuned in to whatever was about to transpire. "I turned my ID badge in to a woman at the end of my last day," I insisted.

"What was her name?" came the quick response.

For the life of me, I could not recall. I don't think I had even noticed it. I had gathered about a dozen signatures from IRS bureaucrats to officially conclude my nearly sixteen-year government career. But I distinctly remembered sitting at the battered government-issue metal desk in her battered battleship gray room as she capably snatched my precious IRS ID badge from the metal chain that hung around my neck. What was all just a day's work to her symbolized the finality of the tough decision the IRS had forced me to make—to resign from the service, rather than be silenced or forced to submit to its will.

I asked the IRS agent detaining me to straighten out this whole silly thing with Dave Junkins's office, in time for me to see my friend Dave Madden. As she listened to my request to go outside and find Junkins—who, as it turned out, had mysteriously vanished, as had Steve Raisch—she motioned to a fellow agent to join us in our private powwow. After conferring briefly, he slouched off to check out my story—I assumed—with a higher-up in headquarters support and services. The minutes ticked away before he sidled back over to us and whispered something urgent in her ear. The woman's face hardened into an icy mask. "It's confirmed," she muttered darkly. "You did not turn in your badge. You are not allowed in the building."

Out of the corner of my eye, I could see Lee, Dave Madden's assistant, engaged in a mild altercation with yet another internal security agent, from whom she was struggling to retrieve her own ID badge. She later told me that the agent who interrogated her had been trying to confiscate her badge, and had only reluctantly returned it to her when she expressly—and firmly—demanded it back.

"Everyone was watching me closely during my last few weeks here," I told my impassive IRS interrogators. "Believe me, they made sure I was properly signed out on my last day."

For a moment, that stupefied them. But after a brief huddle, the female agent—who appeared to be the more senior of the two—had a brainstorm.

"You had *two* badges," she concluded.

"What are you talking about? This is absurd!" I protested, as loudly as possible, stopping just short of actively resisting arrest.

Without offering any further explanation of the dual-badge accusation, the agent stared directly into my eyes, seeming to take great pleasure in speaking her next sentence. "If you don't leave the building immediately, I will call FPS [Federal Protective Service] and have you arrested for trespassing." She was not taking this matter lightly.

Visions of spending the night in jail flashed through my head. Would they really follow through on what I assumed was probably an idle threat? A night in jail, Henry David Thoreau style, might help me make the point I was trying to make—to anyone who would listen—about the destructive yet routine pattern of ethical and legal abuses and the arrogant abuse of power I had witnessed during my years at the IRS. But if I went to jail, there would be no one home to let my three dogs out. Priorities.

I opted to leave. But not before the IRS special agent repeated her preposterous threat. "You must leave right now or you will be arrested for trespassing."

I walked away, steaming. Before that day, my feelings about being forced to resign my post at the IRS had hovered more around sad than mad. But after this grotesque charade, I was fighting mad. Those bastards hadn't even given me a chance to call Dave Madden and let him wish me a happy birthday! So much for turning forty.

Dave told me the next day that he had received a visit from a pair of internal security special agents, who informed him that I had been banned from the building, that he was "not to attempt to let me attempt to enter," and that if I tried to reenter, he was to report immediately my attempt to trespass on government property.

Until Tax Day 1996, I had only the slightest inkling of how threatened the IRS was by my campaign to force it to obey federal law. But after this little episode, for what it was worth, any remaining reservations about taking on the IRS were swept aside by anger at the absolute arrogance on display. You know those government whistleblowers you sometimes read about in the newspapers? Well, meet Shelley Davis, thorn in the IRS's side. Despite all my best self-preserving instincts, I had become a government gadfly.

Nearly twenty years earlier, my hyperliberal college professor father had wished me well when I took off from my Nebraska home to start my first job in Washington—as a historian for the Air Force. "Keep an eye out," he'd said. "Pay attention to every little detail, because that's the only way you'll ever figure out *why* so many things go wrong inside the government."

Still in shock that the child on whom he had tied black armbands to protest the Vietnam War could go to work for not just the government, but the Defense Department no less, he had taken solace in the idea that I would at least achieve a privileged insider's view of our government in action. Following my father's advice, I'd done what I could to keep my eyes open. What I found in those early years had impressed, not distressed, me. As I loyally served in a variety of positions at the Defense Department, I never perceived the place as an enemy camp. Especially when it came to what had become "my" issue—government record keeping. Despite blunders, botched operations, and political infighting, the Defense Department didn't haggle over saving its records—good, bad, ugly, or indifferent.

But now the tables had turned. You know that old saw about the son thinking at twenty his dad is an idiot, then at forty realizing how much the old guy must have learned in the intervening years? Well, something like that happened to me. Here I was, being threatened with arrest by my own government—your government—on utterly false pretenses for daring to try to have an innocent birthday visit with an old friend. They were treating me like a spy in the enemy camp, not a law-abiding, loyal citizen.

For seven frustrating years, I loyally served as the first and last IRS historian. The following is what I call the secret history of the IRS because the IRS would never have permitted me to write it for you. Even though that was my job.

It is the story of inept and clubby IRS executives who have forgotten what their job really is, what public service really means. It is the story of how unethical behavior thrives in the highest ranks of the IRS bureaucracy. It is the story of how the IRS runs from its past, evades its responsibilities, coddles criminals, lies to Congress, retaliates against whistle-blowers, and squanders the billions it receives in taxpayers' funds on incompetent management schemes, cushy off-site management seminars at top-notch resorts, and computer systems that don't work and cost plenty. It shrouds all these actions in a culture of secrecy that makes disclosing what goes on inside its marble halls a federal crime. Unlike its sorry subject, what you are about to read is an open book, the first time an IRS insider has dared to tell the truth about what really goes on at the IRS.

No wonder they tried to arrest me.

1

FIRST IMPRESSIONS ARE RARELY WRONG

AUGUST 1988

In the dog days of summer, about the last thing I wanted to do in swampy downtown D.C. was to find a parking space close by the IRS National Office Building at 1111 Constitution Avenue. Worrying about rush hour gridlock, I nearly missed a car pulling out of a metered space directly across from the official Temple of Doom.

I pushed as many quarters into the meter as I could fish from the bottom of my purse and sallied forth into the great bureaucratic unknown, trying not to think too long or too hard about what in God's name I was doing there. Instead I waltzed in, pausing momentarily inside the public vestibule for my eyes to adjust from the sparkling summer sun outside to the dim recesses of the inner lobby.

I was surprised to see, off to one side, an armed guard station. A standard-issue rent-a-cop was vigilantly minding the store. In my naïveté about the unexplored territory of civilian government agencies, I had fondly imagined that security-consciousness, so oppressively prevalent at the Defense Department, would not be such a high priority here. Wrong.

After working for the last year and a half at the hyper hush-hush Defense Mapping Agency—one of a handful of low-profile organizations like the National Security Agency and the National Reconnaissance Office which few people know to associate with our national intelligence effort—and after eight years of service as a historian for the Air Force, I had had my fill of writing secret histories of government projects so highly classified that they probably wouldn't see the light of day before the turn of the next century.

Sure, I enjoyed certain aspects of my job, but I really needed a change. To that end, I treated myself to periodic outings to the DMA personnel office, where I could scan the list of available government jobs, keeping a weather eye peeled for that key word "historian." One day in February 1988, I caught the key word attached to the bone-chilling name Internal Revenue Service.

As would most Americans at that time, I felt my brain seize up at the mere mention of the intimidating initials IRS. But from a purely professional standpoint, I harbored something more than mere idle curiosity at the prospect of doing whatever an official IRS historian might actually do. Compose a history of taxation in the United States starting with the Boston Tea Party? Compared to compiling reports on the latest state-of-the-art Global Positioning System, dashing off some brief, breezy account of the Whiskey Rebellion sounded like a day at the beach.

Even better, the job would be a promotion, a step up the Civil Service ladder from my current position. The possibility of being granted a 30 percent pay raise was no small consideration as I contemplated the job, I can assure you.

I dialed the number on the posting to request a complete job description. After opening the packet that arrived surprisingly shortly thereafter, I was impressed by the language used to describe the newly created position of IRS historian. It seemed as though the official responsible for filling the position had actually taken the time and trouble to think about what the new historian's duties might encompass. How was I to know that those impressive-sounding phrases had been cribbed from similar job listings at the Smithsonian Institution, conveniently situated catty-corner across the street?

Without hesitation, I entered my name as a candidate for the job of official IRS historian. And received not a peep out of them for seven months. Not even so much as a standard form letter—of which I'd seen plenty—acknowledging my interest in the job or advising me that they had filled the position with another candidate.

By the time anyone got around to calling me, I'd all but forgotten about the IRS and its historian job. At eleven or so on a slow summer morning, my office phone jangled. A bored-sounding voice on the other end asked if I could come for an interview the next afternoon. No apologies for short notice.

All I could think of was what an incredible pain it would be to drive to downtown D.C. from DMA, located at the Naval Observatory at that time, also home to the Vice President's residence. Not to mention what an even bigger pain it would be to turn right around an hour or so later to head back to suburban Virginia, at the height of rush hour. Why not blow the whole thing off? After giving the matter another second, I reminded myself that yes, I did need a change. Of course the IRS was no doubt a very strange place. But I would never know *how* strange unless I checked it out myself.

The particular bigwig I was to meet had the unusual name of Orion Birdsall. I knew nothing about him, except that he carried the impressive title of deputy assistant commissioner for human resources and management support, a post that apparently had some oversight responsibility for the new historian.

As I stepped off the elevator on the third floor—where the head IRS honchos hang out, I was soon to learn—and hurried down one of those interminably long federal hallways, I was struck by the degree of drabness achieved by those dusty corridors, lined with innumerable Philip Marlowe–style frosted-glass doors. Not that the fabled fluorescent-lit corridors of the Pentagon are anything to write home about. But if you ever set foot inside a Defense Department installation, you become unwittingly enrolled in armed forces history, mainly by the ever-present display of historical artifacts, like a sports hall of fame. A feel for the past and for a long, proud tradition exudes from those trophies in glass cases, vintage documents, framed drawings, certificates, photographs, portraits—all that wonderful old junk historians love, and most people at least glance at as they walk by. But, I'm convinced, even the most fleeting glancers imbibe some subliminal historical effect—a sense of the power and majesty of the past.

Judging by the bleak, barren walls of the IRS corridors, there was no institutional memory around here. No pride, no tradition, no echoes of victory or defeat. Where were the portraits of IRS commissioners? The framed hand-calligraphed documents, engraved certificates, hand-tinted photographs of famous revenuers? Nowhere in sight. I strongly suspected that, if given half a chance to poke around in the nooks and crannies of the building, I would dig up a few things. The IRS hallways, in short, needed me. Whether the rest of the place did remained to be seen. And so, on to Orion Birdsall.

The remarkable drabness of the public spaces made the pleasantly painted, plushly appointed executive suite of the deputy assistant commissioner for human resources and management support look all the more like an oasis of civilization in the desert. A well-dressed secretary greeted me with a perfunctory hello before silently seating me on a comfortable couch, which lined the wall of an attractive anteroom. The mellow mood was enhanced by indirect lighting, elegantly draped windows, tasteful pile rugs—discreet touches, I later learned, that all came courtesy of a sizable staff of IRS in-house decorators, who dash around those drab, decor-poor halls with swatches of cloth and chips of paint, polling the mucky-mucks on whether they'd like their office walls painted teal-green to coordinate with their cordovan carpeting.

When the intercom buzzed on the secretary's desk, she ushered me into Deputy Assistant Commissioner Birdsall's inner sanctum. I found myself gripping the hand of a soft-spoken, rather tentative Virginia gentleman, whose most striking physical feature (for a man in his fifties) was a shock of straw-colored hair, lending his round face an oddly boyish air. And he wore his hair long—by government standards. I took it as a sign that the IRS, at least in the upper echelons, might not be the boot camp it was so famously cracked up to be. And a welcome contrast to the close-cropped, starched dignity of the Defense Department personnel with whom I'd spent the last decade. How was I to guess that this modish style was more a sign of his oddball status at the agency?

The next thing that caught my eye upon entering that spacious office was the handsomely framed, three-by-two-foot Senior Executive Service (SES) certificate above Orion's expansive, solid wood executive desk. This document signified the owner's exclusive membership in good standing in the club of "SESers," also known to cognoscenti of Beltway bureaucratese as "Above GM–15s." These high-level paper pushers—there are, believe it or not, thousands of them—take home upward of $100,000 a year. Many make $125,000. Despite all the moan-

ing and groaning about pitifully low government salaries and self-serving reports in the press, I've been surprised by how ludicrously high
many government salaries are. Forget all the talk about those fabulous
benefits—which *are* pretty fabulous. The money ain't bad either.

I had only a moment to take in the glossy, wood-veneer, glass-
front bookcases and the polished hardwood furniture before two
other middle-aged men, conservatively dressed like Orion in drab
department store suits, rose politely to shake my hand. When they
resumed their seats, they arranged themselves like ducks in a row on
the couch. This peculiar formation gave them the look, at least from
my point of view, of a judicial tribunal. Had they taken a sneak peek
at my most recent 1040? Was I in for an audit? What else was I to
think? This was the IRS after all.

After clearing his throat, Orion introduced me to his two compan-
ions: John Ader from "Examination" and Paul Harrington from
"Collection." My ignorance of the meaning of both terms presented
me with a golden opportunity to ask both of them precisely what
they did for a living. They seemed somewhat astonished to find
themselves kicking off the interview by answering my questions. All
the same, it made a pretty good ice-breaker. "Examination," John
Ader—a younger, dark-complexioned fellow—explained, was the
IRS euphemism for "audit."

"'Examination' sounds like a test in high school," I volunteered.
John agreed that it was a peculiar term, dating back to the dim
recesses of IRS history—Lord only knew how long ago. He
shrugged in resignation.

"That's why you need me!" I replied. John Ader chuckled politely.

Paul Harrington, a tall, balding, stoop-shouldered man, explained
that his department, Collection, was the division that gets all the bad
press.

"We seize people's cars when the owners don't pay their taxes." He
grinned. Coming from such a seemingly mild-mannered guy, this
Rambo talk seemed a trifle incongruous. But even this sharp incon-
gruity reinforced my growing perception that the IRS, like the Defense
Department, was perhaps getting a bad rap, based on bad press. I could
help them with that, I thought to myself, because a key aspect of the
government historian's job is to present a more human side to an organization by providing a glimpse into its past. In the IRS's case, of

course, I would have my work cut out for me. But that was precisely the reason, I assumed, that they had decided to create the position.

"So you're the bad guys?" I prodded Paul Harrington, perhaps unnecessarily.

"I'd prefer to call the folks whose property we seize the bad guys," he demurred. Harrington, I suddenly noticed, had truly big feet.

"Do you squish tax evaders with those shoes?" I asked, Lord knows why, except that I was feeling mild embarrassment. To his credit, he didn't bat an eyelash. He chuckled and nodded, as though the thought had never occurred to him. Ader and Birdsall, for their part, took my lame attempts at humor in stride. About halfway through the interview, I began to feel surprisingly at ease, particularly compared to similar interviews with the armed forces.

My interviewers also seemed relaxed, with John sprawled out on Orion's couch, Paul's large feet brushing the edge of the coffee table, and Orion himself leaning back pensively in his soft sofa, studying the ten-foot ceiling with a distracted air, as if he were attending a graduate seminar.

I decided to cut the chitchat and launch into my professional pitch. Here's the gist: After earning my bachelor's and master's degrees in American history, and being persuaded by an unusually charismatic history professor that I should consider embarking on a career in military history, I had—with all due reservations—accepted a summer internship in historical research at the United States Air Force History Office.

It was 1979. I was twenty-three. Among other projects, the Air Force asked me to prepare a comprehensive chronology of the U.S. military intervention in Cambodia. At that early stage in my government career, I didn't have a security clearance, but I did what I could with the materials at hand, drawn from unclassified sources. The man I worked for, a senior Air Force historian on the verge of retirement, couldn't have been more considerate of my situation. Operating under the assumption (which turned out to be correct) that I represented the next generation of government historians, he went out of his way to teach me the ropes before sailing off into the wild blue yonder, on the golden wings of a government pension.

Among the important things that he taught me was a deeper appreciation of the critical importance of government history.

Government historians, he confided with palpable pride, were official journalists. We keep track of details and decisions as they occur. We—he always used "we," intentionally including me, an intern, in his intellectual corps—lay the factual groundwork for future historians. We help an agency avoid repeating terrible mistakes, because we're there to ensure that mistakes aren't covered up. Or shredded.

Above all, he impressed upon me that history has a life-and-death impact on society. Without official history, so much of what went on in the corridors of power would have gone unrecorded, from the Battle of Bull Run to the Bay of Pigs, from the New Deal to Hiroshima to the Cuban missile crisis. Not every government agency, of course, takes its history as seriously as do our uniformed forces. But after just a few days at the Air Force, I was hooked. I found the work fascinating, the people interesting and, most surprisingly—given my background as the daughter of a liberal college professor father—well worth respecting.

When the summer was up, rather than return to school to get my doctorate—I had my sights set on Duke, University of North Carolina at Chapel Hill, or Ohio State, three top campuses for military history—I stayed on at the Air Force. I rose steadily through the civilian ranks, spending the better part of the next decade roaming around the country, from base to base, acting as the official eyes and ears of posterity on the ground and in the air.

When John Ader pressed me for more details, I swung into a brief verbal dispatch of the history I'd written for an obscure (and since disbanded) Air Force command known as the Air Lift Communications Division. They'd been called in to take up the slack as—to be blunt—government scabs during the 1983 civilian air traffic controller's strike. President Ronald Reagan had successfully broken the back of that strike using Air Force air traffic controllers as his reinforcements. Whatever the political and social issues involved in that struggle, the Air Force had kept the civilian aviation industry in the air during an exceedingly tension-filled time.

Orion's last question was the most obvious: "Why are you interested in leaving the military for the civilian sector?"

"I think that I'd benefit from a change of atmosphere."

How true. After just under a decade of being a captive audience for high-level military men and women saluting and sirring each other to death, I felt a breath of fresh air when I heard these three men address one another—and me—on a first-name basis.

The interview lasted maybe half an hour. I walked out totally convinced that I'd blown it. "Do you squish tax evaders with those shoes?" Why did I say that? There had been no call to be flippant and silly when historians should be serious. Still mentally chewing myself out, I could hear my phone ringing as I turned the key in the lock of my front door and rushed to pick it up.

"Shelley?"

I took a deep breath. It was Orion Birdsall on the line. He cleared his throat.

"We were just sitting here wondering how much time you might need before starting your new job."

Stunned, I hesitated. Orion jumped in.

"We were hoping you could start in two weeks."

Two weeks! I would have liked to give the DMA a month's notice, but I knew from experience that two weeks would be a respectable interval to give notice to a government agency. The sole question remained: Did I want the job?

Frankly, it was a no-brainer. I was crying out for a change. Practically any change would do. Even from frying pan to fire.

That image didn't occur to me at the time. I had a dramatically different picture. This new IRS gig felt not only like a genuine change, but like a genuine challenge. The *first* IRS historian. I might even get a shot at substantially influencing a major federal agency. Opportunities like that come rarely if ever in Washington.

"Two weeks would be fine. Thank you, Mr. Birdsall."

"Thank *you*," Orion replied, ever the perfect gentleman. "So let's see, I guess we'll be seeing you on"—he paused to check his desk calendar—"Monday, August 29."

DISORIENTATION SESSION
Monday, August 29, 1988, A.M.

I'm sitting at a plastic-topped desk in a dank, dark basement room, bored utterly out of my gourd. I'm doing my damnedest to listen—but at least half the time, not succeeding—to the employee orientation required of all new IRS hires. I've been issued a thick three-ring notebook of rules and regulations all IRS employees are expected to follow without question. I've been told that I'll be responsible for all of it. Every last word.

I sit through a tortuous explanation of conduct befitting an IRS employee. Before I get a chance to back out, I'm fingerprinted and sworn in. Dutifully I raise my right hand and repeat a solemn oath to uphold the Constitution, defend my country, protect the rights of the taxpayer, so on and so forth, into eternity. Orientation makes me sick.

What most disturbs me about this particular underground session is that it all seems so rote, so routine, so insanely lacking in substance. I'm a Girl Scout in one key respect: I expect people to have some sense of purpose and passion about their work. If they don't—or if their managers don't let them—that's sad.

Carved in stone above the entrance to 1111 Constitution Avenue is a statement correctly attributed to former Supreme Court Justice Oliver Wendell Holmes: "Taxes are what we pay for civilized society." Truer words were never written. But here in this basement room, I find myself mentally gagging as one long-term IRS drone after another shows up at the podium and goes through the motions of letting us in on the IRS's deep, dark secret—that it can be a social embarrassment to work here. More from a sense of institutional loyalty than disloyalty, more from fidelity than a need to dissent, I begin revising the orientation program on the spot. I conjure up an inspiring image of a Holmes-like IRS higher-up (in real life, they're much too busy to bother) standing proud and tall at the podium, delivering a stirring speech about what a grand mission it is to collect taxes. Not these monotonous voices, meaningless words, robotic body language. The overall tone, the thrust of the message, is one of shame and discomfort about working for the IRS, collecting taxes. "Hang down your head, Tom Dooley, hang down your head and cry, 'cause you poor federal stool pigeon, one day you're bound to die."

Of course, I know that tax collectors have never been popular, not in the days of the pharaohs, not during the reign of the Caesars, nor during Charlemagne's time, or Napoleon's, or, for that matter, Savonarola's. But this message strikes me as over the top.

"You'll have an easier time of it," an odious woman smarmily levels with us, "if you tell people you work for the Treasury
Department." Now, that's a bit like CIA agents telling people they
work for the State Department, except that the CIA has a national
security rationale. This casual habit of deception at the IRS exists
strictly to alleviate social distress.

Being the official historian for an organization is basically about
building up pride in the institution. But "when outsiders hear you're
with the IRS," she says with a smirk, "most of the time they'll harass
you, hassle you, make you feel bad, or, worst of all, ask for help in
tracking down their refund." That's orientation.

PIZZA PARTY

A few hours later, having been duly sworn in, signed in, hole-
punched, and tagged as the latest willing recruit to the cause, I find
myself a guest at a farewell pizza party for the outgoing assistant
commissioner for human resources. Mike Dolan's being sent south to
take over as the regional commissioner for the Southeast Regional
Office, based in Atlanta. Until he's officially out the door, Dolan is
my boss Orion's boss.

Therefore, it seemed very PC for me to go. Earlier that day, Ann
Pope, who heads up the staff office serving both Orion and Mike
Dolan, tentatively invited me to the party. I've been—temporarily, of
course—attached to her office because at this point Orion Birdsall
has not had the time or expended the effort to figure out what else to
do with me. Or, for that matter, where else to put me, much less
what I'm supposed to do when I get there.

A touch self-conscious about attending an intimate gathering for a
guest of honor whom I've never met with a bunch of people I don't
know from Adam, I view it as an opportunity to get to know a few
people and introduce myself. At least these people will be bemused
by the sheer novelty of my position, right? The party occurs in a
small conference room directly adjoining Mike Dolan's capacious
office.

Try as I might to be the cheery, perky, outgoing individual that I
normally am, within the first five minutes, I find the socializing

much harder going than I had any reason to expect. The blank stares, the baffled gazes, the looks of thinly veiled disdain with which I am greeted by one and all startle me. These people display so little curiosity about my new job, much less about me personally, that I get the distinct impression that I'm being given the cold shoulder.

"Shelley," Orion calls over to me at one point. "I'd like you to meet Mike Dolan.

"Mike," Orion says, "I'd like you to meet Shelley Davis, our new historian."

"Oh," Mike Dolan grunts, all three-hundred-odd pounds of him, seemingly more interested in another slice of pizza than in this innovation for the IRS staff. "So you're Orion's historian," he mutters, as if that's my official job title. An IRS office mate once described this guy as "a tight-collared, fleshed-faced Irish beefeater."

Before I even screw up enough courage to reply, Dolan dashes off to scarf up some seconds. Not to worry. He'd be back in IRS headquarters a few years from now with a huge promotion to the highest career position: deputy commissioner of the IRS.

ORION'S BRAIN TRUST

Months later I figure out that I was to be part of a long-range master plan dreamed up by my boss Orion, who had this "vision"—possibly on the road to Damascus—of founding a creative brain trust at the IRS. Ideally—Orion had a tendency to live in the world of ideals—he'd form a collective, innovative, forward-looking group of really smart people who might, if given a fair shot, hatch some original solutions to the innumerable problems dogging IRS management. In theory, not a bad idea at all. And I do give Orion full credit for coming up with some pretty neat, cool, even unusual ideas. But the problem at a place like the IRS is that the word "creative" is about the farthest thing from a compliment that you can get. In fact, it's an insult—a total put-down. The word "creative" is used against him, as a way to sling mud, as a way to convey that in a fundamental sense—the IRS sense—Orion is a tad unsound. It is perhaps unfortunate that his very name, Orion, makes it sound as if he's from outer space.

That's why Mike Dolan's derisive reference to me as "Orion's historian" hit home, because it became a moniker until Orion retired a few years later. "Orion's historian," in the eyes of many IRS executives, made me his entertainment, a diversion. What the people at the top of the IRS respect more than anything else, not surprisingly, is go-for-the-gut, turf-defending, infighting skills. To put it mildly, that is not Orion's bag. His greatest handicap at the agency, functionally speaking, is that he's not a tax man, either by temperament or by training. He's a management-training, personnel guy—a people person. He's worked his way up the ranks on the personnel side for a few decades until attaining his present post, heavy with prestige but remarkably free of the burden of power.

How was I to know that I would end up being lumped together in the institutional collective unconscious with Orion's "environmental scanner"—more popularly if derisively known around 1111 Constitution Avenue as "Orion's futurist." His job, if you could call it that, apparently consisted of clipping articles, virtually at random, from a vast assortment of newspapers and magazines, and laboriously assembling them into cute collages that reminded me of nothing more than eighth-grade current events projects. From these rooster's entrails, the futurist divined "social trends" of presumed interest to the IRS hierarchy.

Then there was "Orion's ergonomicist," who—as his title suggested—kept track of "ergonomic" issues—does your chair fit right?—at the headquarters. Orion was stymied when it came time to hire an anthropologist to fill out the crew. They drew the line there. The happy compromise: they hired an official historian.

DAY TWO

On my second morning, Orion kindly, though not without some visible trepidation, shows me my gunmetal desk, tucked away in the corner of a busy office on the third floor, down the hall from his office.

"This is all we've got for you at the moment," he says, eyes cast downward, embarrassed for me. "Don't worry, we're going to get you slotted in somewhere better real soon," he says reassuringly.

Ann Pope, the master of Orion's small support staff, I soon learn has an infinite number of bosom buddies scattered across that huge building, which houses some three thousand employees. Most of them seem to know Ann not only by sight, but personally, and seem to have standing invitations to come sailing by with their cups of coffee at the start of the day and spend most of the morning endlessly gossiping about internal IRS affairs.

For the first few days, I have to admit, I get a kick out of it. I consider these endless, pointless, circular anecdotes relating who's in and who's out at the upper levels of the IRS hierarchy a form of primary research. While it may not be historical, the gossip helps to clue me in to the wily ways of my new employer. Yes, I will listen in, damn it—Ann's loud explanations leave me no choice about that—and make sure I glean something of interest from my involuntary eavesdropping. When not pursuing my anecdotal research, I try not to be driven out of my mind by the incessant jangling of Ann Pope's jewelry. An attractive fortyish woman, she wears more high-decibel jewelry than any woman I've ever met.

Acutely aware of how little I have to do, especially without any guidance, I decide to interrupt one of Ann's gossip sessions to ask if there might be anything in the office I might read to teach me about the IRS. Ann Pope briskly escorts me to a wall covered with shelves and lateral files, where she points me toward the multivolume *Internal Revenue Manual*, which I think she hopes might keep me busy and quiet for the next thirty years. The manual, Ann informs me, is the official guide to IRS rules and regulations. I later learn that at the IRS, the tax laws passed by Congress are known as "the Bible," while the manual is "the Catechism."

While it's no masterpiece of prose style, the *Internal Revenue Manual* turns out to be my literary lifesaver. Compliantly pulling a thick, bound volume (filled to the edges with tiny print) off the shelf, I take it to my seat, plug my ears, and eagerly begin scanning the table of contents.

In a matter of minutes, I find what I'm looking for. An innocuous entry for Records Management. From my years at Defense, I know how closely government historians typically work with government records managers in a joint effort to make sure that important documents generated in bulk by government agencies are saved for posterity. Professional historians are skilled at identifying what might be important to preserve for historical purposes, but records managers are technically adept at making sure that key documents aren't thrown out or destroyed. The ultimate repository, of course, for all government documents deemed worthy of permanent preservation is the National Archives in Washington.

The records managers, institutionally speaking, should be my allies at the IRS. In so many areas, our tasks and responsibilities overlap. With mounting interest, I read at random a few entries regarding the IRS records management program. Judging by the manual, at any rate, the IRS seems totally on top of the case.

1. The Records Management Program involves the management of all records of the Internal Revenue Service from the time they are created or received until they are finally disposed of.

2. The Records Management Program provides for the application, on a continuing basis, of sound management principles and techniques to the creation, maintenance, use, retrieval, preservation and disposition of records . . . and includes records documentation, correspondence management, records systems, records retention and disposal, microfilming, records equipment and supplies, and administrative mail management.

Clearly, my best course of action is to make contact with Records Management, ASAP. If nothing else, they'll at least know where the voluminous IRS records are stored. I can't wait to get my hands dirty, going through reams of real paper in some dank, airless vault. Getting hold of the records managers should be the shortest, swiftest route to the buried IRS historical payload.

I flip open my handy IRS telephone book (which was next to impossible to get) and look for the name of the chief of the Records Management office. Susan Heine. I dial the number listed, explain why I'm calling, and, before not too much time has elapsed, find myself in real-time, person-to-person conversation with Susan Heine herself.

"I've heard about you," she says flatly.

Something in Susan Heine's tone of voice sounds defensive. I find it hard to credit that any negative information about me—even admitting that such existed—could have wormed its way through the grapevine to her in such short order.

Susan volunteers that she would be more than happy to meet with me—but not for two weeks. She's too busy managing tons of records to see me even for a two-minute chin-wag until then. Disappointed, because I can't figure out where else to begin, I agree to wait. She knows, I reckon, where the bodies are buried. Of course, I mean that only as a figure of speech.

ORION'S BELT

Toward the end of my first week in office, Asst. Dep. Comm. Orion Birdsall finds a few minutes to sit down with me. Now that he's gone and created this position for me, I've detected a certain pattern of avoidance and evasion in his attitude toward me, which I tend to ascribe to a moderate degree of discomfort regarding the burning question of what he is to do with me now that I'm here. And what I am to do.

"We have arranged"—Orion displays a real genius for delving into details—"to transfer the position of official historian to Human Resources Technology."

I gaze back at him as if he just gave me a case of institutional leprosy. Human Resources Technology is not only one of Orion's pet projects, but also a standing joke around the organization, known by its acronym, HRT, pronounced "hurt." As I learn more about HRT, I actually laugh so hard that it does. Maybe it's because the HRT staff has an utterly undefinable mission.

I wonder aloud—in Orion's general direction—why this radical step is being taken, and so precipitously. To myself, I try to make the connection between history—my job—and Human Resources Technology, whatever that is. But I can't.

Orion responds with a conspiratorial wink. "The main reason we're shooing you downstairs to HRT is that on the first floor, you can have your own cubicle."

Being sent from the third-floor "power center" to the third-class deck on the first floor means a loss of the status and prestige automatically conferred by proximity to power. In exchange for my very own cubicle.

"Okay," I say, "I'll take the cubicle."

"Now keep in mind," Orion sternly advises, "that you will be part of the HRT staff in name only. You will be attached to them for care and feeding. I will continue to be your supervisor."

After a decade in the Defense Department, I know that "care and feeding" means foisting a troublesome posting off on someone else's departmental budget so that you don't have to take the charge on your own account. Typically a case of horse trading between departments. Over my years at the IRS, I would be traded more than any horse ever should be. A couple of years later, I would actually be traded to a different department in exchange for a copy machine. A co-worker told me that in this case my value was validated because the copy machine in question came with a collator.

"Could you, if possible, fill me in so I don't say something stupid, about what Human Resources Technology does around here?"

Before the question is even out of my mouth, I realize that it was not the right question. A look of acute distress, verging on pain, crosses Orion's lightly lined face. He mumbles something vague about "support staff for technological change with regard to personnel management." Basically, he gives me the brush-off. If this had been Defense, he could have mumbled "national security" and been done with it. Instead, he dismisses my parochial concerns with a wave of an authoritative hand.

"Don't get too hung up on what they do. They do all sorts of things. This is just a way for you to submit your time card and make sure you get paid, okay?"

Before vanishing in a puff of smoke deep into the obscure bowels of the lower levels, I decide to throw caution to the winds and ask Orion, point-blank, why on earth he saw fit to create the august post of official IRS historian in the first place.

Orion looks down at the ground, at his desk, at his hands, at the walls. Everywhere and anywhere but directly at me. I've just about given up on his ever spilling the beans when he reluctantly levels with me.

"I was sitting on an airplane," he starts out, in a don't-tell-anyone-I-told-you tone. "I happened to stumble upon an article in the in-flight magazine, describing how some corporations reap substantial rewards from the work of professional historians who write company histories."

I wonder what might have happened if Orion had taken a different airline.

A trifle impatiently, Orion recalls how impressed he was that "historians conduct all sorts of interesting research into specific questions, develop museums and displays, serve as staff advisers. . . ." His words trail off uncharacteristically. He seems positively peeved at me, as if I'm forcing him to consider something he would rather leave alone.

"Would any of the activities you read about in that article be appropriate in the IRS context?" I ask.

Orion opens his mouth, closes it again, and ponders his response for a remarkably long time. At last, he opens his mouth to speak, like the oracle at Delphi. I am on the edge of my seat here.

"I really wanted to make sure that all the various projects now under way in the national office are accurately recorded," he says, spreading his hands to convey all-inclusiveness.

Now all I have to do is hone in on *which* projects currently under way at the national office might be worth pursuing, and I'm home free.

"There's so much going on at the IRS right now," Orion blurts out. "Things are changing so fast," he mumbles distractedly, gesturing out toward that dangerously drab hallway, where things might well be morphing, even as we speak. "I thought that better records should be kept. . . ."

I ask for the names of a few projects he thinks might be worth documenting for posterity.

"Personally," he responds without hesitation, "I'd say the action around here is in information system upgrading and enhancement."

Hauling himself back on familiar ground, he clicks off a dizzying array of alphabet-soup names—AES, ICS, EFS—in rapid succession. "I'd say that most if not all of them could probably stand being more closely documented."

Ironically, I walk away from that first meeting with my supervisor with the nagging feeling that what he is really looking for is a records manager. This is a little disconcerting, since he has several already. I'm wondering why he doesn't know that.

JUST BIDING MY TIME

After making my move to the first floor, I keep reading my manual and minding my own business, preparing—so I tell myself—for my big meeting with the IRS records managers. I've only been at my new desk a few minutes when a wadded-up ball of paper lands on my desk. I can't see past my partition, so I have no idea where that harmless missile might have come from. I return to my handy manual, but it isn't long before a second lobbed ball lands on an open page, obscuring a key passage that I've just marked for closer inspection.

> Materials should not be withheld from the public simply because they may be subject to misinterpretation, because there is no public benefit to their release, to avoid embarrassment or hide instances of errors or wrongdoing by Service officials or employees.

Standing up, cagily circling my desk, I successfully track down the perpetrator: a short, dark, balding fellow with a New York accent, a motor mouth, a wry smile, and a deep chuckle.

"You were so quiet," he says out of the corner of his mouth, "I started wondering if you were still alive."

"I'm just trying to get through the manual," I respond with a smile that I hope conveys that I know how dopey a goal that must seem to him.

"Why on earth would you be bothering with that? Nobody uses it anyway. I don't think anyone's ever read it—at least not all the way through."

Shrugging, I admit—much as I hate to admit—that that's all I can think of to do at the moment, until I have a meeting with people I desperately need to see before getting into gear. He greets my admission with the snort and the chuckle I'm beginning to believe my title deserves.

"Oh, I've heard about you," he says.

By the way he says it, I know that he doesn't mean any harm. My newfound friend informs me that his name is Fred Fallik, and he is a psychologist. What a bizarre handle, I think, for a psychologist! I figure he must be part of Orion's brain trust. Why in God's name would the IRS hire a psychologist?

"So why does an IRS need a historian?" he taunts me.

"Why on earth do they need a psychologist?" I taunt back.

Fred shrugs, a shrug that speaks volumes, a shrug that seems to come from somewhere deep inside himself. "You know," Fred says philosophically, "I've been asking myself that for a couple of years now. Recently, I've stopped asking."

Fred, I soon learn, is by nature an existentialist. For an existentialist, being stuck at a desk in Human Resources Technology at the Internal Revenue Service confirms all of one's basic instincts about the absurdity of the workaday world.

"Since you're so smart," I challenge Fred, "can you tell me what the following three words—Human Resources Technology—strung together mean in the English language?"

Fred sits back and laughs, a deep belly laugh. "Shelley," he says, gently dressing me down, "take my advice. Don't waste your time trying to look for deep inner meanings around here. Human Resources Technology means just what it says—absolutely nothing at all."

Fred and I become fast friends. I learn soon enough that at forty-two, Fred has only recently returned to work, having recovered from bypass heart surgery. Once upon a time, he admits, he was your typical two-pack-a-day man. Nowadays, of course, he throws wadded-up balls of paper on people's desks. Pent-up tension seeking an outlet.

Since, as he can no doubt ascertain, I'm not overwhelmed with work at the moment, I decide to enlist Fred as—to deploy a sociological term—a key informant with regard to my short-term investigation of the organizational culture of the IRS. Orion hasn't succeeded in hiring a staff anthropologist, so in the meantime, I figure I'll pick up the slack.

Fred tells me that by both training and temperament he's an

"industrial psychologist." He holds a Ph.D. from Michigan State and worked for Booz, Allen (the large management consulting firm) before taking a lower-pressure job with the IRS. An industrial psychologist's job, he explains, consists mainly of designing surveys, evaluating tests, and doing what sounds to me like a lot of boring statistical work. Fred is a crackerjack evaluator of surveys and a top-notch statistical analyst, but at the IRS nobody pays the slightest attention to what he's doing or his unique talents. He evaluates surveys for departments, who thank him for his input and then totally ignore his suggestions. It's a chronic problem, he says, and seemingly intractable. Fred's long since abandoned hope that he'll make a difference at the IRS. At the moment, he's biding his time, waiting for the right opportunity to move on. He takes whatever pleasure he can in drawing a not insubstantial paycheck, and, given his medical history, he appreciates that his federal health insurance is so comprehensive. A divorced father, he's concentrating on putting his three kids through college. It is an article of faith with him that he'll make his break from HRT some time soon. Until then, he's trying not to get too bent out of shape by "the insanity upstairs."

Extrapolating from Fred's individual situation, I gather that quite a few people nominally attached to HRT are absent from their posts for days, if not weeks, at a time. At first, I chalk this up to chronic absenteeism, until I'm keyed in to the fact—by Fred, of course—that these people are in training. Training for what?

As for the people who do stick around, their tasks appear to be, shall we say, not precisely related to the collection of taxes. There's a guy whose job consists entirely of developing "time planning worksheets." To my observation, he spends countless hours at his desk, reading newspapers and drinking gallons of very weak coffee.

"The major motivating force in human behavior," Fred sternly declares, "is inertia." The longer I stick around here, the more I fear that Fred's Law might apply to me. Unlike Fred, I have found an outlet for my mounting frustrations, right on the premises: the IRS Health Improvement Program, a fancy name for the gym tucked away in a dreary basement corridor. When I invite Fred to join me for a workout, he groans.

"Shelley," he says, "when are you going to get real, okay? Don't you realize that if you're sick enough to need the Health Improvement Program, that they'll never let you in, because you'd never be strong enough to pass the ridiculously strict medical screening they make you take, because God forbid you should have a heart attack working out at their gym."

"Start slow," I advise. "Work your way into it."

"And give them the satisfaction of expiring on the premises? No way—you go have your fun."

ARCHIVES AND RECORDS MISMANAGEMENT

September 13 is my lucky day because I actually have an appointment. I'm just about jumping out of my shoes as I stride across the street to the Records Management office. The department happens to be located in an old post office building taken over by the IRS, called the Ariol Rios Federal Office Building. (I discovered that Ariol Rios was killed in the line of duty while working for the Bureau of Alcohol, Tobacco, and Firearms, which was part of the IRS until 1972.)

I've already said that the IRS National Office Building takes up four square blocks of prime real estate and rises seven lofty stories above the ground. If you assume that it would be plenty large enough to accommodate all the IRS employees in Washington, you'd be wrong.

The main building holds only three thousand people, a tiny percentage of the total Washington metro area IRS contingent of nearly ten thousand bureaucrats, none of whom ever actually touches your 1040. They are policy wonks. Ten thousand strong. The service is in fact heavily decentralized, with headquarters employees dispersed across some thirty buildings, as far afield as suburban Virginia, Maryland, and even West Virginia. In an effort to consolidate some of these scattered employees, in late 1996, the IRS began moving into a brand-spanking-new federal office building just inside the beltway in New Carrolton, Maryland. This new building cost the taxpayers $202.7 million, according to the General Services Administration.

Upon entering the Rios Building, I see the original WPA murals gracing the lobby and upper floors (depicting early postal delivery scenes, including the Pony Express) defaced by vampire fang marks graffitied into the necks of many of the heroic figures. Distressed at this lack of respect for original art, but realizing I'm nearly late for my first official encounter with IRS records management, I forge onward and upward.

Even by my increasingly lax system of categorization, Susan Heine does not strike me as a typical government "type," let alone an IRS one. Maybe it's the aging-hippie, flowing, flower child gauzy garments—the sort of peasant skirts you buy from a street vendor— that make me wonder why she's in charge of IRS records. I soon learn that Susan isn't really a records manager, that she spent most of her career in IRS personnel.

Four of us—Susan and her two assistants, Mary and Tony—sit at a small conference table tucked into a chaotic corner of their office. Tony, who has an eastern twang to his voice (New York? New Jersey?) is in his late thirties and exhibits the fastidious manner one might expect from a professional records manager, even though none of the IRS records managers is certified, the official stamp of the profession.

Tony speaks in a remarkably clipped tone of voice. He strikes me as the bureaucrat's bureaucrat. That is, if you handed Tony a stack of paper and told him to tear off the top right-hand corner of each one, he would likely do so, without ever pausing to think about the worthiness of the task, the ultimate goal, or whether there might be a faster, more efficient way to tear off all those corners.

Mary, the oldest of the three, is also the quietest. Her stony face is lined from years of smoking—you can smell the smoke on her clothes. Judging by first impressions, which isn't always fair, I find these three IRS drones somewhat scary. Even Tony, the youngest, seems dried out and stretched on a rack, mummified and buried alive. The fact that none of them is professionally trained in what they do is, to take a broader view, even more absurd.

Since I'd called this meeting, I launch into my rehearsed pitch for close cooperation between our two offices. I explain that I've worked for the past nine years as a federal historian, and always worked hand in hand with records managers at the Defense Department.

Since we'll be working together in the future, I thought we should get to know one another. That's about it. Nothing too fancy.

To my chagrin, I see them throwing one another private glances, suggesting that perhaps I am being just a little presumptuous there. No one has called ahead and told them to work closely with me, certainly no one at Orion's level. From their point of view, they're busy enough for government workers. Why should they expend extra effort and time "working closely" with the IRS historian, for God's sake?

Because it's their job. Imagine that the National Archives is a gigantic bank vault of information, a huge safe-deposit box, where the government keeps all its artifacts. Since the government is a terrible pack rat, it needs people like me, collaborating with professional records managers at the various agencies, to help separate the wheat from the chaff, the knowledge from the noise, according to protocols called Records Control Schedules. It is the Records Management department's responsibility to draw up these schedules and ensure that they are scrupulously adhered to.

I can hear myself saying, "I hope to be able to make your job easier by helping to identify documents worth preserving for historical value." I can tell by the looks in their eyes that they aren't buying it. There isn't much verbal response. For the most part, they listen politely and nod their heads in unison, but their body language betrays them. They seem to be hoping that when I'm done with my pitch, I'll go away and leave them alone to do whatever it was that they were doing.

The most disturbing part of this first meeting is that they don't seem to comprehend my most basic questions.

Such as:

"Where are the records?"

"How many IRS records are in the National Archives?"

"How often do you send records to the National Archives?"

"Are there places in this building I should be looking to find records?"

I feel like one of those English-as-a-second-language teachers asking questions for non-English speakers to repeat slowly in class.

Tony finally responds—after checking first with Susan by throwing her a fast glance to make sure it's okay to fill me in on the dirty details.

"Shelley, why don't I show you some of the files we keep in this office, so you can get a better feel for what we're up against?"

As I take Tony's lead, Susan eagerly removes herself from the scene. "Well Shelley, it's been nice to meet you, I've got to rush off. I'm sure Tony can fill you in on everything you'll need to know in continuing to work this issue out."

As Susan skedaddles out of there just as fast as her peasant-skirted bootie will take her, I'm still totally in the dark about what "issue" she's talking about, let alone "what they're up against." Mary silently returns to her cubicle without even bothering to say good-bye. Tony, meanwhile, has practically taken me by the hand to lead me—the blind leading the blind—to a row of lateral filing cabinets stacked up against one wall.

"Here," he says, with a yank backed up by surprising force, with which he tugs open a gray steel drawer and starts pulling out file after file after file, and tossing them in a heap on a vacant desktop. "That's only part of the correspondence we've had with the National Archives."

These files copiously document, Tony explains, the "dispute" between the IRS and the National Archives, which has been in bitter stalemate for many years, going on decades.

On the face of it, the very notion of engaging in a "dispute" with the nice, gentle folks at the National Archives strikes me as far-fetched. I know several of the archivists quite well, and there isn't one in the bunch I wouldn't mind meeting up with in a dark alley.

I beg Tony to fill me in on the broad brushstrokes. With a pained expression, he tries. The National Archives, he says contemptuously, has "frozen" many IRS records.

But why would they go and do that? I wonder. In a lowered voice, Tony confides that one primary focus of the interagency dispute is the IRS's vast holdings of criminal investigation case files, including informant files, that date as far back as the critical tax evasion case that sent Al Capone to prison.

Those thousands of case files are occupying miles of expensive space at Federal Records Centers scattered across the country and run by the National Archives, Tony explains. From the IRS's point of view, there's no reason to keep all that paper around. The cases have long since been closed. Why not just chuck the stuff?

Because, the National Archives insists, some of this stuff might have—and here I come in—historical or some unspecified "other" value. The problem is, Tony continues, those hard-assed archivists actually want to look at the IRS case files. Imagine that. Well, of course I can imagine that. Only by looking at a document can the archivists tell whether it has any long-term historical significance. The Archives always reviewed the top secret documents I perused in my years at the Defense Department. It was routine, standard procedure.

"What's the problem with letting the Archives review IRS case files?" I wonder.

Rather than respond, Tony simply snaps shut the file drawer he's holding open and throws me a cold, hard stare. Finally he says something.

"We save the manual. That's our history. The rest of this stuff we should be able to toss."

So now I get it: Rather than being their ally in helping the IRS to demonstrate that this costly stuff is all just a bunch of junk, given my obvious professional bent, I will be far more likely to end up siding with the National Archives!

For weeks afterward, I can't get out of my head my final exchange with Susan Heine. On my way out of her office, I poke my head into Susan's cubicle to thank her for taking the time to meet with me.

"Shelley," she warns me in all seriousness, "you're probably better off not even dealing with those people over at the Archives. Call us first if you have any questions about record keeping at the IRS. Don't call them."

TREASURE CHEST

Bill Sherman's office is filed deep within the National Archives. A small, dark, perennially messy cubbyhole, it's stereotypically similar to most archivists' offices that I've delved into over the years. Bill Sherman is the man responsible for keeping an eye on the records of the Treasury Department, which includes the IRS. Bill appears to be rapidly approaching retirement age. When I look closely at him, I notice that he's pale, almost molelike. I find myself wondering how often he gets to see the light of day—perhaps not very often. For his part, Bill Sherman seems awfully pleased that, at long last, someone official has taken the time and the trouble to poke around in the IRS records.

"We don't get too many people coming over anymore," he says, a bit sadly. I am for a moment reminded of one of those Ottoman Empire bureaucrats who kept fastidious records on certain small Turkish islands, years after that ancient empire had been dissolved.

"I'll be happy to show you what I've got, but I'll tell you right now, it isn't much," he adds apologetically, as if the dearth of holdings is somehow his fault. Wheezing from the multiple layers of dust in his middenlike office, Bill kindly walks me back into the stacks, off limits to the public. I'm relieved to see hundreds of file folders arranged in gray, fold-over archival boxes and properly indexed, occupying the section of posterity—about two hundred feet of metal shelving—allotted to the IRS.

At random, I pull a file or two relating to the Whiskey Rebellion, which fascinates me for no particular reason. Not far from a load of letters from Civil War tax commissioners, I locate leather-bound oversize ledgers filled with beautiful calligraphy listing names of nineteenth-century taxpayers, their addresses, and an exotic assortment of tax assessments for property, such as gold watches, horses, silver plate, and, yes, slaves.

I soak up a few beautifully handwritten letters, in cursive ink on rag paper, from taxpayers to the commissioner of Internal Revenue, mainly requesting the commissioner, in his awesome majesty, to clarify some arcane issue about their taxes. Some want their money back.

For a few blessed moments, I imagine that I've stumbled Indiana Jones–like upon the Holy Grail of taxation. I feel back on top of history. Then the sight of linear foot upon foot of empty gray steel shelving, barren of material, levels me like an archrival. It should be there but isn't.

"You might find this stuff kind of interesting," Bill says, breaking into my reverie with a sympathetic wink, as he hies me down a narrow aisle of gray metal shelving to show me a few cabinets filled with identification badges for Prohibition agents. Of course, they have little or no historical value, but they're kind of fun to see. The solemn faces of the agents during Prohibition belie the fact that bootleggers operated across the country with such notorious impunity. I guess if you were out chasing Al Capone with the possibility of a sawed-off shotgun being thrust in your face, you'd be serious too. All those serious faces doing such serious work. Those were the days—not only when "revenuers" carried shotguns, but also when they took the trouble to store this sort of thing in the Archives. When the place had some institutional self-respect, more akin to the G-men at the FBI.

After checking Bill's list, I realize that the National Archives is holding no post-Prohibition records. Where are the documents that might help tell the story of a federal agency's evolution from a tiny corps of shotgun-toting revenuers into the present eight-hundred-pound gorilla we all live in fear of today? What have they been up to, at taxpayers' expense?

"That's about it," Bill says, shaking his head sadly. For my own sweet sake, and that of my country, I hope not.

2

HISTORY, SHMISTORY

MISSION IMPOSSIBLE

We're passengers on a ship that is sinking. There are twenty-five of us on deck, but the lifeboats will hold only fifteen. What do we do? Which of us should be permitted to jump into the lifeboats? Which of us should stay behind and hope to be rescued? We're a small group. We have to learn fast to make life-and-death decisions. Do we pick old people? Women? Children?

"Maybe we should throw all the auditors overboard," I say, with forced levity. My distressed shipmates laugh, but Lynne Hayes, my putative boss as head of Human Resources Technology, gives me a dark look. Forgive me, Lynne. But at the DMA, I participated in a year-long Executive Leadership Program, designed to identify and train mid-level Civil Service employees with the potential to become executives at the Department of Defense. The program required one week of travel monthly, during which we had to partake in trendy management "trust-building" exercises just like this one. Over the course of the year, I'd rearranged enough deck chairs.

Memo to myself re "Fitting Into Hurt." As Orion Birdsall, assistant deputy commissioner for human resources, has taken great pains to point out, I am attached to HRT for "care and feeding only." Those are his exact words. Lynne Hayes, however, has taken it upon herself, as a personal character-building project, to make sure that I am properly indoctrinated into her group. Orion must never have bothered to tell Lynne that she was only to sign my time card. Instead, Lynne is determined to whittle away at my square edges until I become a round peg.

So far, everything seems to stymie her. I develop an increasingly firm conviction that joining this sorry HRT "team" makes no sense for me. In retrospect, I think that my personal rejection of Lynne's "team" must have threatened the integrity of the group as a whole because, at that time, HRT as a team was drifting into dangerous doldrums. It lacked any real function. How could it possibly play as a team, and why on earth would I want to play for it?

Finding a function, in fact, in the form of a "mission statement" is the central thrust of a cozy three-day off-site retreat at Coolfont, a posh rustic resort nestled in the West Virginia mountains. Granted, it's a tad tough to bitch and moan about having to shack up in my own grandly furnished private cabin in the woods, with my own private fireplace, my own private kitchenette, and, best of all, my own private whirlpool tub. In all my years at the Defense Department, that putative paragon of waste and extravagance, I never once stayed at a fancy cabin in the woods courtesy of Uncle Sam. For this HRT retreat, we obviously needed private cabins so that our mission might come to us in a flash of inspiration while we were sitting in our Jacuzzis around midnight, possibly after downing a bottle or two of well-chilled Chardonnay.

Suffice it to say that Lynne Hayes never did succeed in getting me to join her HRT team, which after those three days drafting a mission statement, was ultimately disbanded anyway—an apparent casualty of being challenged in the mission department.

Unconcerned with the existential travails of HRT, I tried my best to do my job. I began receiving calls, seemingly at random, from IRS employees who had heard about this strange new wonder called the "historian" and were just trying to understand what I was doing. Always friendly and casual, the callers seemed genuinely interested in my position, unlike those in the upper echelons. To many mid-level employees, a historian was a strange and marvelous phenomenon, like having an astrologer on staff, or a soothsayer.

My most frequent calls came from employees who had been told to get rid of documents, but harbored deep reservations about simply deep-sixing their stash. While the *Internal Revenue Manual* stipulated elaborate protocols to handle such routine processing, discarding, and preservation of documents, nobody—and that means nobody—followed them. The Records Control Schedules were a fiction. And most were horribly outdated.

At least once or twice a week, some anxious secretary would call: "My boss asked me to clean out this office"—or "this storage space" or "this file cabinet"—"and I have all these old documents I think may be important. I was told to just get rid of them, but I don't know what to do. Can you help?"

Somehow, these people had a sneaking suspicion that this stuff might be more than just stuff. In many cases, it was evidence of their work over the years, and blithely pitching it didn't seem right. But they didn't know what was the right thing to do. No one ever told them. That was how I initiated my impromptu collection of "Twentieth Century Internal Revenue Service Records," quite possibly the largest single holding of IRS documents outside the National Archives.

My collection began with an empty desk. When the desk drawers were full, I scrounged around the dreary IRS hallways for spare storage equipment. An empty filing cabinet here, a credenza there, a bookshelf there. Sometimes in my searches I'd find piles of documents waiting to be discarded. I carried them back to my office to see if any were worth keeping. Often they were. Before long, my little cubicle began to overflow with surplus paper. Real work, at last.

A trained historian doesn't work this way, but I had no choice. Either that or twiddle my thumbs waiting to be contacted by Susan, Tony, or Mary in Records Management. Occasionally I would refer a caller to them, just to see what happened. Nothing. The records managers were too busy. Invariably the callers were told to try again tomorrow. Or some other time. The message was clear: Don't bother us.

I always made sure to tell my sources to call me back right away if Records Management didn't help them. Usually within a few days I'd get a call back, begging me to "save" their documents from destruction. I was doing them a favor, taking this surplus stuff off their hands, and off their consciences as honest federal employees. Of course they were doing me a favor too.

After a few months I began to feel like the hub of an underground information network scattered throughout the IRS headquarters (and its innumerable satellites), determined to "save" the recent history of the IRS against all odds. I identified with George Orwell's classic dissenter in *1984* whenever allies would murmur quietly to me in the national office's dreary hallways, expressing their support for my efforts.

The call of calls came from a colleague across the street in an IRS satellite office, home of the Information Systems Division where a good deal of the "action" was, according to Orion. So I perked up when this brave employee (who shall, for obvious reasons, remain nameless) whispered—as if her boss might overhear her—that her boss had told her to clean out a small storage room. But she knew, she insisted, that the materials stored in two lateral filing cabinets in that space were important. She was in a quandary. What should she do?

"Don't do anything," I said urgently. "I'll be right over."

To this woman's boss, these piles of old paper were junk. And also, perhaps, not merely junk, but a potential paper trail that might contain embarrassing information. Information that might one day leave a record of IRS action, or inaction. What was the point of leaving a record behind? It could only spell trouble. Paper was bad. Records were threatening. Unless, of course, we're talking about taxpayers' records, which were protected as if they were the Crown Jewels.

I'd been doing some background reading and research—I'd even conducted a few preliminary interviews in preparation for embarking on a full-fledged history of IRS efforts to upgrade its computer systems. But so far I'd been stymied by a near total lack of documentation, relying on the spotty memories of a few veteran IRS employees. Could this be the booty I'd been looking for?

Yes. I arrived to find her cabinets chock full of documents dating from the 1970s through the mid-1980s. They were not nearly as redolent of history as the lovely calligraphic works in Bill Sherman's rival collection, but they were original documents all the same, tracing IRS efforts to upgrade its computer processing systems—the one consisting of woefully outdated computers that might crash any day and spew forth garbage instead of refunds, despite decades of throwing billions of dollars into a black hole. These records tracked the creation of that black hole.

I expected Orion's approval. Since getting in to see him was practically impossible, I'd developed a strategy of lingering in his outer office, bugging his secretary, waiting for him to get a free moment so that I could poke my head in the door. It took me most of the next day before I got the high sign to enter his inner sanctum.

"Orion." I burst in, bubbling over with enthusiasm. "You're not going to believe what I found! Most of the documents about IRS computers dating all the way back to the sixties! Minutes of meetings, correspondence, contracting documents, the works! Everything I need to start digging into my history of how the IRS got itself computerized."

"Not so fast," Orion said gloomily. "We're hardly out of the woods yet."

"I know that." I dismissed this as mere caviling. "But now I've got the story!"

I'd expected a reaction like that of an editor hearing that a hungry cub reporter has just stumbled upon a major scoop. Orion looked as if he'd just sat on a rat. He screwed up his face, wrinkled his nose, and frowned. I didn't get it. How could he so obviously fail to share my glee and joy at making such a momentous discovery? These were documents I thought had vanished, lost to history. Now, through a fluke, they had been recovered.

After one of the endless, painful pauses I was beginning to get used to, Orion cleared his throat to speak.

"Shelley," he said in a sad tone, as if breaking a bit of bad news to a child. "I think that's wonderful. I really do. But . . ." Another pause. "I honestly think, for your sake, that this is probably not the best time for you to pursue this subject, or necessarily the best subject for your first research project."

I was flabbergasted. Hadn't it been Orion who'd said this was where "all the action" was? After a long pause, I asked, "Would you mind telling me why?"

"It's just too controversial," he said impatiently, clearly resentful at having to explain the obvious reason that one just doesn't delve into "sensitive" matter of this sort, not unless one is looking for trouble. I'd never thought of myself as looking for trouble, just looking for truth.

"There's far too much politics involved. This is a very sensitive issue around here. A lot of careers and a lot of money are on the line with this one. If I were you," he concluded, "I'd shy away from this one like a hot potato, until you've gotten your feet wet around here. I'm sorry if you had your heart set on this, but Shelley, I'm really just trying to protect you."

At least he didn't say "trust me."

Though it all made sense in the IRS context I had come to know and despair of, it still amazed me that a project as dry and technical as computerization could possibly be such a hot potato. In a larger sense, I was only just starting to imbibe the full implications of my professional position. Here I was, Orion's creation out of whole cloth, and my sole sponsor, my only backer, my single reason for being in the IRS, didn't have the faintest idea of what an official historian's proper role should be at a major federal agency.

Orion was really looking for a records manager but didn't know what such a person was supposed to do. The fact that he already had a records manager in Susan Heine, and her loyal minions Mary and Tony, was beside the point, because clearly they didn't know what they were supposed to do either. I'd come to the IRS wanting to write history, not manage records. Particularly not to help mismanage records, as seemed to be the case around here.

"Well, if you say so," I mumbled, trying as hard as I could to conceal my sense of deep disappointment, in him personally as well as in my increasingly awkward position. "If you don't want me to start work on the history of computerization, are there any other areas you'd like me to pursue?" Yeah, and any other wild-goose chases?

"Oh," he answered vaguely, "you're still so new here. Why don't you spend a little more time just meeting people, scrounging around for background materials, familiarizing yourself with the organization in general?"

I think he could tell by my crestfallen look that that just wasn't good enough. That if he was going to throw me off the scent of what I really wanted to do, he'd better come up with something a little more concrete—on the spot.

"Okay," he said finally. "I've got an idea." As you can probably tell by now, Orion was big on ideas.

"There's this committee . . ."

Goose chase.

"This committee meets throughout the fall to prepare for the upcoming 1989 tax filing season," Orion was saying. "It's called the Filing Season Readiness Group, and it's made up of a small group of IRS executives and other staff members who meet every two weeks to talk out what the IRS is doing to make sure everything is on schedule for the kickoff starting January 1."

These preparedness meetings were scheduled to begin that very week, which is probably why Orion, clutching at straws, thought of them as a quick substitute for pursuing my true calling. Who knew, I thought, maybe there'd be something in it. In any case I didn't seem to have much of a choice.

That afternoon Orion took me to meet John Hummel, an executive who, when he wasn't in Washington chairing the readiness group, was IRS district director in Detroit. We found him setting up operations in a conference room on the third floor, which had been designated the readiness group's headquarters for the duration of its short-lived existence.

Though he was in his fifties, John Hummel was boyish and gangly, with a ready smile and a quick mind. He quickly grasped what my role was, kept telling me what a neat job I had, and more than once during our initial contact told me that he was "a real history buff."

"I think this is a great idea Orion had to create this job," he said excitedly. "I think you could be a real asset to the organization."

I felt somewhat buoyed by Hummel's apparent grasp of what my job ought to be. My hopes for the future rose even further as he proceeded to fill me in on the background of the computer modernization program—then known as Tax Systems Redesign (TSR). The new program had been launched in early 1986. Here, I thought to myself with no small satisfaction, Orion had steered me away from the history of computerization, and now I was being filled in on that very subject.

"It all started with the Tax Filing Season from Hell," he began, and let out a loud groan when I asked what that was.

"Let's just say that's when the all hell broke loose around here.

Don't you remember when the entire tax collection system of this country just about self-immolated?"

I'd been living in Texas at the time, working for the Air Force as a historian. I couldn't recall experiencing any IRS problems that year. But within the blinkered world of the IRS bureaucracy, the perception was that the agency's massive 1985 screw-ups would have lingered in the public's memory banks for decades. What the IRS didn't realize was that while the specifics of what went wrong at the IRS at the time had faded, a perception remained that the IRS was inept and bungling. A deeply traumatized IRS had spent much of the last few years climbing from "hell," and as Orion conceded, it was still far from grace. The IRS was left with an increasingly dim, fast-fading memory of a total disaster—the organizational equivalent of a nuclear meltdown. In fact, one IRS veteran later told me that only the news of the space shuttle Challenger blowing up wiped their screw-ups off the front pages.

A few mornings after my initial meeting with Hummel, my office phone rang. The gruff voice on the line barked at me, "Are you the one who calls herself the historian?"

Not even knowing whether this was an IRS employee, I responded simply: "Can I help you?"

"My name is Don Curtis," he said urgently, "and we need to talk. Can you come over now?"

The tone was so urgent that I dropped everything and dashed across the street to an office in the same building as the Information Systems Division and the recently rescued files. I assumed he was among the rank-and-file like all the other callers and was surprised to find him behind a frosted glass door and beyond an anteroom, complete with secretary, who made me cool my heels while he finished a phone call. I soon learned that it was typical of Don not to tell me who he was, his title, or even that he was an IRS executive.

Don's secretary eventually led me into his office, which was not nearly as plush as Orion's, but was by no means shabby. Don was a short, tightly wound man in his mid-fifties, with a build that looked as if he might have been compressed in a metal compactor. He thrust his hand out at me, grasped my hand in a tight, firm grip, and waved me into a seat on a nicely upholstered couch, while he seated himself in an armchair directly opposite.

The walls were covered with old engraved prints depicting Revolution-era scenes of early Virginia. A colorful array of glossy brochures advertising local historic sights such as the Manassas Museum near the Bull Run battlefield sat on the coffee table directly in front of me. I picked up a brochure on Leesylvania State Park and casually asked him where it was.

"And you call yourself a historian?" Don upbraided me. "Are you telling me that you don't even know the location of the original home of the Lee family? You know the Lees, don't you?"

I sat there dumbfounded, not knowing how to respond to this blunt frontal assault on my friendly query.

"You probably don't even know," Don pressed on with his campaign, "who Light-Horse Harry Lee was." He sat there glaring at me triumphantly, daring me to come up empty-handed.

I redeemed myself by correctly identifying Light-Horse Harry Lee as Confederate General Robert E. Lee's grandfather, Washington's Revolutionary War general, and the man who led Washington's troops into Pennsylvania to suppress the Whiskey Rebellion, the first all-American tax protest just a few years after the War of Independence had been won.

Don snorted and thrust out his hand.

"I guess you can call yourself a historian," he said, welcoming me into his private club.

To Don Curtis, Virginia history *was* history. Except for the history of the IRS. I was left to my own devices to learn that in his capacity as a member of the Prince William County Historical Commission, Don had spearheaded the preservation of the Lee family property and the surrounding area by organizing a grassroots effort to turn the entire vicinity into a state park.

Getting down to brass tacks, Don leaned forward in his armchair and began seriously debriefing me. If Orion Birdsall was not willing to give me anything specific to tackle, his fellow Virginian Don Curtis had no hesitation about informing me of my responsibilities as the new IRS historian.

"How much have you heard about the evolution of IRS computer systems?"

"Well," I said, "just a few days ago, I heard about the Filing Season from Hell."

Don smiled knowingly. "I'd call that a beginning. Let me just preface my remarks on that subject by stating that when I retire, I'm going to write a TV sitcom"—he pronounced that term as if mouthing a curse word—"about the bureaucratic bumbling around here. It's so tragic that the only way to properly deal with it is to turn it into a farce."

He chuckled at the thought, but that chuckle conveyed a definite edge of despair. Don, I would soon learn, cared deeply about the IRS and its myriad foibles, like a father when his children have done something terribly wrong. The one hour I spent with Don Curtis that afternoon convinced me that despite Orion's concerns, I would forge quietly ahead with my research into the IRS's faltering campaign to modernize its computer systems.

"The American people have a right to know about the shenanigans that have gone on inside this place for too long," Don said, reminding me of my duty as a professional to tell the truth even if it made some people look bad, or feel worse. Don inspired me every step of the way as I progressed in my quiet investigation into that "charade and a shambles and a bumbling farce," in pursuit of yet another pocket of history I had a sinking feeling would probably never see the light of day. I consoled myself that Don Curtis was there in his office, chuckling to himself as I filled him in— "debriefed," we would say—about every new misadventure I turned up as I did my spadework.

When something came up that he wanted me to hear, as it did several times a month, Don would call immediately. If he reached my answering machine, he'd leave an urgent message instructing me to get back to him without delay.

"Mayday, mayday," he'd holler, "the ship is sinking. SOS."

That was our secret code letting me know that something was up. We were indeed passengers on a sinking ship. And there were not nearly enough lifeboats to go around.

3

REIGN OF ERROR

IRS Secret History, Volume I

Within the next five to ten years we will have a totally redesigned tax administration system. Paper tax returns can largely be a thing of the past.

—1984 IRS annual report

BUDGET BUST-UP

On March 14, 1996, the Treasury Department (of which the IRS
is a part) conceded to Congress that after spending well over $4 bil-
lion over five years, the IRS's most recent effort to upgrade its computer systems was "badly off track." Four months later, in June
1996, the House Appropriations Subcommittee approved deep
spending cuts at the IRS, calling for heavy layoffs of two thousand
employees assigned to what the *Washington Post* charitably called the
IRS's "troubled computer modernization project."

Representative Jim Lightfoot (Republican-Iowa) expressed the
frustration of millions of taxpayers, even a few employed by the IRS,
when he blasted IRS senior management for badly bungling its highly
touted computer modernization. "The bottom line is that I'm fed up
with excuses," Congressman Lightfoot thundered indignantly. "If you
can't get it right in eight years, you might as well forget about it!"

In his capacity as chairman of the House Treasury, Postal Service,

and General Government Subcommittee, Lightfoot had every reason to be upset. Among a handful of elected officials, he asserts oversight of the otherwise all-powerful IRS. This power gives
Congressman Lightfoot a substantial degree of influence over the
fate of an agency that seems to have drastically lost its way. By 1996
IRS critics were finally realizing that the systematic malaise affecting
the computer modernization program symptomized a larger afflic-
tion.

Under Lightfoot's proposed bill, Congress would slash funding
for the IRS by a staggering 11 percent, including a resounding reduction of $270 million targeted specifically at the mismanaged com-
puter modernization project. This represented a cut of nearly half
the $700 million appropriated for the 1996 fiscal year. The sheer size
and broad scope of this cut, aimed not merely at the faltering computerization efforts but at the agency as a whole, "appeared to shock
agency officials," the *Washington Post* reported. In the ultimate slap
in the face to senior IRS management, Lightfoot's bill called for
putting the Defense Department in charge of writing contracts for
all future IRS computer modernization efforts. The message was
clear: You screwed up guys, big-time. We can't even trust you to buy
your own computers.

"The computer modernization project found few defenders yes-
terday," the *Washington Post* concluded. "Critics say the project has
been poorly managed and does not link the new technology to the
latest tax collection task." Sounding perhaps like an information
technology specialist in business, one IRS computer expert (who preferred to remain anonymous) put it to me this way: "We lost sight of
our mission. We thought we were supposed to be on the leading edge
of technology. But we have no business being on the leading edge.
We have no money for that. We need to be able to be flexible enough
to adapt to new discoveries, not to discover new ways of doing business."

Rather than maintaining itself on "the leading edge of technology," Don Curtis claimed that the IRS hemorrhaged along on "the
bleeding edge of technology." The IRS spent the better part of the
eighties convincing itself and Congress that it could march proudly
into the twenty-first century using innovative and emerging tech-

nologies to process the millions of tax returns it receives every year. But amid all the heady hubbub and buzzwords like "image recognition" and "network linkage," the IRS forgot—as it has a lamentable tendency to do, and not unlike large corporate bureaucracies—that its basic mission is to collect money from taxpayers. It failed to ask taxpayers, arguably its customers, what they were ready or willing to accept in new ways of getting their money to the IRS. It failed to consider the uncertainties that go along with developing new technologies. It ignored its own history. In particular, it ignored recent history. It ignored the lessons of the Nixon years. It ignored the nearly fatal Filing Season from Hell.

REMEMBRANCE OF THINGS PAST

TAX RETURN BACKLOG GROWS IN WAKE OF COMPUTER WOES
TAXING TALES OF THE IRS
BEWARE THE IRS COMPUTER: NOT EVEN A BOY SCOUT IS SAFE!

—Philadelphia Inquirer, Spring 1985

On April 26, 1985, a janitor cleaning up the remains of an unusually chaotic and frenetic Tax Day in Philadelphia found envelopes containing unprocessed tax returns (many with undeposited checks still attached) in a trash barrel on the loading dock of the IRS's sprawling Philadelphia Service Center. After he turned this embarrassing find over to his supervisor, a desperate weekend-long search ensued of all trash barrels at the center. The search turned up, much to center management's horror, 109 envelopes still containing unprocessed tax information, all of which nearly ended up as Philly landfill.

Out of those recovered 109 envelopes, ninety-four contained checks made out to the federal government, totaling $333,440. Thirty-six contained unprocessed 1040s. Twenty-four contained estimated tax payments. On April 30—just four days after the discovery of the first cache of buried treasure—an IRS internal auditor pulled at random three brown envelopes from yet another trash can inside the center. One of the three contained a check made out to the IRS for $2,500. The General Accounting Office (GAO) would later report that IRS officials found between fifty and a hundred unprocessed tax returns stuffed in a wastebasket in a women's restroom in the Philadelphia Service Center.

"THE NEW IRS COMPUTER SYSTEM CONTINUES ITS REIGN OF ERROR," trumpeted a headline in the *Philadelphia Inquirer,* which disclosed that in January 1985, the same apparently dysfunctional center had erroneously seized the bank account of a Boy Scout Council in rural Pennsylvania. The Boy Scout troop's missing money was just one of ten thousand accounts, scattered throughout the mid-Atlantic region, adversely affected by an IRS employee's failure to properly post a computer tape reflecting tax payments withheld during the 1984 tax year. These reflected some $300 million prepaid to the government. The growing backlog of unprocessed returns clogging IRS service centers across the country threatened to burst badly strained digital dams. Though the scope and depth of the backlogs varied from region to region (with Pennsylvania by far the worst hit), few regions remained utterly unscathed by the bugs.

Even on the already dismal PR front, there were nightmares and horrors to come. On May 6, 1985, the IRS disclosed that a supervisor at the Austin, Texas, service center had ordered the destruction of several thousand letters from corporations requesting adjustments or protesting errors in their tax bills. Service center employees anonymously quoted in the *Wall Street Journal* blamed "a desperate attempt to reduce a rising backlog of complaints and to maintain a high production rating."

There were plenty of candidates to lay blame for the Great Tax Meltdown of 1985: the data processing executives at the national office who arrogantly yanked a woefully antiquated yet still functioning system and replaced it with an inadequately tested new one; a tightfisted Congress that for years had put off IRS requests for funds to update its data processing facilities, based on mounting concerns that an all-electronic system might not include adequate safeguards to maintain the security of taxpayer information; the IRS officials who failed to allay those concerns and neglected to address them or even acknowledge their legitimacy—even after having been put on notice that security issues were paramount not only on

Capitol Hill, but on Main Street as well. Unfortunately for American taxpayers, none of these culprits was ever held accountable for the massive IRS mishap of 1985.

SCURZE AND URPS

In mid-1984 Ray Keenan was the director of the Memphis Service Center when the IRS national office bestowed upon him and his highly automated facility the honor of test-driving a brand-new IRS data processing initiative: the Service Center Replacement System. SCRS (pronounced "scurze" by IRS insiders) was the primary operational component of the Equipment Replacement Program (ERP)—fondly called "urp," as in Wyatt. The ERP program mandated the installation of all-new equipment and software to replace the huge, still functioning, digital dinosaurs dating back to the "golden age" of the IRS in the mid-sixties. Many of these old machines still served as workhorses in the IRS's ten regional service centers.

"I was getting reports that the new system wouldn't work," a still-traumatized Ray Keenan told me five years after the fact, when I interviewed him about the debacle. "I lost patience and said to myself, 'This stuff costs a lot of money. Now if I went out and bought a new car and it didn't work, I'd take it back.' So I told the representatives from Sperry [the contractor] that I was running out of time and that I didn't understand why a brand-new machine shouldn't work."

In response to Keenan's mounting anxieties, Sperry compliantly pulled out the troublesome equipment and installed new machines—but the problems didn't go away. Computer runs took far longer than anticipated, causing backlogs (of the sort later to bedevil the Pennsylvania Boy Scouts) and in general foreshadowing to an astonishing degree practically every glitch and technical difficulty soon destined to produce the Tax Filing Season from Hell.

To make matters worse, the new Sperry machines were programmed in a computer language different from the original ones, so that IRS programmers were faced with rewriting more than one thousand internal software programs in an emergency mode—with not nearly enough slack cut into the schedule to iron out all the inevitable bugs.

Ray Keenan believed that, as field tester, his job was to provide Washington with regular updates on system failures as well as successes. He dutifully provided periodic progress (or lack thereof) reports on the growing scourge of Scurze to his superiors in Washington. Despite his less-than-glowing reports of problems with the equipment, senior data processing officials in the national office responded that they were working on "optimizing the system."

"I didn't want to contradict them," Keenan later explained, though he repeatedly advised them, "As of now, this system is not ready to roll." They might have been busily optimizing the system in Washington, but back in Memphis, the system was performing, at best, according to minimum specifications. Ray Keenan's reputation as a good tax collector was on the line, but if he didn't get word through to Washington, he believed his ass was grass. He was a reluctant Paul Revere riding through the night—but instead of looking for beacons, IRS executives in Washington covered their eyes.

At an annual conference of senior IRS executives in Washington, Ray Keenan courageously demanded a meeting with his Washington counterparts to discuss the underperforming computers. He was determined to get through to them or else go down trying. "I shouted and pounded my fist on the table," Keenan later told me, still noticeably astounded at his own temerity. "But all they wanted from me was assurances that the system would be operational by January 1985." In all good conscience, Keenan couldn't do that. Instead he raised the red flag and personally waved it in front of their faces, faces within months to be covered with egg. But, like the occasional corporate executive when faced by potential public humiliation, shame, or embarrassment, Ray Keenan's counterparts in Washington simply tuned out the bad news and stuck their heads in the sand.

Another deeply distressed veteran of the Great Memphis Meltdown would later confirm Keenan's version of events. "It's like a train you can see coming down the track and you're going to be run over by it, and you keep telling people and nobody hears you." Until it's too late.

Just as the Washington contingent had pushed for, the new SCRS computers went into national operation in January 1985. The results, as we have seen or experienced firsthand, were catastrophic. As desperate supervisors were confronted with destruction of unprocessed tax returns and harassed employees began frantically stuffing unprocessed returns into wastebaskets and ceiling ducts, barely a word emerged from the highly touted systems managers in Washington. But Congress heard the screams of outraged taxpayers. On the floor of the Senate, Pennsylvania senator John Heinz solemnly decreed the Philadelphia Service Center "a chamber of horrors," the bureaucratic equivalent of Madame Tussaud's.

"The IRS appears to be in total confusion," Heinz hollered, demanding an immediate investigation by the General Accounting Office of the entire disgraceful debacle. The GAO published a scathing report on the fiasco in a matter of months, which one Delaware newspaper colorfully described as "shredding Philly's IRS Office." The report blasted the Philadelphia Service Center for shoddy management, poorly trained employees, overloaded computer programs, and disgracefully high employee turnover. It was a nightmare. A snafu. And a perfect excuse to wring even more computer money out of a reluctant Congress, which is exactly what the IRS did.

WIDE OPEN SECRET

My own overt investigation of the Great Meltdown of 1985 resulted from an innocent bit of subterfuge. Rather than write a comprehensive, blow-by-blow account of the sorry saga of IRS computerization, I decided to keep a low profile and do an utterly noncontroversial history. The Memphis Service Center, which was to celebrate its twentieth anniversary in 1992, gave me the ultimate front: It asked me to compile a commemorative history of two decades of data-processing service for its anniversary celebration.

Couching the sordid saga of the dispute between Memphis and D.C. in the innocuous context of an official twentieth-anniversary history of the Memphis Service Center achieved a form of stealth advocacy. I even went so far as to bury Ray Keenan's blunt reflections on the deaf ear he was given in Washington in the center of the pamphlet, where I suspected none but the most dedicated IRS history buffs (or a few unfortunates afflicted with chronic insomnia) would ever stumble upon it.

Once I realized that one could trace the Filing Season from Hell to the national office's failure to heed Keenan's Cassandra-like warnings, I emphasized Ray Keenan's courage to deliver bad news rather than the national office's failure to avert the disaster.

What happened to Keenan in the end? This tough-talking, straight-shooting New Yorker—nicknamed "Brut" by his secretary in Memphis—ended his thirty-year IRS career alone in a small, windowless, stark office buried in a satellite building miles away from 1111 Constitution Avenue, playing an ill-defined oversight role in computer modernization. What better way to shoot the messenger?

BIG BROTHER?

Since average taxpayers worry about the IRS's becoming an Orwellian Big Brother, they may be relieved to know that no single system stores every piece of the puzzle yet. That's why, when you call the IRS to ask why it sent you some weird-looking form letter, one office may be totally unnerved by your questions, while another might be able to help you immediately. The trick is figuring out whom to call for what purpose. The IRS certainly doesn't make that easy.

After you seal your 1040 in an envelope and drop it in the mail (ideally by midnight on April 15) it goes to one of ten IRS service centers. These are huge processing facilities, the size of multiple football fields, where your return is removed from its envelope and sent into the maelstrom of the IRS processing system. Remarkably, despite all the cries of woe (and cries of wolf) from the IRS about its antiquated computers, those old monster machines still handle the task fairly well. Believe me, if they didn't, you'd hear about it—if not from the public or the press, from the IRS itself. Sometimes there's something to be said for keeping an old clunker going as long as possible.

If you attach a check made out to the IRS* to your 1040, it's pulled off immediately and sent down another chute to be deposited within twenty-four hours. In the meantime, your 1040 meanders along its own serpentine processing path. Data entry operators transcribe information from your tax returns into the IRS computers. If you could visit an IRS service center in late April, you'd see row upon row upon row of data transcribers furiously tapping keyboards to transcribe data from hundreds of millions of tax returns.

Surprisingly, only about 40 percent of the information you dutifully record on your 1040 is transcribed into the IRS computerized database of taxpayer information. That's yet another reason it's so hard for the IRS to answer your questions. Depending on whom you end up talking to, the person may have only a small piece of information about your return. It takes weeks to pull an actual paper copy of a tax return from a National Archives warehouse. If you need to know something about information from your return that wasn't keyed in to the IRS "master file" (the IRS term for the vast database encompassing all transcribed returns), you may just have to wait. That's why the IRS loves it when you can come up with your own copy of your 1040.

The survival long beyond its built-in obsolescence of this remarkably antiquated system is the main reason that it takes so long for your refund check to arrive in the mail. The General Accounting Office has castigated the processing of tax returns by the IRS as "slow, cumbersome and predisposed to error." Although the IRS has developed an electronic filing program so that you can avoid the long line of tax returns in the service center "pipeline," electronic filing is little more than a costly novelty to the taxpayer, used primarily by the IRS as a public relations tool.

Problems with fraud in the electronic filing program have caused the IRS to take a second and a third look at its rapid expansion of this highly touted tax filing innovation. Experiments with telephone and home computer filing are under way, but years from widespread

---

*Actually, the IRS asks that you make your check out to the Internal Revenue Service rather than the IRS to avoid the possibility of miscreant employees altering IRS into MRS and cashing your tax payment check.

availability and acceptance. Considering the state of information technology in the nineties, the IRS is woefully behind the power curve. When most of our other financial transactions are efficiently automated and information about our credit and other accounts is available with a simple phone call, the IRS looks more and more like a dinosaur stumbling through the Renaissance.

THE GREAT IRS

It wasn't always this way. When computers were young and the IRS was in the glory years of the "great IRS," the merging of tax processing with emerging technology was carried out with an astounding degree of panache. In the sixties the IRS rightly earned a reputation as a federal agency at the head of the pack in the efficient use of computers. What went wrong between the 1960s and the 1990s is a story of bad decisions, pigheadedness, bad timing, sheer stupidity, and advancing entropy.

Processing millions of tax returns has never been an easy job. As far back as 1918, a mere five years after the modern income tax era began, IRS Commissioner Daniel Roper reported that the name, address, and amount of tax from each taxpayer had to be recorded seven times for various parts of the processing operations. Roper proudly announced an innovation that year to dramatically speed up processing operations. Installation of machinery for "duplication of records by mechanical means" allowed the IRS to print stencils at the rate of one hundred per minute.

New developments in technology were not overlooked by the IRS. In 1927 Commissioner David Blair announced the purchase of sixteen folding-and-sorting machines. This eliminated much work done by hand by IRS clerks. Blair boasted that these new machines could accomplish in seven hours what three employees could do in the same period.

It wasn't until the dramatic broadening of the tax base during World War II that the IRS found itself desperate for some way to speed up the processing. The sheer number of returns was staggering, having increased from a mere 6.4 million returns in 1939 to more than 48 million returns by 1945. The income tax had graduated from a "class" tax to a "mass" tax. By 1945 just about every wage earner in the country was sending a 1040 to the tax collector.

The IRS conducted experiments in offices around the country, using tabulating and punch card equipment. In dramatic contrast to its overblown predictions of the 1980s and 1990s, the IRS was surprisingly cautious in taking its first stumbling steps toward automation. The 1950 IRS annual report reflected this caution in the statement, "Some of the newer types of mechanical equipment tested were found unsuitable—while others, still in the trial stage, give preliminary indication of increased production."

Compare this to the bold proclamation of the 1984 IRS annual report, which predicted that "within the next five to ten years we will have a totally redesigned tax administration system. . . . Paper tax returns will largely be a thing of the past." More than ten years have passed since that bright shining statement, and the IRS is still clunking along with the same outmoded, obsolete data processing technology. Somewhere in the years between the cautious optimism of 1950 and the outrageous arrogance of 1984 lies the mystery of what went wrong with the IRS. We are nowhere near the day when we will see a paperless tax system. And as Congressman Jim Lightfoot pounds the bully pulpit in distress, we remain billions of dollars poorer as a nation.

The fifties and sixties truly were the good old days for the IRS. With the massive increase in the number of tax returns during World War II, sometimes it took as long as a full year for the IRS to issue refunds. But by 1952, refunds were issued in about a month, faster than today's standard tax return processing. Tax returns were due on March 15 and taxpayers generally delivered them in person or mailed them to their local tax office. All IRS work related to tax returns, whether it was reviewing the 1040s for accuracy, auditing returns, collecting unpaid taxes, or answering questions from taxpayers, was handled in local tax offices. Back then, the IRS offered one-stop service.

The first large-scale experiment with automated processing came in 1955 when 1040A returns from ten district offices in the Midwest were bundled and shipped to Kansas City for centralized handling. The following year, what was then called the Processing Branch was renamed the Midwest Service Center in the Kansas City IRS office. By 1957 three service centers were processing tax returns from twenty-nine states with large volume-tabulating equipment.

By 1959 the IRS had developed a broad-based plan to automate all tax return processing. The plan called for removing the job from local tax offices and centralizing it in seven service centers around the country. Each service center would be filled with the new modern computers just becoming widely available. A "national computer center" in West Virginia would serve as the central hub for all accounts. In February the IRS submitted its plan to Congress, which approved the whole concept four months later.

Even apocalyptic visions of the Orwellian world of *1984* couldn't derail the IRS's all-systems-go effort to centralize its tax return processing. In 1962 *Time* magazine reported in an April Tax Week issue that "the IRS has in the works a system calculated to scare the daylights out of every taxpayer in the land." *Business Week* covered the same story, adopting a similarly paranoid tone, calling the new IRS computer "the net that will eventually pull in many big and little taxpayers who are now slipping through the relatively crude net of the IRS."

Despite these dire warnings about the growth of an omniscient, centralized federal bureaucracy, armed with state-of-the-art computers capable of tabulating and sorting just about every bit of available information about every United States citizen, most Americans accepted the notion of centralized filing. Nobody noticed any difference in their routine other than having to write their Social Security number on their tax return for the first time.

Mortimer Caplin, commissioner during the first years of implementation of the automated system, later attributed its surprising success to a combination of positive social factors. "There was an undercurrent of respect and cooperation in the country. We had budgetary support. All these things were coming together. The economy started turning around. We were polite to taxpayers, encouraging our agents to go out into the schools and become part of the community."

The origins of the mess the IRS finds itself in today can be traced back to 1967, the first year the original computer system went into nationwide operation. Just as it put the finishing touches on its masterpiece of automation, the IRS announced grandiose plans for a "long range study of the Data Processing System to meet the needs of the Seventies." That same study, under a different name and after many generations of IRS and congressional leadership have come and gone, is still under way today, while its conclusions remain as vague and intangible as ever.

The crying needs of the seventies have evolved into the desperate needs of the twenty-first century, yet the IRS is still trying to figure out how to improve its original system. The early effort was dubbed "System of the Seventies" and was envisioned as a dramatic step forward from the still functional system of the sixties, expected to be obsolete in a few years. Perhaps the success of that first effort went to the IRS's head. In retrospect, there may not have been a crying need to make major changes to the system that had just been installed to such fanfare. In fact, to the credit of the IRS computer geeks of the late fifties and early sixties, that original system still chunks along pretty well today. IRS executives don't seem to grasp the inanity of pleading "the sky is falling" when begging for more money to buy newer, sleeker, faster systems, and at the same time proudly proclaiming that they've concluded yet another "successful filing season" remarkably devoid of major glitches and crashes.

But why stop at centralizing taxpayer accounts in one large computer center when you're on a roll? The new plan shifted gears, calling for decentralizing account maintenance to seven service centers. As an afterthought the IRS added plans to build three more service centers to bring the total to ten by 1972.

In 1969 the IRS teamed up with MITRE Corporation to design the specifications for this spanking new "System of the Seventies." But with the decade itself drawing fast upon them, the System of the Seventies was hastily renamed the Tax Administration System, or TAS for short. The IRS took six years to refine and present the TAS concept before the Office of Management and Budget put its stamp of approval on TAS in September 1975. TAS carried a price tag of $649 million and a promise of being in full operation by 1982. But TAS was never to be.

The IRS presented its concept for TAS to Congress in 1976. Bad timing. The country was still reeling from Watergate, and the IRS was still being hounded to come clean on its dubious course of action during the Nixon years. Watergate had exposed the IRS as an agency capable of initiating politically-inspired audits, a realization that some say permanently tarnished its reputation as an agency "above" political hanky-panky.

The main problem with totally upgrading the IRS computer systems, from the nation's perspective, was that the IRS had already demonstrated its incapacity to fully insulate itself from the hurly-burly of political infighting. With public trust in the IRS plummeting, selling increased computer capabilities so that IRS employees would have faster and easier access to taxpayer account information was foolhardy. Plain dumb may be a better description.

In a classic duck-heads-and-run maneuver, Congress dilly-dallied on its decision to fund TAS until the IRS could come up with better arguments for needing this massive new system, with all its bells and whistles. Congress finessed its delay by asking the IRS to provide "a more refined cost/benefit analysis," which really meant, in time-honored Beltway parlance, "Come back next year, when the heat will be off."

Congressional oversight committees tormented the needy IRS officials coming to Capitol Hill with all sorts of awkward questions regarding its plans to digitize information on its tax returns. Did the IRS plan to computerize each taxpayer's religious affiliation based on charitable deductions? Did the IRS plan to computerize medical data from medical expense deductions? Did the IRS plan to computerize membership in unions or other organizations off individual tax returns?

Even though the IRS strongly denied plans to extract this type of information from every tax return, the IRS neither appeased nor convinced Congress. In 1977 the Office of Technology Assessment issued a report on TAS that noted simply that the availability of increased computerized capabilities might "make the temptation to misuse the information irresistible, or worse, its actual use undetectable." Case closed.

Basic distrust of the IRS's ability to handle increased computer capabilities properly, coupled with the IRS's utter failure to demonstrate a genuine need for enhanced capabilities, caused Congress to submerge the agency's grand plans for TAS in 1978. Stripped of its grandiose dreams, a humbled IRS began to slouch to its worst reputation so that, nearly twenty years later, a 1996 House Appropriations Committee member denounced repeated funding requests for IRS computer programs as a classic case of "throwing money down a rat hole."

In the wake of the 1978 TAS debacle, the IRS began promoting its computer improvement program under a new name: the Equipment Replacement and Enhancement Program, or EREP for short. The word "tax" was nowhere in the promotional materials touting this zealous project. Perhaps the IRS thought it could fool Congress by leaving out the dread "t-word." But the term "enhancement" tipped off IRS-bashers: The IRS was still getting too big for its britches. Congress informed IRS that it could only replace worn-out machines. No enhancement would be allowed.

The Equipment Replacement and Enhancement Program was soon truncated to the Equipment Replacement Program, or ERP, of which the SCRS (Service Center Replacement System) that crashed in 1985 was a key component. By 1983, about midway through the ERP, the IRS announced yet a new twist, which it self-styled the Tax Systems Redesign, or TSR. The price tag was estimated at $225 million. The IRS told Congress it could complete the program within eight years of program approval and funding. IRS honchos figured enough time had gone by since Watergate to make it safe to beg again for more and newer computers.

While visions of Tax Systems Redesign danced feverishly in IRS programmers' heads, they forged ahead with SCRS—the good old Service Center Replacement System. The setbacks of the seventies had left the IRS determined to prove it could pull off a computer modernization program without endangering the tax system. It wanted to bring SCRS in on time and within budget. Executives in Washington, D.C., wanted SCRS to be operational on schedule, no matter what. The January 1985 deadline became the value driver for the SCRS program.

In evaluating what went wrong with SCRS during the Filing Season from Hell, the General Accounting Office claimed the IRS "took actions inconsistent with Congressional and Office of Management and Budget guidance and with its own system sizing assumptions." Determined to do something right, the IRS did just about everything wrong. By focusing on meeting the January 1985 deadline above all else, the IRS rained trouble upon itself.

From the depths of 1978 to the sloughs of 1985—the year of the Great Meltdown—the IRS had been desperately seeking new ways to convince an increasingly stubborn Congress that it needed more computers, more money for more computers, and more staff to run more computers. Luckily for the IRS, the bad press on the Tax Filing Season from Hell turned Congress around. Elected officials don't like irate calls, lots of them, from constituents demanding action. Giving more goodies to the IRS probably wasn't what voters had in mind.

During the flush decade that followed the Tax Filing Season from Hell, Congress tried to make sure that it would "never happen again" by pumping money into the IRS, which the IRS used to buy lots of plans, lots of consultants, lots of new employees, lots of new equipment. What it didn't end up buying was a new tax processing system good enough to replace the original sixties system.

In the late eighties, IRS appearances before congressional committees to ask for money for Tax Systems Redesign projects became a showcase of computer projects—AUR, ACI, ICS, AES, FAISR, IMS, ALSS, among others—all complete with fancy new jobs and job titles. The IRS even concocted the new post of assistant commissioner for information systems development to manage the growing menu of computer programs. These were the "projects" that my first supervisor, Orion, wanted me to document when I arrived at the IRS in the fall of 1988.

The rhetoric began to flow freely with the fast funds from Congress that very year. The 1988 IRS annual report claimed that the new computer system—whatever it was called—would be "flexible and easier to modify so that it can be updated periodically without having to change the entire system." Much less its name. "ISD is trying to standardize the components or 'building blocks' of the system. If the blocks are basically the same, they can be interchanged or rearranged to form different structures without causing major changes to the function of the system as a whole." Say what?

No one in Congress knew then that the many IRS projects were incompatible systems, each designed independently to meet the needs of different factions within the far-flung organization. IRS auditors wanted their own computer system. So did the collection officers. And management. And if the senior managers got their own system, then by God the lawyers wanted one too. The IRS computer chefs tried to please everyone, and so everyone had his own decentralized computer project.

In 1989 *Financial World* magazine reported that "after three failed attempts and $70 million, IRS officials have finally settled on a long-range program for overhauling the tax information system." The article revealed that after ten years of debugging and deglitching, Tax Systems Redesign was "still in the embryonic stage" and would reach a probable cost of $4 billion over the next decade.

By 1990 the IRS changed the name of its program again, this time from TSR to TSM, from "Redesign" to "Modernization," yet the computer skeptics were growing weary of the same old IRS tune sung with new words. To appear interested in outside feedback, the IRS humbly asked the National Research Council to review and analyze the feasibility of its plans. The IRS also began pumping out a series of hefty documents with impressive titles, including one released in 1991 called a Draft Master Plan for Tax Systems Modernization. Unfortunately, the report preparers forgot to pay even lip service to protecting the privacy and security of tax returns. Big oversight. Privacy issues—the hottest of hot buttons as far as the public was concerned—had been simply ignored altogether.

The General Accounting Office quickly pointed out the omission, noting that "concerns over security of taxpayer information helped doom an earlier attempt by the IRS to modernize its systems" and suggested that the IRS consider this issue for the next version of this document. How the IRS, which had already struggled for more than a decade to upgrade its computers, could forget or disregard the very issue that brought down its earlier efforts is nothing less than mind-boggling.

By 1992 the IRS had whipped up a Final Design Master Plan, which this time included a section on the Privacy and Security of Tax

Information. The price tag for Tax Systems Modernization had by then swollen to a staggering $8 billion. Still, the IRS blandly assured Congress that all systems would be go by the year 2001.

At one point an IRS spokesperson actually compared TSM to the effort expended by the nation in putting a man on the moon. What the spokesman missed in drawing this preposterous analogy was the salient fact that the United States did, in fact, succeed in putting a man on the moon. The IRS, for its part, had not succeeded in drastically or dramatically improving on the tax information system installed during the glory years of "the great IRS" thirty years earlier. While NASA actually succeeded in at least taking "one small step for a man, one giant leap for mankind," IRS has been too busy scrambling in different directions to take many small steps, let alone leaps.

Admittedly, the IRS tried. The nineties unfolded as the decade of myriad reports: new Technical Systems Architecture, a Security Architecture, a Disaster Recovery Plan, and a Near Term Transition Reference Report. Descriptions of an emerging "business vision," short on substantial detail and long on trendy management buzzwords, filled attractive four-color brochures published to promote the IRS and its slick new computer system.

By 1992, CFOL, TIES, DPS, SCRIPS, AICS, EF, and TRIS had mutated into two species of projects, an "interim" strain containing ACI, AICS, AUR, CHEXS, CASE, CFOL, ICS, SCRIPS, SERP, TSIS, TRIS, and TIES, and a second, "long-term" strain containing CPS, CMS, CAPS, DPS, EMS, and WMS.* To fund both strains, Congress would have to shell out $23 billion. IRS to Congress: Are you buying? The IRS pushed the implementation date to 2008, well ahead of the average congressman's "long-term" vision, and well past his or her expected tenure in Congress.

---

*ACI (Automated Criminal Investigation); AICS (Automated Inventory Control System); AUR (Automated Underreporter); CHEXS (Check Handling Enhancement Expert System); CASE (Counsel Automated Systems Environment); CFOL (Corporate Files On Line); ICS (Integrated Collection System); SCRIPS (Service Center Recognition/Image Processing System); SERP (Service Electronic Research Project); TSIS (Taxpayer Service Integrated System); TIES (Totally Integrated Exam System); CPS (Case Processing System); CMS (Corporate Systems Modernization); CAPS (Corporate Account Processing System); DPS (Document Processing System); EMS (Electronic Management System); WMS (Worldwide Management System); EF (Electronic Filing); MIA (Mirror Image Acquisition); ALSS (Automated Litigation Support System); OCRSR (Optical Character Reader System Replacement); TSAW (Taxpayer Service Advanced Workstation).

One IRS information system analyst I interviewed described this methodology as a classic case of "taking a piece of this one and a piece of that one and saying it's something new and different so you show progress. When projects fail, they're combined with others or simply renamed. One year you have XYZ and ABC programs. The next year you announce the MNO project, which features elements of XYZ and ABC. The next year you announce a new program, FGH, which has parts of MNO, XYZ, ABC, and maybe something new. They never have to do what they originally set out to do. It's a shell game."

And a pretty costly shell game at that. The General Accounting Office reported in 1993 that IRS efforts to improve its computer systems since 1988, just five years, had already cost $831 million. But a bigger problem was that the IRS could account for only $530 million of the total. What happened to the remaining $301 million was something of a mystery. The IRS could pinpoint $240 million as spent on the "interim" projects and $290 million on its "long-term" projects. The IRS couldn't explain the missing millions. The General Accounting Office couldn't find it. Surely the answer lurked in the IRS records, right? What records?

In early 1993 the General Accounting Office began prancing around a "difficult and sensitive issue that has been with us since the early days of Tax Systems Modernization," that of management competence in IRS computer modernization efforts. How qualified were "career" IRS employees to handle a multibillion-dollar advanced technology acquisition? some began to ask indirectly. In testimony before the House Committee on Appropriations, the GAO finally came out and said it: "the evidence points to the need for stronger Tax Systems Modernization technical management."

GAO urged the IRS to create yet another new position for a senior executive who would be solely responsible for directing this overall, broad-based modernization effort. Claiming it could not find anyone outside the agency willing to take on this awesome responsibility (which paid well over $100,000 in salary), the IRS once again elevated one of its own inner circle to the new position and gave him the title "Modernization Executive." Larry Westfall brought nearly thirty years of IRS loyalty to the job. With a business degree from

Indiana State University, Westfall joined the IRS in 1963 immediately after finishing school. His early IRS background was in administration and personnel. Westfall worked his way up through the system, ending up as the director of the IRS Austin Service Center before returning to the IRS headquarters in 1991 to work with Tax Systems Modernization. While he had three decades of IRS experience, Westfall was not an expert in the implementation of advanced technology. He was an IRS bureaucrat.

The IRS's own testimony before Congress during the early nineties presented an unsurprisingly rosier picture than the GAO's, one that promised to realize massive benefits in the very near future—as long as Congress continued to feed it with enough funds. In March 1993 Dep. Comm. Michael Dolan—yes, the same Mike Dolan whose farewell pizza party I attended on my first day as an IRS historian in 1988—returned to Washington to take up the highest career position at the IRS. Dolan proudly informed the House Ways and Means Committee that the IRS had just awarded a contract worth nearly $90 million for something called SCRIPS (Service Center Recognition/Image Processing System) along with a second contract for a "Federally Funded Research and Development Center" valued at nearly $80 million—I particularly liked the "federally funded" appellative. Part of the latter procurement would cover a "Tax Systems Modernization Institute" to provide "high level technical assessment, strategic planning, and acquisition support" for the modernization program.

Mike Dolan's Service Center Recognition/Image Processing System was designed to provide an "interim" system between the keypunching technology of the sixties and a more pie-in-the-sky, long-range planning effort formally denominated the Document Processing System, or DPS. But within two years of Dolan's grandiose pronouncement, SCRIPS was in jeopardy, beset by problems privately attributed by one IRS executive to software that was neither sophisticated nor sturdy enough to handle the large workload presented by the tax processing job. As problems with SCRIPS gradually surfaced, the IRS continued to press forward with its rosy predictions and scenarios, hoping to keep Congress and the public in the dark about the blood running in the gutters behind the scenes.

One can almost imagine them handing out rose-colored glasses to Congress before beginning each presentation on the "progress" of Tax Systems Modernization.

At the ribbon-cutting ceremony for a SCRIPS pilot project at the Cincinnati Service Center on January 11, 1994, IRS Commissioner Margaret Richardson proudly proclaimed that "with the start of the SCRIPS pilot today we can truly say that Tax Systems Modernization is off the drawing board and a reality." The commissioner duly predicted that the SCRIPS and DPS programs would be combined and operational by the year 2000.

At long last, the heady days of touting future successes to obscure current troubles were numbered. On February 28, 1994, the IRS awarded a fifteen-year contract valued at $11.3 billion for DPS—the all-new, highly promoted Document Processing System—and boldly predicted that DPS would be installed in all processing centers by 1996 "if testing goes well."

It must not have. 1996 has come and gone. The IRS did not announce the setbacks by holding a press conference, or issuing a bold, proud pronouncement. Instead it began to wind down the project, scale back efforts, and backpedal quietly, far less dramatically.

Just as old-style Kremlinologists could detect subtle shifts in the internal balance of Soviet power by carefully analyzing May Day photographs, so too can we pick up internal shifts in IRS plans by studying its internal documents, at least those few that remain intact. In an employee newsletter published in early 1995, the service candidly conceded—to its own people, of course—that "while the IRS aims to be on the leading edge of technology, our mission leaves no room for unnecessary risks. Because our plans for changing the way we process tax returns involve many risks, we've decided to minimize them by adding an extra testing phase to the DPS development schedule." Translation: DPS has been back-burnered, perhaps permanently.

One IRS employee, whose project stumbled through the Three Stooges years, chuckles when he hears the telltale words "high level" from "high-level" IRS officials, like many a middle manager in the corporate world.

"If they're looking to create a new project, they always claim to be doing it at a 'high level,'" he says. "That way, the employees in the middle are never responsible for meeting program milestones, because it's being done at a 'high level.' They explain what a new program will do at this 'high level,' but never explain how they're going to get there."

Despite these farcical about-face fandangos, the IRS still appears utterly oblivious to the obvious: The American public is becoming more, not less, concerned about safeguarding personal privacy in the emerging high-technology information age. A recent *USA Today* "Snapshot" survey compared the percentage of Americans who professed to be "very concerned" about privacy issues in 1977 and 1993. In 1977, some 25 percent of those surveyed indicated they were "very concerned." By 1993 the number of techno-anxious Americans had more than doubled, to 53 percent.

It wasn't so long ago—1978—that the IRS's first fledgling computer modernization effort went down in flames because of doubts about the IRS's ability to protect taxpayer information. Today, though more than twice as many Americans profess to be "very concerned" about precisely this issue, IRS continues to ignore its own history. If American citizens have a short memory, then the IRS appears to have the attention span of a gnat.

ELECTRONIC FILING (EF): BOON OR BOONDOGGLE?

For one brief, shining moment in the troubled history of IRS computerization, one program stands out as, if not an unqualified success, at least tangible evidence of progress: electronic filing of tax returns. When electronic filing began back in 1985, the IRS didn't consider it part of the overall Tax Systems Modernization effort because it emerged from the Taxpayer Service office. Once the IRS belatedly realized that electronic filing was its one promotable success story, the system became a "cornerstone" of TSM.

Though the early history of electronic filing remains frustratingly foggy because of—surprise—very few written records of early planning sessions, what little evidence has survived strongly suggests that the concept sprang from the increasingly intimate bond between the IRS and the tax practitioner community. In other words, EF came to life as both an IRS program and a potential profit center for the ever-burgeoning tax preparation industry.

H&R Block, the largest single tax preparation "practitioner," has also been the largest single transmitter (and proponent) of electronic tax returns since the program's inception. Though rival tax preparers and accountants have been quick to log on, if only to realize the positive economic benefits of charging their customers for the "convenience" of offering electronic tax filing, the convenience is mainly the IRS's and the tax preparers'.

When a Washington journalist requested background documents on electronic filing through a Freedom of Information Act (FOIA) request, the IRS replied that it could not find any records relating to the inception of electronic filing. The IRS has no records about its electronic filing program? Of course not—since for decades the agency has routinely "disappeared" its records.

The disconcertingly close connection between the IRS and the tax practitioner community is nowhere more evident than in the sudden promotional push behind electronic filing. As initially developed, electronic filing forced a financial link between taxpayers and tax practitioners that never existed before. When the program began, the only way to electronically file a 1040 was to pay a private tax preparer for the privilege. Never before in the history of the tax system had the IRS required taxpayers to use private tax preparers to take advantage of one of "its" programs. Which strongly suggests that its belated adoption as an "IRS" program, part of the overhauled TSM, is nothing more than a clever sham.

If the IRS had taken a bit more time in the early 1980s to think through the concept of electronic filing, it might have developed an electronic filing program that gave taxpayers an option of filing on their home computers, visiting local IRS offices to file on government computers, or, if they desired, hiring someone to do it for them. The IRS now struggles to develop these options itself, but more than a decade after launching the program—which is more than enough time for taxpayers to associate electronic filing with H&R Block and other paid tax practitioners and for savvy computer firms to produce their own tax prep products. During that window of opportunity lost to the IRS, the tax preparers successfully snared their market niche.

Initial projections for the growth of electronic filing followed the overly optimistic pattern of previous rosy IRS projections. The 1992 IRS annual report predicted that the IRS would receive 100 million electronically filed returns by the year 2000, or about 75 percent of all returns filed. By the end of 1993 the commissioner quietly downgraded that estimate to 80 million electronically filed returns. But for even this lower projection to stay on track requires the IRS to believe in miracles. From a starting point of about twenty-five thousand electronically filed returns in 1985, ten years later the IRS was up to 12 million returns. But the growth rate had slowed. In fact, it represented a marked decrease from both 1993 and 1994, when the IRS received 12.3 million and 13.5 million returns filed electronically. Whatever the number, it's a far cry from the boldly projected 100 million or even 80 million returns projected just a few years ago.

No one in the IRS seems prepared to ask whether most American taxpayers feel comfortable with electronic filing. While some people might view filing their tax returns electronically as an innovation, the vast majority of willing taxpayers are hardly high-techies. Those who remain wary about the IRS's ability to protect their paper tax return may not be quite so quick to merge onto the electronic filing superhighway. My own CPA refuses to offer electronic filing to his clients, failing to see any advantage in asking his clients to pay an additional fee to save a few weeks in receiving their refund.

In reality, the sole tangible advantage to filing a tax return electronically is receiving your refund slightly faster. If you file a paper return early in the filing season, the difference may be only a few weeks. Many taxpayers legitimately ask themselves whether it's worth paying an additional fee to earn a few extra weeks of interest payments on their money. In the case of the average tax return, the fee to file electronically is far greater than any potential interest earnings. The IRS touts the fact that a taxpayer receives an acknowledgment that his or her return has been "received and accepted" as an additional advantage of electronic filing. But for years, taxpayers have been putting a postage stamp on an envelope, dropping their tax returns in a mailbox, and waiting for their refunds without this "advantage." If they wanted or needed such an assurance, they mailed their 1040 with a return receipt attached, which costs a few bucks at the post office, far less than the electronic filing fee.

The sad fact is that most electronically filed returns originate with taxpayers who can scarcely afford to pay the price of electronic filing—those with incomes low enough to file exceedingly simple tax returns, 1040As and 1040EZs. They've been snared by the electronic filing web due to well-financed marketing campaigns mounted by the tax practitioner community. Perhaps the most seductive form of inducement has been the introduction of "refund anticipation loans" (RALs) by tax practitioners, which only intensified their marketing of electronic filing.

When a taxpayer applies for a Refund Anticipation Loan from say, H&R Block, he or she can receive a loan against an "anticipated" refund in a matter of days, as opposed to weeks. Of course, in addition to charging the fee for electronic filing, there is an RAL fee on top of that, ranging from $20 to $60, depending on the amount of your refund. That can bring the amount you have to fork over for the privilege of getting your tax refund quickly—that's money you've already paid to the government, on which you've earned no interest—up into the $100 range. You'd better have a loan shark breathing down your neck to justify spending that kind of money.

The RAL was hardly the financial innovation that the IRS anticipated when it launched electronic filing. But anyone with even a remote grasp of American business ingenuity could have predicted that new twist. One can't really fault the practitioners for finding a new business opportunity and running with it. That's the American entrepreneurial spirit at work. If the blame lies with any particular party, it lies with the IRS for not developing its electronic filing program as a stand-alone program, capable of functioning independently of the practitioner community.

The increase in RAL fees, plus all those new customers eager to file "with a push of a button," opened up new opportunities for tax fraud. In the eighties the IRS gave remarkably little thought to this pesky problem. Not until 1990—five years after the program was launched—did the IRS try to grasp the dimensions of this burgeoning underground industry. It hired Harvard University criminologist Dr. Malcolm Sparrow, an expert in tracking credit card fraud, to prepare a report on electronic filing fraud. Sparrow's report, submitted in late 1993, estimated the cost of electronic filing fraud at between $5 billion and $9 billion per year in lost revenue.

The IRS had previously estimated the cost of electronic fraud in the $1 billion range. Sparrow also revealed that 98 percent of the fraud schemes he uncovered involved tax returns claiming the earned income tax credit, a special program to provide low-income taxpayers with a refund of up to $3,560 based on their earnings and family size. He warned of the potential for ever larger problems with tax compliance, fearing that if taxpayers see the IRS as unable to catch all these people collecting fraudulent refunds, willingness to comply with the tax laws would decline.

Inevitably, Congress began pressuring the IRS to "do something" about the fraud problem. And so, without bothering to consult or inform the tax practitioner community, the IRS developed and implemented a "Revenue Protection Strategy" for the 1995 filing season. This strategy was to stop fraudulent refunds before they landed in taxpayers' hands. Although one IRS employee defended the IRS action by claiming that "we told the practitioners to be sure that Social Security numbers were correct," she admits that the IRS never alerted practitioners that any additional emphasis was going to be placed on refund fraud in 1995. "We were under fire for fraudulent returns," she maintains. "We had to do something."

The IRS waited well into the filing season to drop this noisome bomb on the tax practitioner community. On February 3, 1995, the IRS announced that it was giving extra scrutiny to all returns filed electronically that claimed the earned income tax credit. This meant that refunds from these tax returns, mostly from low-income taxpayers (those who needed their refunds most desperately), would inevitably be delayed—possibly even longer than if they had filed a paper return in the first place. Taxpayers with little money to begin with paid an extra fee to get their money faster, only to find their money held back while the IRS checked for fraud.

The most significant step the IRS took in its Revenue Protection Strategy was to eliminate the "direct deposit indicator" or DDI for electronically filed returns. The DDI was a computerized acknowledgment that let practitioners know whether their clients had any prior tax problems or outstanding student loans or child support obligations that would require the government to withhold their refund. Without the DDI, tax preparers had no way of knowing whether their customers were deadbeats and whether their refunds would come through. And so issuing customers a loan based on an anticipated refund became risky business for the practitioners because the lender would ultimately be held responsible for returning the "loaned" refund money to the IRS if it was discovered that the taxpayer was not eligible for the claimed refund.

Beneficial Corporation (one of the nation's leading issuers of Refund Anticipation Loans) was so distraught at being sandbagged by the IRS that it filed suit against the agency, claiming that more than $300 million of its funds had been put at risk because of an irresponsible IRS action. Though Beneficial dropped its suit when the IRS promised to make changes before the 1996 filing season, the company made its point. The IRS had burned it and its competitors; nobody was pleased. The IRS needed the electronic returns filed by Beneficial and other large practitioners to keep its numbers up, so that it wouldn't lose support for the one program it could even remotely term a success.

Ironically, the new Revenue Protection Strategy was successful in reducing electronic filing fraud. A fair number of dependents mysteriously vanished when Social Security numbers were more closely checked. Fraudulent tax preparers were more effectively screened through fingerprint and criminal record checks, a new initiative at the IRS. But the agency's unshakable belief that it must keep all such "sensitive" information inside the agency hopelessly undermined any positive publicity it might have reaped from the success of its Revenue Protection Program. The success came after the damage had been done.

In 1995—the same year that a New York City tax expert happened to notice that the cover of an IRS publication for tax practitioners referred to "practitioners" as "practioners"—the IRS boldly announced that it was working on a strategic and marketing plan for its electronic filing program, something it had never done before. What for-profit business would put a program in operation for ten years and develop a marketing plan only after major problems arose? Ten years later?

If the IRS didn't have enough problems of its own making, another huge computerization problem looms just around the bend. It is a problem that faces government and private industry computer systems alike—the need to reprogram systems to adjust to the turn of the century, the year 2000—but is even more critical at the IRS because of the tax system's dependence on very specific dates. In the fall of 1996, the *Los Angeles Times* reported that a potential breakdown of the tax processing system lay ahead if the IRS did not take immediate action to confront this dilemma. The reporter wrote, "A computer meltdown at the IRS would ripple through the rest of the government and through the economy" and "will throw the government's financial operations into chaos." Even Arthur Gross, the latest in a string of executives hired to manage the IRS computer modernization effort admitted, "A failure would mean a major disabling of the Internal Revenue Service." By late 1996, the IRS had surveyed what it would take to implement the necessary conversion by January 1, 1999, in just one of its four major groups of software. For just that single group, the IRS says it will take 1,800 staff years, the equivalent of nine hundred people working full time for the next few years. It's time for the IRS to take off its rose-colored glasses and get to work.

A "high-level" IRS computer executive I interviewed sums up the frustrating thirty-year effort of the IRS to modernize its data processing systems in the following words: "The history of tax systems modernization is a history of bravado and attack—promising what you can't hope to deliver and attacking what you promised when it doesn't work."

Another employee, frustrated and appalled by IRS wastefulness, bitterly explained: "The sad thing is that if the thing had been managed properly, we might not have had all those whistles and bells, but maybe we would have had a workable system."

Don Curtis, who often enjoyed putting a classical spin on these things, once compared the IRS's bumbling efforts to correct its own mistakes and clean up its own blunders to Hercules cleaning up the Augean stables. To complete this classical analogy, I'd as soon compare the IRS effort to tango into the Information Age to Sisyphus pushing that stone up the hill, only to see it roll back down, again and again, into an absurd eternity.

4

WATERGATE

IRS Secret History, Volume II

In the spring of 1989, some six months into my seven-year tenure at the IRS, I was standing in the agency's crowded, chaotic Disclosure office, hoping for some guidance on how best to handle an FOIA (Freedom of Information Act) request when a man in his mid-fifties approached me with a pensive look on his face. His opening remark was straightforward: "You look kind of confused, is there something I can help you with?"

After recovering from my shock at being so cordially received by anyone in that slum of an office, I introduced myself.

"Oh, so *you're* the new historian," he said with a welcoming wink, and a smile that told me that he must be one of the good guys. By "good guys," I mean merely those IRS staffers who didn't feel threatened by finding a certified past-recorder in their midst.

"I'm Earl Klema," the man said, reaching out to shake my hand with a warm, firm grip, "I'm deputy director around here."

For the record, Earl Klema looks just like what he is: a guy from the Bronx. His disheveled clothes and somewhat absent demeanor reminded me of Detective Colombo, right down to the crafty, squinty eyes, the charming smile, and a disarmingly New York-ish way of posing a seemingly innocent—or deceptively dumb—question.

"Why don't you come back to my office?" Earl offered, "and I'll see if I can track down what you need on the phone."

We made our way through the din of Disclosure's outer office, which gave me a brief chance to reflect on how deeply most federal agencies resent having to respond to so-called Foya (FOIA) requests. To be truly responsive seems always to involve painstaking searches through mounds of records, which takes time, money, and even—if the documents in question ever do see the light of day—a potentially high toll in PR terms for the agency concerned. There's not much incentive for federal agencies to cooperate fully with FOIA requests, or to make doing so a high priority. Still, it's the law.

But nothing in my experience in handling FOIA requests at the Defense Department prepared me for the level of contempt with which the IRS held its congressionally mandated duty in this regard. It clearly took out its frustrations on its own harried Disclosure staff.

Earl Klema's minions sat squeezed like sardines into cubicles so small their swivel chairs could barely swivel. To my relief (since we were both hoping to squeeze in there), Earl Klema's personal domain was, by comparison, like the captain's quarters on an aircraft carrier. Two bored-looking secretaries occupied a spacious reception area, through which Klema quickly ushered me, making a point of shutting his office door behind us.

Once comfortably ensconced in his executive-style high-backed chair, Earl had more than enough room to swivel. He could have rolled back and forth and ricocheted off the walls, for all anyone outside would have known—or cared. He even had room to spare for a few bookshelves, which held weighty works of greater substance than volumes of the tax code, with which many IRS executives chose to garnish their shelves, hoping to achieve that appropriately sober "executive" decor.

Earl had a few history books, a few books on government, a few books on current affairs. Here was a man, I thought, who'd miraculously retained a capacity for independent thinking despite his numerous years at the agency. Without any further ado, he launched into an entertaining reminiscence of a multidecade career as a revenue agent during the glory years of the "great IRS," back in the mid-sixties.

Earl had earned his federal stripes working in the trenches, along with the tough characters who seize cars and other property in lieu of tax payments, reputedly at the drop of a hat. Within those few minutes of idle chitchat, Earl happened to drop a revealing fact about himself: On his last day as a field agent, before coming to Washington to take a well-paid desk job at headquarters, he took it upon himself to preserve his own briefcase, intact and untouched since the very last time he snapped it shut and slipped home its latches.

What on earth, I wondered, could have possessed a guy like Earl Klema, an ordinary, plainspoken guy from the Bronx, to do a weird thing like that? As I got to know Earl better, the incident came to symbolize for me the essence of the man, both as an individual and as a government official. Like Don Curtis, Earl had developed a true fondness for the IRS, despite its myriad foibles and faults. And like Don Curtis, Earl happens to be one of those fortunate souls blessed with an innate sense of the past—a natural historian, if you will.

A few weeks before he retired in 1993, Earl gave me—in my official capacity as the IRS historian—that plain, heavily scuffed brown leather briefcase, which contained everything an IRS revenue agent would take with him on his daily rounds, circa 1968. I opened Earl's cherished case to find tax forms, audit sheets, ledgers, and notebooks still covered and filled with carefully scribbled No. 2 pencil marks. There were no portable computers in those days. Not even an adding machine compact enough to take with him on the road. Earl had made do with pencils and legal pads. Inside that briefcase were artifacts of a career IRS-er, and a major addition to my fledgling collection of IRS documents and memorabilia.

At our first meeting Earl didn't take long to cut to the chase. He quietly asked if I'd ever heard of something called the Special Services Staff, or SSS. As a matter of fact, I had not. But I couldn't help remarking on the obvious resemblance of the name to that of the Nazis' feared shock troops, the SS.

"Well," Earl said thoughtfully, not being one to beat around the bush, "seeing as how you happen to be our first official historian, you probably should know something about the most controversial episode in our recent history."

His appraising eyes told me that he was gauging my reaction to this revelation. Could he trust me with sensitive information about a scandal that had rocked the service from top to bottom, and made the Filing Season from Hell look like a day at the beach?

Earl crouched down in front of his desk and began yanking on a lower left-hand desk drawer, from which he hauled folder after folder of documents and files, dating back to the turbulent time when the country was being torn apart by riots and civil disturbances, when cities were burning and college campuses were under siege.

"You can start with these," Earl said, dumping a vast pile of paper in my lap. "Go right ahead, take them back to your office for review. Just get them back to me by the end of the week."

A few days later, I dutifully returned all of Earl's material. I think he could tell by the look in my eyes that I was still dazed by the depth of the find. With a barely discernible twinkle of the eye, Earl asked if I'd found his little cache interesting.

"*Interesting?*" I said, in this hey-you've-got-to-be-kidding tone. "This stuff is *unbelievable*." I told Earl I wanted to hear everything he knew about the amazing, shocking, outrageous SSS of the IRS.

After my enthusiastic response, Earl paused for a long time, apparently pondering his next step. As with Don Curtis, I got a feeling that he was contemplating whether to initiate me further into the mysteries of this secret society. "If you find all this stuff intriguing," he mused aloud, carefully secreting the piles of files I'd just returned to him back in his desk, "then I've got something that you'll find even more incredible." He paused again. "I need to show you our room upstairs. You'll really get a kick out of that."

Earl snagged a serious-looking set of keys from yet another drawer in that messy desk, and whisked me out of his office and onto an elevator, which lurched us up to the fifth floor. We walked wordlessly down one of those endless, dreary, drab IRS hallways until, suddenly, Earl stopped short. A sign next to the frosted glass door identified it as Room 5120.

Easing those hefty keys out of his hip pocket, Earl—a trifle furtively—opened the door. I was surprised and somewhat disappointed to find myself in an ordinary-looking IRS conference room. Moving to the far end of the room, Earl stopped in front of a curtain on an obviously windowless wall. After a dramatic pause, Earl yanked open the curtains to reveal an imposing heavy steel vault door, recessed into the wall, that bristled with two heavy locks. In awe, I stepped back to make way for Earl, who began sliding those big keys in sequence into the locks, which held two big steel bars in place. Earl had to pull hard on the thick metal door to drag it over the pile carpet, which had been installed without regard to the occasional need to open the vault. With the door finally open, I eagerly gazed into a dark, dusty cavern, in which I could just barely make out row upon row of government-issue filing cabinets, fading off into the shadows.

"These," Earl announced, "are the IRS Watergate files. The SSS records."

Earl had previously confirmed that I had a top secret clearance, so when I asked if I could sneak a peek at a few files, he could scarcely object.

"Why not?" Earl shrugged. "Be my guest."

Flipping through a few file folders at random, I could see at a glance that the cache contained FBI reports, printouts from the IRS master file of tax information, and newspaper and magazine clippings concerning the still highly sensitive Watergate era at the IRS. I was looking at a vast collection of historical material documenting the sixties. A quick glance through a few of the files convinced me that someone could write a social history of that turbulent decade just from the massive amount of data stored in Room 5120 of the IRS national office. Here was documentation on the much-feared, top secret IRS Special Services Staff, which operated much like the infamous White House "plumbers" in a covert dirty war against suspected dissidents, all assumed to be tax evaders as well. Thanks to Earl Klema, the explosive legacy of the SSS had been, at least until then, preserved. I can only hope that Room 5120's collection remains intact to this day.

The IRS issue made Watergate explode.

—Nixon White House aide Charles Colson

Our public memory tells us that the IRS sat at Richard Nixon's knee, auditing his enemies and going easy on his friends. Our public memory tells us that these shenanigans continued until White House counsel John Dean gave the country a shocking wake-up call with his testimony before the Senate Watergate committee in mid-1973, which preceded by barely a year Nixon's abdication from the throne in disgrace.

The surviving legacy of the Watergate years is reform, reform, and more reform. Unfortunately, the reforms have not provided results, results, and more results. An irate Congress and a deeply disillusioned public became determined to "open up" government so that never again would the country be confronted with a White House shrouded in secrecy. But to a startling degree, at least with regard to the IRS, Congress's attempt to "open up" the government has been a dismal failure. The irony is that by taking steps designed to "protect" tax returns from the wandering eyes of politicians, an unwitting Congress handed the IRS both a weapon and a shield that the tax collector has since used to fend off public scrutiny and evade public accountability.

Our collective memory tells us that Nixon and his henchmen, Haldeman and Ehrlichman, sent "enemies lists" over to the IRS, and that the IRS compliantly did their bidding by calling in those unfortunate souls for tax audits. In 1976 Texas senator Lloyd Bentsen reinforced that popular impression by sternly denouncing all the president's men for turning the IRS into a "lending library" of tax returns. He vowed to prevent future political abuses of a nonpartisan government agency by clamping down on access to tax returns, restricting even the President from viewing them. The unintended result of this crackdown was that Congress gave the IRS a blanket in which to cloak itself, providing almost total armor-plated protection from the public eye. Whenever anyone wants to know what really goes on inside the IRS—including members of Congress trying to investigate problems with IRS management—IRS higher-ups can cite "taxpayer privacy" as a way to avoid spilling the beans. That's why Earl Klema and his Disclosure office always had to tread on eggshells when trying to respond to Freedom of Information Act requests—because the way the IRS chooses to interpret the relevant statutes, "protecting taxpayer information" has turned into a tool to protect the IRS itself, far more than the innocent taxpayer.

THE SPECIAL SERVICES STAFF

On Wednesday, June 18, 1969—six months into the Nixon presidency—the Permanent Subcommittee on Investigations of the Senate Committee on Government Operations held a series of hearings on civil disorders and disturbances in Room 1202 of the New Senate Office Building, with Senator John L. McClellan, Democrat of Arkansas, presiding as chairman. Focusing on the increasingly violent anti–Vietnam War movement, the subcommittee wanted to find out who was provoking the commotion at home.

That day's hearings centered on the Black Panther Party, the radical organization founded in Oakland, California, in 1966 by Huey P. Newton and Bobby Seale, in close cooperation with Stokeley Carmichael, the former chairman of the Student Non-Violent Coordinating Committee—popularly known as SNCC. Under "Prime Minister" Huey Newton, the Black Panther Party had evolved into an armed gang, as nonviolent as a SWAT team. The BPP became notorious in Oakland when members began carrying loaded shotguns and rifles in that city's mean streets, vowing to protect the black community from police brutality. Their motto: "police the police."

Newton and Seale were skilled political propagandists who popularized the term "pigs" as an epithet to apply to uniformed law enforcement, as in the following inflammatory statements excerpted from the Panther newsletter: "The pigs entered Father Neil's church in Oakland where the Panthers were holding a meeting. . . . The pigs, about twelve of them, burst in holding 12-gauge shotguns in front of them in a menacing manner, inexplicably accompanied by a white minister. . . ."

Huey Newton, also the party's "Minister of Defense," was fond of rhyming slogans that foreshadowed today's rap, such as "Buckshots Will Down All Cops" and "If You Don't Believe in Lead, You're Dead."

The lead witnesses at the day's session were Jean Powell and her husband, Larry Clayton Powell, a couple of ex-revolutionaries disillusioned by the movement after the arrest of party cofounders Huey Newton and Bobby Seale on conspiracy-to-commit-murder charges, and the subsequent elevation of David Hilliard to the position of BPP de facto war chief.

Under Hilliard's stewardship, Jean Powell testified, Black Panther fund-raising efforts supposedly targeted at raising bail for the two imprisoned Panthers quickly degenerated into extortion tactics designed to accumulate cash for the personal use and pleasure of David Hilliard and his cohorts in the party.

"The party is financed from a flow of funds generated by barbecues, donations, and intake from robberies," Jean Powell insisted, before going on to estimate that the proceeds from these activities brought in "anywhere from fifty to one hundred thousand dollars a month."

John L. McClellan, a conservative Dixiecrat of the old school, led the questioning of Mrs. Powell. "How much of this $50,000 to $100,000 a month actually went to feeding hungry schoolchildren?" McClellan sternly inquired.

"None of it," Mrs. Powell replied.

"Was any of this money ever taken out of the treasury and used to do anything for the community that you know of?" McClellan pressed on.

"Not that I know of," replied her husband, Larry Clayton Powell. "Not even for other party members, let alone the community."

That remark touched off a fury in the room, and later on in the press, only fanned when Senator McClellan rhetorically asked the Powells if, to their knowledge, any individual Black Panthers, or for that matter the Black Panther Party, had ever filed a tax return. The answer, not surprisingly, was no. Even more disquieting to critics of the IRS, the tax agency had not, as far as anyone could recall, ever asked the Black Panthers for a 1040 either.

The news that these known criminals and rogues—at least from the point of view of the predominantly white senators on the panel—had never filed a tax return hardly came as any great surprise to anyone. But that the IRS, in its wisdom, had neglected to "go after" an organization that openly called for the armed overthrow of the government and the killing of cops didn't look any better for the IRS than it did for the Panthers. Some senators, recognizing a political football perfectly poised to support their claims that they were "doing something" about armed revolutionaries running amok in the streets, began pressuring the IRS to "go after" these subversive organizations that were tearing the country asunder.

This incident, then, and not the famed Nixon enemies list, was the genesis of the IRS's covert operations. Even as these inflammatory hearings got under way, an Atlanta lawyer named Randolph Thrower was taking office as President Nixon's first IRS commissioner. Thrower, a tall, serious tax attorney who still practices at the Atlanta law firm where he worked before his brief stint in the Nixon administration, says he met Richard Nixon only once before his appointment, at a campaign fund-raiser. Thrower did know Charles McClain, one of Nixon's former law partners, who suggested Thrower to Nixon as a prime candidate for the chief post at Internal Revenue. Thrower was duly sworn in as IRS commissioner on April Fool's Day, 1969.

Just six weeks into his new job, the commissioner hired a man named Roger Barth to be his "special assistant." Unlike Thrower, Barth did have very strong personal ties to the President. He was so close to the family that he had served as "front man" for Nixon daughters Julie and Tricia during the 1968 campaign.

Once established inside the commissioner's office, Barth became a conduit between the IRS and the White House. The White House joined Congress in pressing the IRS to "do something" about dissident parties and organizations soon after Barth's arrival at 1111 Constitution Avenue.

On June 16, barely two months into his new job as commissioner, Thrower was visited by Dr. Arthur Burns, one of Nixon's top domestic policy advisers, and the future chairman of the Federal Reserve Board. Burns (who later denied any memory of this meeting) conveyed—according to Commissioner Thrower's own written record of the event—"great concern over the fact that tax-exempt funds may be supporting activist groups engaged in stimulating riots both on campus and within our inner cities."

The reason for the visit from someone as high-level as Arthur Burns was obvious: the White House was seeking to reinforce its demand that the IRS "do something" about these tax-flouting radical organizations—and pronto. Just four days later, on June 20, 1969, yet another young presidential adviser eager to curry favor with the President penned a brief note to Roger Barth, quantum-upping the political pressure on the new commissioner.

"The President is anxious to see some positive action taken against those organizations which are violating existing regulations," Thomas Charles Huston sedulously stressed. "I have advised him that I will keep him advised of the efforts that are presently underway." Translation: Efforts to take "positive action" against subversive organizations had better be under way, or else.

Just five days later, on June 25, 1969, the Senate Committee on Government Operations reiterated its earlier message when an IRS executive named Leon Green, deputy commissioner for compliance, found himself "raked over the coals"—as he later put it—by the more conservative senators on the panel for evading a clear course of public duty. With eyes fixed firmly on the public's perception of their role in the affair, the committee members directed their ire at Green's lack of assertiveness in dealing with exempt organizations. Still, no enemies list. Neither congressional leaders nor White House officials had asked for tax returns; both branches simply wanted the IRS to crack down on these groups.

The official Senate Watergate report would later include the intriguing tidbit of information that on July 1, 1969, White House aide Tom Huston called Roger Barth at the IRS to insist that the IRS take a close look at the activities of some specific activist organizations. Huston copied a memo to top White House aide H.R. Haldeman advising him that Nixon had "indicated a desire for the IRS to move against leftist organizations taking advantage of tax shelters," and that he had sent word to Roger Barth to see to it personally that this high-level directive was carried out.

On the same day that Huston called Barth to relay Nixon's insistence that the IRS actively pursue activist organizations, an IRS alcohol, tobacco, and firearms special agent* named Eddie Hughes was urgently dispatched from Atlanta to IRS headquarters in Washington to brief top IRS officials on his personal expertise in tracking the financial records of various subversive, dissident, and militant groups.

In the empty white box on his official travel voucher labeled "pur-

---

*Until 1972, the Bureau of Alcohol, Tobacco, and Firearms was part of the IRS.

pose of trip," Hughes wrote: "My presence in Washington, D.C. is required to assist the National Office with a report on militant organizations and the financial funding thereof, as it relates to violations of the Internal Revenue Code. This report was requested by and will be submitted to the White House." When the IRS later tried to deny any pressure from the White House to go after radicals, Hughes's travel voucher provided contradictory evidence.

The day after Hughes's arrival in Washington, a select group of high-level IRS executives (but not Commissioner Thrower) convened at 10 A.M. in the office of Donald Bacon, Leon Green's boss as assistant commissioner of compliance. The subject of the meeting, according to the official minutes, was "Ideological Organizations." After special agent Eddie Hughes filled them in on his method of attacking the problem, the IRS formally launched a secret effort to target dissident individuals and groups for tax audit. The meeting concluded with a formal decision to establish "a task force or group" at the IRS to "collect basic information on all these organizations." The sinister Special Services Staff was born. The IRS didn't need an enemies list from the Nixon White House. It was formulating one on its own.

Don Virdin, an upper-level IRS staffer who attended these meetings, became the unofficial secretary of the group. Through a series of Virdin's memos, the burgeoning efforts of the IRS to act as a strike force against radical groups gradually reveal themselves, in all their repugnant, ideologically charged odor. Virdin's notes of the first meeting focused on one of the major obstacles the new organ would face before it could launch its covert operation. Before it could start targeting anyone, the group needed an operational definition of the term "ideological organization," to define its opponents. The group's failure to define this term precisely would come back to haunt it, but the members resolved to proceed with their perceived mission: to rescue the country from dangerous radicals who were assumed to also harbor desires to undermine the tax system.

The as-yet unnamed group would be primarily "an intelligence gathering operation," Virdin wrote. If Don Virdin's group was looking for a working definition of an "ideological organization," it needed only to look in a mirror.

The shadowy organization-within-an-organization's next meeting took place on July 18. By that time, the group had been officially christened the Activist Organizations Committee. An obscure IRS bureaucrat named Paul Wright was anointed its official chairman. More than any other person inside or outside the IRS, Paul Wright would create the legacy of official deceit that linked the IRS, Watergate, and the Nixon White House in an unprecedented and unholy alliance.

As the leader of this super secret strike force, Paul Wright wielded tremendous, unchecked power to incite audits and otherwise target politically unpopular groups and individuals. But twenty years later, remarkably little is known about Wright the person, or Wright the bureaucrat, except what little has survived in his own incendiary words. The role of the IRS in the Watergate fiasco had everything to do with an unknown bureaucrat named Paul Wright and little to do with the famed enemies list. In fact, it's quite probable that Wright learned of the "enemies list" along with the rest of the United States when John Dean delivered his damaging testimony during the 1973 Watergate hearings, four years after he took charge of the Special Services Staff.

From the surviving record, Wright appears to have come from nowhere to become one of the most powerful men, if only for a short time, at the IRS. The commissioner at the time, Randolph Thrower, would later claim not only to have never heard of him, but to have had next to no knowledge of what he was up to.

According to an affidavit later filed in a court case against him, Paul Wright joined the IRS in 1942 and held a "variety of line and administrative positions" before being picked for the XD—the Executive Development Program, which prepared career service employees to join the executive ranks. In 1967 he became a staff adviser to Harold Snyder, director of the Collection Division. In July 1969 he "was informed by Mr. Snyder that at the direction of Donald Bacon, Assistant Commissioner of Compliance, and his deputy Leon Green, a committee was being formed to deal with certain apparent abuses of the tax laws by activist organizations and individuals."

After his appointment to the committee, Paul Wright revealed himself as a zealot, a fanatic, a loose cannon eager and willing to be deployed by higher-ups who were less willing to take the heat than he was, in fulfilling both broader and lower purposes. Under Paul Wright's driving leadership, the Activist Organizations Committee quickly evolved over the course of a series of 1969 meetings into the Special Services Staff, slated to coordinate all IRS activities involving "ideological, militant, subversive, radical, and similar type organizations."

Virdin's memo recording the July 24 secret session carried the strict warning, "Disclose On Need-To-Know Basis Only." "This is an extremely important and sensitive matter in which the highest levels of government are interested," Virdin stated, for the record. "Highest level of government" was an obvious reference to the White House, possibly even to Nixon himself. The memo went on to advise those who read it ("For Your Eyes Only") that the activities of the committee "should be disclosed generally only to those persons who need to know, because of its semisecret nature. Indeed, action is being taken to obtain top secret clearance for the full-time Committee members. Our files will be protected with the usual intelligence type security. We do not want the news media to be alerted to what we are attempting to do or how we are operating because the disclosure of such information might embarrass the Administration." Adopting an alarmist tone well suited to the mission, Virdin further maintained that "some of these organizations may be a threat to the security of the United States and one of our principal functions will be to determine the sources of their funds, the names of their contributors." The IRS had launched its own secret enemies list.

In his first staff memo, Paul Wright wrote, "From a strictly revenue standpoint, we may have little reason for establishing this Committee or for expending the time and effort which may be necessary, but we must do it. We have gotten too much adverse publicity about exempt organizations."

Wright seemed aware of his team's irrelevance to tax collection and tax law enforcement. He must have recognized that the Activist Organizations Committee, soon renamed the SSS, was primarily a public relations–driven enterprise, albeit a secret one. So certain was the IRS of the moral authority of its position in this regard that

Virdin expectantly wrote in a memo to his boss, Harold Snyder, on July 31, 1969: "I visualize the day—perhaps three years from now—when Paul and his group will be called to the White House to receive a Special Award from the President for the tremendous job they have done!"

There was no special White House ceremony three years later. In fact, almost exactly three years later, on June 17, 1972, five armed men—the soon-to-be world-famous White House "plumbers"—were arrested for breaking into the headquarters of the Democratic National Committee at the Watergate complex in Washington, D.C., an incident which, as its ramifications evolved, would permanently shed a harsh, unwelcome light on the Nixon administration's dubious tactics.

The IRS officially activated the AOC on August 5, 1969. One of its initial actions was to contact the FBI and get itself on the FBI's distribution list for reports and materials concerning activist organizations and individuals. The FBI obliged, and FBI files began flowing freely into the IRS. By the end of August 1969 Wright proudly reported that the AOC was "operating under 'Red Seal' security precautions" in a room on the third floor of the IRS headquarters building. The meaning of "red seal" was unclear. In all my years with a Top Secret Defense Department security clearance, I had never heard such a term. The relative security of AOC operations was questionable at best.

Wright's self-serving memo defined the group's purpose as follows: to "collect relevant information on organizations predominantly dissident or extremist in nature and on people prominently identified with these organizations. Many of the organizations are controversial, all are newsworthy, and a large number are known to be militant, revolutionary, and subversive." Nothing about tax evasion.

Throughout the next year, Wright's handful of employees amassed files. Most of the repository came from the FBI, although the staff culled newspapers and other media for articles on trouble-making members of American society, a far wider variety than Nixon's list of influential journalists, politicians, and heavyweight contributors to George McGovern's 1968 Democratic campaign. Suspected tax cheats, by dint of their association with some "radical" cause, included actress Shirley MacLaine, New York Mayor John Lindsay, and Nobel Prize–winning scientist Linus Pauling. Folk singer Joan Baez had her very own IRS file. There were thousands of other alleged, less-renowned subversives. Suspect organizations included the National Urban League, the American Civil Liberties Union, *Rolling Stone* magazine, and the National Education Association, an outfit not known to be particularly violent or threatening to the national interest.

By mid-1970 the White House asked aide Tom Huston for an update on the progress on the ideological organizations effort "since July 1, 1969, when we first expressed our interest in this matter." Huston's request for this update landed on Commissioner Thrower's desk on August 14, 1970. Thrower maintains that he had never heard of the Activist Organizations Committee or the SSS before this request. When I asked him about Paul Wright, Thrower had no idea who he was or what he was doing. *Paul Wright was doing whatever forwarded his goal, acting almost entirely on his own volition.*

In September 1970 Thrower sent a status report to Tom Huston at the White House on the work of what Wright now called the Special Services Group. The report stressed that "knowledge of the existence and operations of this Group should be carefully limited" although the report revealed no results beyond the accumulation of 1,025 files on organizations and another 4,300 on individuals. But, of these five thousand-odd files, the Special Services Group had referred only sixty-nine cases to IRS field offices for audit.

The White House wasn't satisfied. Two days after receiving the bland IRS report, Huston told H.R. Haldeman that the IRS report was "long on words and short on substance." Huston wrote a memo to Haldeman: "Nearly 18 months ago, the President indicated his desire for the IRS to move against leftist organizations taking advantage of tax shelters. I have been pressing the IRS since that time to no avail. What we cannot do in a courtroom via criminal prosecutions to curtail activities, the IRS could do by administrative action. Moreover, valuable intelligence-type information could be turned up by the IRS in field audits." The heat was on.

Paul Wright marched forward to identify subversive and radical elements in American society. In a meeting with Justice Department officials on June 25, 1971, Wright boasted that the Special Services Group had dispatched a high percentage of its files for further IRS field investigation and possible criminal prosecution, even though the actual referral rate was less than 2 percent. Justice Department officials were quite interested in these possible criminal cases, and Wright agreed to give them a list of "those individuals considered by the IRS to be the most significant extremists." One Justice Department official reportedly at this meeting later denied any memory of it. Assistant Attorney General Robert Mardian said that, as far as he knew, Wright had never followed through on his promise.

When all was said and done, no more than a handful of criminal prosecutions ever resulted from information gathered by Wright's cloak-and-dagger Special Services Staff. To the benefit of a larger American public, despite his grandstanding, Wright never displayed any great talent for manipulating the IRS's field operations, a bureaucratic ineptitude that made his boastful claims all the more ludicrous.

Nevertheless, the important thing from the IRS institutional standpoint was to foster an illusion that the IRS was doing something about the problem, so that the White House would get off its back. The SSS, for all of Wright's puffery, was evolving into more of a smoke-and-mirrors monstrosity than an actual breaking-and-entering team complementary to the White House plumbers.

By late June 1971 the Special Services Group had moved into a larger, more secluded room in the basement of IRS headquarters. Wright noted that he now possessed the FBI's list of all underground newspapers and editors throughout the United States, and schemed to match the list against the IRS master file of taxpayers to make sure that the underground papers and personnel were filing tax returns.

In July 1971, Commissioner Thrower resigned, eager to return to private practice in Atlanta after a series of run-ins with the Nixon White House—of Thrower's experience, more later. In August of that year tax attorney Johnnie Walters, the former assistant attorney general for the Tax Division in the Justice Department, assumed command at the IRS. Walters would later claim that he knew nothing of a Special Services Staff until a disgruntled ex-FBI agent leaked information on the operation in January 1972, six months after Walters took office.

Robert Wall, a thirty-three-year-old former FBI agent and naval officer, had resigned from the FBI in April 1970, fed up with his experiences at the bureau, during which he had been forced to spend—from his apparently liberal perspective—an inordinate amount of time pursuing fruitless cases against black radicals. Wall eloquently pleaded his case before the public, and vented his frustrations about his abruptly terminated federal career, in a blistering January 27, 1972, cover story in the *New York Review of Books.*

After wasting months trying to nail a former member of SNCC (Student Non-Violent Coordinating Committee), Agent Wall was advised by his superiors that "the IRS has requested his arrest record from the Identification Division of the FBI." Wall was told to work closely with the IRS on closing a possible tax case against this individual.

"When I went up to the IRS I found that it had secretly set up a special squad of men to investigate the tax records of a list of 'known militants and activists.' The FBI was supplying the names of the persons for the IRS to include in this list. After talking to several IRS officials, I was sent to a locked, sound-proofed basement room of the IRS headquarters in Washington, where I found a file on my subject, among hundreds of others piled on a long table. . . ."

That was it. But by God, that was enough. Articles in the *New York Times* and the *Washington Post* quickly appeared blasting the IRS for setting up its own squad of dirty tricksters, a full six months before the ill-fated Watergate complex burglary. The IRS could no longer deny the existence of what was now called the Special Services Staff. For the first time, the IRS provided official acknowledgment of the SSS by including it in the rarely-read *Internal Revenue Manual* on April 14, 1972, innocuously describing the staff as "a central information gathering facility consolidating data and making appropriate dissemination of information relevant to tax enforcement." No mention of the SSS focus on ideological or extremist organizations. Despite the press leak, no one in the media or Congress pursued the story after the initial revelation. Most eyes were fixed on Nixon. The American public would have to wait for over a year for a more complete description of the Special Services Staff from White House counsel John Dean during the nationally televised Watergate hearings in mid-1973.

And so Paul Wright continued to hoard files. By November 1972 the count reached eleven thousand, containing twelve thousand classified documents, according to a staff memo. Wright wrote, "It takes considerable naiveté not to recognize that we are confronted with highly organized and well financed groups bent on destroying our form of government and they are moving very carefully, step by step, following well laid plans. . . . Probably their number one goal at this point is to erode and eventually destroy our entire tax system."

The targets of his Special Services Staff, according to Wright, were "organizations and individuals, who through insidious methods have collaborated to form a revolutionary force, which if allowed to develop gradually will become well established before becoming apparent. Perhaps the only way to combat a tax rebellion growth or movement in our society is for the IRS . . . to expose the hard core leaders and fringe element in our nation who advocate tearing down our present system."

In reality, outside the sheltered halls of 1111 Constitution Avenue, sixties rebels waged their war against the primary sponsors of the Vietnam War: the Pentagon and its purported partners-in-crime, the CIA, Dow Chemical, and assorted other warmongers and profiteers. The tax man was never a primary target for their angst.

Wright urged heads of IRS offices around the country to follow up on his staff's referrals, divided into two major categories so that the field executives could understand the gravity of his effort. The first included "violent groups" that "advocate and practice arson, firebombing, organize prison riots, skyjacking, those who print and distribute publications advocating revolution against the government of this country." The second covered the "so-called Non-Violent Groups," those who "by alleged peaceful demonstrations oftentimes deliberately initiate violence and destruction. Included are those who publicly destroy and burn draft cards, destroy Selective Service office records, participate in and organize May Day demonstrations, organize and attend rock festivals which attract youth and narcotics." So there it was. Youthful attendance at a rock concert was enough to convince Paul Wright that someone might be a tax cheat. Forget about the notorious and well-known names of those individuals who actually made it onto Nixon's famed enemies list. Regular guys might end up with an IRS file under Paul Wright's criteria. The IRS enemies list was much less selective than Nixon's list.

Wright also told IRS executives that he had access to a "computerized printout" from "another agency" listing people who posed "a threat to the security of this country" and including "16,000 entities where tax violations would appear probable." The assumption was that, if someone made this list, obviously from the FBI, then that person must also be a tax cheat.

A hapless field executive in New York exposed Wright's inflammatory rhetoric inadvertently. John J. Flynn, an IRS regional commissioner for the North Atlantic Region, based in downtown Manhattan, took Wright's plea for more field support of Special Services Staff activities seriously—so seriously that he edited Wright's lengthy memo to a more reasonable size, put his own signature on it, and sent it throughout his region on December 18, 1972.

Several months later, in April 1973, IRS Commissioner Johnnie Walters resigned, like his predecessor Thrower, fed up with White House pressure and interference as he attempted to administer the tax system impartially. More on Walters' experience later. Cincinnati tax attorney Donald Alexander became Nixon's third tax commissioner shortly after Walters' early departure. Just weeks later, White House counsel John Dean broke open the floodgates of Watergate when he began testifying before Congress about his activities in the Nixon White House. Unlike his predecessors, Donald Alexander learned about the Special Services Staff almost immediately—on his second day on the job. Years later, Alexander recalled that he didn't much like the sound of this operation even then, but with the advent of the Watergate hearings, there was worse, much worse, to come on his watch.

During his first day of nationally televised testimony before the Senate Select Committee on Presidential Campaign Activities, John Dean alleged that the White House had attempted to bend the IRS to serve its own partisan political purposes. In his June 25, 1973, testimony, Dean further alluded to a "special group in the IRS which collected information on extremist individuals and organizations," without providing its name. Then Dean dropped the bombshell: He revealed the existence of the President's "enemies list."

Amid the media frenzy surrounding Dean's disclosures, the "special IRS group" and the enemies list became inextricably linked in the public mind. Yet no solid link existed between the enemies list and the Special Services Staff, except the proximity of the two in Dean's testimony. Yet in a stunning case of dismal PR, no one at the IRS seized the initiative and saw fit to enlighten a reeling American public about this important distinction.

The IRS could at any time have denied culpability when confronted with allegations of harassing the people on Nixon's enemies list with tax audits. Perhaps the reason the IRS remained stonily mute was that what it did do—on its own initiative—was more excessive and far-reaching than the White House effort. The IRS hit list was more than ten times longer than Nixon's enemies list. It's one thing for a President to go after his perceived political enemies. It's something else altogether for a nonpartisan federal agency to target innocent citizens purely on the basis of their ideological bent. Both are wrong, but one is definitely scarier than the other.

On June 28, 1973, the House-Senate Joint Committee on Internal Revenue Taxation announced that it would investigate charges of political use of the tax system by the Nixon White House. Shortly thereafter, someone from inside the IRS leaked poor John Flynn's rewrite of Paul Wright's memo to *Time,* which trumpeted its scoop in appropriately Gilbert and Sullivanesque tones in its headline, "KEEPING A LITTLE LIST AT THE IRS." On August 9, just days after the *Time* article, the IRS announced it was abolishing the Special Services Staff, effective immediately, claiming that IRS Commissioner Alexander had reached the decision to disband the SSS following an in-depth, "two-month study" showing that "the functions of the SSS could be "carried out by other units of the IRS."

Despite claims that this decision was based on an "internal study," in my historical sleuthing I found no evidence that any such study was ever conducted. Even Alexander in 1996 admitted having no memory of such a study. It seems as if the IRS was attempting to put an official spin on its hurried efforts to clean up the mess created by Paul Wright. In abolishing the Special Services Staff, Alexander pledged that the IRS would continue to pay close attention to tax cheats, but claimed that "political or social views, extremist or otherwise, are irrelevant to taxation."

RALPH NADER VERSUS THE IRS

In October 1973, with the Special Services Staff on its way out, Ralph Nader's Tax Reform Research Group filed a FOIA request with the IRS pressing for the release of information on the disgraced and disbanded IRS strike force. Characteristically, the IRS simply ignored Nader's letter. Nader's group called and wrote more letters. The IRS continued to stonewall. Fed up, Nader's outfit filed suit against the IRS on July 22, 1974, to release the material it had asked for nine months earlier. Finally, on October 21, 1974, the IRS released a few select Special Services Staff documents, but deleted the names of individuals and organizations listed in Special Services Staff files. Nader protested the deletions. A month later, the IRS released a few more documents. It took thirteen months for Nader's Tax Research Reform Group to get a response from the IRS, which was by no means complete.

The IRS's reluctant November document release included the names of ninety-nine organizations with files in the SSS collection. Although this was a very small percentage of the eleven thousand Special Services Staff files, the documents gave Nader enough information to claim that the Nixon White House was behind the establishment of the Special Services Staff. A banner headline in the *New York Post* (then a liberal daily) trumpeting "IT'S ANOTHER ENEMIES LIST" only fueled the confusion that still exists between Nixon's enemies list, with fewer than eight hundred names, and the Special Services Staff list, with its broad membership base of more than eleven thousand.

In a move eerily comparable to the mysterious discovery of Rose Law Firm billing records in the Clinton White House over twenty years later, the IRS announced—just a few weeks after Nader broadcast the link between the White House and the IRS's formation of the SSS—that it had belatedly "discovered" documents purporting to "prove" that the IRS had established the Special Services Staff on its own initiative, not at the behest of the White House. Another comparison might be to the intensified effort to release Nixon-era documents after release of the Oliver Stone pseudohistorical feature film *Nixon*.

In a parting shot, aimed at itself, the IRS duly conceded that it had by this disclosure accorded itself the "dubious distinction of earning credit for setting up a special unit to investigate activist organizations and their members." Despite concerted IRS efforts to downplay Nader's remarks by releasing the "newly discovered" internal documents, the AP reported that "there remains a potentially critical gap in the document series, because files that might show what role the White House played at the IRS apparently have been destroyed." Indeed. The SSS files I viewed in my capacity as IRS historian were woefully incomplete, considering the enormity of Paul Wright's covert efforts.

WALTER TEAGUE VERSUS THE IRS

Commissioner Alexander abolished the Special Services Staff, but he couldn't trample the inconsiderable fruits of its labors. Walter Teague was one of the cases referred to the field by Paul Wright's staff. A political activist from the New York City area, Teague had been active in the antiwar movement since 1964. He had an FBI file. He had a Special Services Staff file. Three years had passed since Walter Teague's file left the Washington, D.C., offices of the Special Services Staff on its way to the field. The day after Alexander's announcement that the SSS would live no more, the IRS moved in on Walter Teague.

The IRS claimed that Teague's name was randomly selected from the thousands of Special Services Staff files to be checked against a master file of all taxpayers. IRS computer printouts showed a Teague tax return only for 1968, with no records for years before and after 1968. The FBI report in Teague's Special Services Staff file showed that Teague had sufficient income through the 1960s to warrant his filing a tax return.

Based on this unaudited data, the Special Services Staff sent Teague's case to the IRS Manhattan District Office on July 30, 1970, where it sat for six months before being assigned to a revenue agent. Another year passed before Teague's file was transferred to the Audit Division. In the interim, the IRS found evidence of Teague's missing 1965 tax return. The Audit Division began to reconstruct Teague's earnings for the still missing years, without Teague's knowledge or input, looking back ten years.

Once finished with estimating Teague's income, the Audit Division referred his case to the Intelligence Division to explore potential charges of criminal violation of the tax law. The Intelligence Division didn't see any criminal activity and returned Teague's case to the Audit Division. Audit recreated Teague's 1040s for 1961 and 1962, the only years for which it had enough data on Teague's income to develop tax returns.

On August 8, 1973, the IRS sent Teague a letter with a "proposed" tax deficiency of more than $3,000 for the years 1961 and 1962. The IRS told Teague that he could either dispute the IRS claim by requesting an appellate conference or else settle his case by sending the IRS money. The IRS was trying to collect taxes that were twelve years old, even though the IRS advises taxpayers to keep copies of their returns for only ten years.

Teague chose to dispute the IRS claim and requested an appellate conference. In his personal records, he found copies of his 1040s from 1961 and 1962, plus a canceled check dated April 15, 1963, matching the amount due on his 1962 tax return. Teague took these documents to his appellate conference on November 9, 1973. When confronted with this evidence, the Manhattan office quickly informed him that his case was closed. Teague owed nothing. How many taxpayers can find twelve-year-old tax records and cancelled checks in their personal files? Teague, the sixties activist, turned out to be a much better record keeper than the IRS. But without his own records, the IRS would have nailed Walter Teague for that $3,000 tax deficiency.

Several years later, the Senate Watergate report would soberly conclude: "So long as the IRS has the power to be a potential harassment for the average citizen if audits are not conducted on an objective basis, this procedure of developing files on dissenting citizens must be questioned. The more important point is that IRS duties and responsibilities are spelled out by Congress and such an intelligence operation is not one of them."

5

THE LEGACY OF WATERGATE

IRS Secret History, Volume III

If the abuses that have been brought to light erode the faith of the taxpayers in the system, it may be the most damaging legacy of Watergate.

—1974 editorial in the Washington Star-News

Congress and the American people will have no one to thank but themselves if they do nothing about it.

—1974 editorial in the Boston Globe commenting on allegations of misguided IRS behavior

NIXON, CAULFIELD, AND LIDDY VERSUS THE IRS

So what was the link between the White House and the IRS? The White House turned its attention to the highest level of the IRS, the commissioner's office. In early 1970 Nixon aide H.R. Haldeman asked Clark Mollenhoff, special counsel to the President, to handle a request that Haldeman claimed was from the President. Nixon wanted to know about the income tax situation of Gerald Wallace, brother of Alabama governor George Wallace. The White House apparently sought to substantiate information indicating that

Gerald Wallace had unreported income and links to illegal contributions made to the 1968 Wallace presidential campaign.

Mollenhoff took the matter to Commissioner Thrower. On March 20, 1970, the White House received an IRS report signed by Donald Bacon, the assistant commissioner for compliance, who hosted the first meeting of the Special Services Group. Mollenhoff delivered the report to Haldeman the next day.

Three weeks later, Thrower opened his *Washington Post* to read the headline "IRS PROBES WALLACE." Investigative journalist Jack Anderson reported that the IRS was questioning alleged kickbacks from state highway contracts to Gerald Wallace and checking to see whether this money landed in brother George's campaign chest. Anderson also said that the IRS had sent confidential tax information to the White House, and he cited "confidential field reports made available to this column" by the White House as his source.

Thrower believed that these "confidential field reports" were the IRS reports, namely Bacon's March 20 memo. The livid commissioner accused Mollenhoff of leaking information from Bacon's memo to the press, but the President's counsel denied that he had taken any such action. "He said it wasn't him, that it was over him," recalled Thrower in 1996. The commissioner told Mollenhoff that he still had to hold Mollenhoff responsible for the leak unless "it was so high that he had no control." Mollenhoff confirmed that someone with much greater authority made the call.

Thrower couldn't allow the White House to leak sensitive information about tax investigations for its own political purposes. He demanded to meet with White House aides Haldeman and Ehrlichman. Suspecting that one of these men leaked the information, Thrower reminded Haldeman and Ehrlichman that disclosure of tax information was a crime carrying stiff penalties. Haldeman and Ehrlichman appeared to take him seriously and "promised to cooperate," according to Thrower.

The next White House encounter did not pass so easily. It involved the Alcohol, Tobacco, and Firearms Division, which had been a part of the IRS since its birth in the 1790s with the whiskey tax. While the passage of a series of gun control laws drove the two parts of the revenue service into different spheres, they both remained under the direction of the commissioner of Internal Revenue. According to Thrower, "the IRS had responsibility for enforcing the gun laws. That was a job I took very seriously. The law enforcement side were known as the Revenuers. They were tough, hard-boiled, very fair minded people."

In the summer of 1970, the position of director of the Alcohol, Tobacco, and Firearms Division was up for grabs. Charles Walker, undersecretary of the Treasury, informed Thrower that the White House had a candidate for the job. His name was Jack Caulfield and he came with the President's blessing as well as the support of "top people in the White House."

After reviewing Caulfield's résumé, Thrower told Walker that he didn't believe Caulfield was qualified to head the ATF. Since the chief of the ATF Enforcement Branch planned to retire soon, Thrower suggested that Caulfield might be better suited for that position. Thrower was told the White House had dropped the issue of putting Caulfield in ATF.

But before Thrower filled the ATF director's job, he received another White House inquiry about the position, with G. Gordon Liddy as the new candidate for director of ATF. Liddy was working in the office of the assistant secretary of the Treasury for enforcement and operations, and Thrower had met him through an organized crime council for the White House. Thrower recalled that: "Liddy made one or two reports to that group. It was evident to me that he was not someone we wanted. He needed close supervision."

Thrower told Walker that Liddy wouldn't be right for the top ATF job either, that Liddy's work with the IRS on gun law issues had already damaged his reputation among ATF personnel. Appointing Liddy would be like "putting the fox in charge of the henhouse," Thrower recalled. He asked Walker to help him find Liddy another assignment, but Walker retorted, "We all have a cross to bear." He reminded Thrower that the commissioner himself must make the assignment and that Liddy was a White House favorite. Thrower held fast and told Liddy that he couldn't have the job. The request was withdrawn. But not for long.

In November 1970 Thrower heard that the White House staffers had reconsidered his earlier offer and now wanted Caulfield to take the chief enforcement job—with one caveat. Thrower would have to remove the Enforcement Branch from the Bureau of Alcohol, Tobacco, and Firearms and have it report directly to him, bypassing the ATF director.

"That didn't smell right," Thrower recalled. "I feared he would end up reporting directly to the White House, by going around me. I thought it would be a very bad signal throughout the IRS." Thrower again said no to the White House. The pressure mounted.

"The more they pressed, the more suspicious I became. I thought I should talk with the President, but I was told the President had heard of my position through the attorney general." Walker finally told Thrower that despite his objections, the commissioner was stuck with Caulfield.

Thrower replied that he would resign before hiring Caulfield. "I let it be known that if they forced me to go through with this I would consider my effectiveness as commissioner to be terminated." He later told the Watergate committee that he was concerned about the potential for creating a "personal police force which would not have the protection and insulation of the career staff." On January 26, 1971, President Nixon accepted Thrower's resignation.

That was apparently just fine with the White House. Thrower considers his demise at the IRS a direct result of a turf battle "in which the President was clearly a participant." Retired IRS executive John Johnson confirms Thrower's account of events, maintaining that despite public perceptions that the IRS commissioner was working hand-in-hand with the Nixon White House, nothing could have been further from the case. "The commissioner was more of a wall against political intrusion and not a conduit for political intrusion during those years," Johnson later recalled.

As an epilogue to this little-known episode of Watergate-era history, G. Gordon Liddy moved to work in the White House in 1971, having missed his chance to head the ATF Division of the IRS. Caulfield stayed at the White House until March 1972 when he joined the Committee to Reelect the President (CREEP). When the Bureau of Alcohol, Tobacco, and Firearms gained its independence from the IRS on July 1, 1972, Caulfield quickly slid into the slot of assistant director for enforcement for the BATF. There he stayed until his name surfaced in Watergate-related investigations in early 1973. While Caulfield finally got his BATF job, it took the resignation of an IRS commissioner and removal of an entire organization from the IRS to accomplish this single goal. Thrower returned to his Atlanta law firm. To this day, his courage in standing up in the face of intense pressure from the Nixon White House is not widely known.

South Carolina tax attorney Johnnie Walters, Thrower's successor at the IRS, fared little better at the hands of the Nixon White House. Before moving just two blocks down Constitution Avenue to take up the IRS commissionership in early August 1971, Walters had served the administration as assistant attorney general for taxation in the Justice Department. Within weeks of Walters's appointment, on August 16, 1971, White House counsel John Dean affixed his signature to a memo entitled "Dealing with Our Political Enemies." This, as it so happened, was the real genesis of the Nixon White House "enemies list." Paul Wright, head of the Special Services Staff inside the IRS, had been actively cooking up his own list for more than two years by this time.

Dean was soon preparing a "talking paper" with ideas on how to make the IRS more "politically responsive" to the White House. Dean's "talking paper"—which he later claimed was based on information provided by Jack Caulfield—dismissed the IRS as a "monstrous bureaucracy, dominated and controlled by Democrats."

Dean and his cohorts at the White House were not all that interested in cutting down on the monstrous bureaucracy; they were far more interested in transforming the agency's putative political persuasion from liberal to archconservative. Charging that the IRS was "unresponsive and insensitive to both the White House and Treasury in many areas," Dean went on to derisively describe the recently departed Randolph Thrower as a "total captive of the Democratic assistant commissioners. In the end, [Thrower] was actively fighting both the Treasury and the White House."

Dean then refocused his lens on the newly appointed IRS commissioner, complaining that Johnnie Walters had not yet exercised enough "leadership" in responding to the wishes and whims of the White House. Dean listed four areas in which he felt the IRS had fallen short: that it had failed to crack down on the multitude of tax-exempt organizations that fed left-wing political causes; that the White House was having trouble obtaining "information in the possession of the IRS re our political enemies"; that the White House had been "unable to stimulate audits"; and that the White House had, as yet, been "unsuccessful in placing Richard Nixon supporters in the IRS bureaucracy." It's a good thing John Dean never met Paul Wright.

"Walters must be made to know that discreet political actions and investigations on behalf of the Administration are a firm requirement and responsibility on his part," Dean insisted in his Jack Caulfield–influenced "talking paper." Walters's political acid test began in earnest on September 11, 1972, when John Dean called him into his office in the old Executive Office Building and handed him a list of names. The list prominently included the names of members of George McGovern's campaign staff and numerous campaign contributors. On the list were statesman Clark Clifford, Congresswoman Bella Abzug, journalist Pierre Salinger, Senator William Proxmire, and actor Gene Hackman, among others. Here, at last, was the first increment of the soon-to-be-famous Nixon enemies list. Paul Wright had a three-year head start on the Nixon White House, having already amassed thousands of names for the Special Services Staff enemies (of the tax system) list.

Dean told Walters he wanted the IRS to open tax investigations of the people on his list. Dean warned Walters "not [to] cause ripples" as he moved ahead with this assignment. Walters told Dean he would recommend that the IRS ignore the list of names and maintained that doing anything with the list of names would "be a disaster for the IRS and would make Watergate [the break-in] look like a Sunday school picnic." Walters took the list, returned to his office, and privately pondered his dilemma.

Two days later, Walters showed the list to Treasury Secretary George Schultz. Schultz agreed with Walters that the IRS should ignore it. Walters then sealed the list in an envelope and locked it in his office safe. Four days after Dean first turned over the list of White House enemies to Walters, Nixon met with his aide H. R. Haldeman. Their conversation rolled around to what John Dean was doing with the IRS. Dean also joined the meeting. What happened at the September 15, 1972, White House meeting did not become public until nearly twenty years later, when the National Archives released the tape in June 1991.

During their meeting, Nixon archly suggested that someone could get his hands on the IRS records of George McGovern. "We have to do it artfully so that we don't create an issue by abusing the IRS politically. . . . And there are ways to do that. Goddamn it, sneak in in the middle of the night," Nixon told Dean in the self-bugged Oval Office.

Walters hadn't gotten back to him about the McGovern supporters and contributors yet, Dean responded, clearly concerned about the IRS commissioner's obvious stonewalling. Upon being advised of Walters's inaction in this critical area, Nixon exploded.

"Well, they're gonna get it," he scolded Dean. "We've got to do it, even if we've got to kick Walters's ass out first and get a man in there!"

Ten days later, on September 25, 1972, Dean called Walters to ask how the investigations of the names on the list were going. Walters responded that he had done nothing about it, and repeated his earlier warning that for the IRS to do anything with the list would be "inviting disaster." Dean pressed Walters to check at least a few names on the list, which contained nearly five hundred names. In an effort to fend Dean off for a while, and buy himself more stonewalling time, Walters responded that he would reconsider the matter with Treasury Secretary Schultz.

Four days later, Walters and Schultz again agreed to do nothing about the White House enemies list. It remained locked in the safe. Walters resigned the following year, fed up with his experiences at the IRS and unrelenting pressure from the White House to use his vast powers against Nixon's personal and political enemies. When he left the IRS on May 21, 1973, Commissioner Walters cleaned out his safe and took the soon-to-be-famous list home with him to South Carolina.

Barely a month after Walter's departure, news of a Nixon "enemies list" splashed across front pages around the country as John Dean began testifying before the Senate Watergate committee. Two weeks after Dean's bombshell revelations, on July 11, 1973, Walters turned the list, along with his handwritten notes of the ordeal, over to the Joint Committee on Internal Revenue Taxation. The joint committee was given the job of investigating whether the IRS had really audited Nixon's political enemies while protecting his friends from audit.

The joint committee issued its report on December 20, 1973. The "enemies list" had by then become part of the political language. During this same period, the revelation of something at the IRS called the Special Services Staff was also making headlines. As a result, the enemies list and the secret IRS list-making unit became inextricably linked in the minds of the American public, even though they were totally unrelated. Though there was some coincidental overlap between the two lists, most of the names on the Nixon enemies list given to Johnnie Walters did not also appear on the list of names compiled in the more than eleven thousand IRS Special Services Staff files.

The results of the joint committee investigation into whether the IRS audited the 575 names on the White House list verified Johnnie Walters's claim that he locked the list away and did nothing with it. The committee found "no evidence that any returns were screened as a result of White House pressure on the IRS." As part of its investigation, the committee compared the audit rate for names on the enemies list with the audit rate for the total population in similar income brackets. One of the first things the committee found was that the majority of the people on Nixon's enemies list had incomes above $50,000. The average audit rate for this level of income in the early seventies hovered around 14 percent, while the names on the Nixon enemies list enjoying this income level found themselves audited at the rate of 22 percent. The committee report noted that names on the enemies list included journalists, politicians, and professionals who tended to have large business deductions. This factor alone would further increase their chances of being audited, the committee maintained. Therefore, an audit rate of 22 percent was considered "normal" by the joint committee investigators.

The conclusion? The Nixon White House very much wanted to use the tax system as a weapon against its enemies and a shield to protect its friends. But the politically-appointed IRS commissioner successfully resisted. The career IRS civil service staff cannot share this position with Johnnie Walters.

While Walters can look back on his IRS years with a sense of pride in doing the right thing, the IRS staff cannot. They never told the commissioner about Paul Wright and his odious Special Services Staff. The work of the Special Services Staff resulted in many vain audits, such as that of Walter Teague. The size of the Nixon enemies list pales in contrast to the thousands of names of taxpayers gathered by the IRS on its own initiative.

In effect, the IRS subverted itself for political purposes. A commissioner of weaker backbone than Thrower or Walters could have easily acquiesced to the White House's desire for political manipulation of the tax system. Twenty years later, suspicions of similar misuse of IRS power for political purposes were raised in the Travelgate scandal. But in contrast to the 1973 Nixon revelations, there has been no publicly released congressional investigation of the IRS's unusual audit of Ultrair, a small travel agency in Smyrna, Tennessee, that was providing air charter services to the White House Travel Office at the time the Clinton administration fired seven Travel Office employees and tried to shift Travel Office business to a company owned by a longtime Clinton crony. In contrast to its rapid, five-month investigation of the Nixon administration's attempt to politically subvert the tax system, the Joint Committee on Internal Revenue Taxation has remained publicly mute on the controversy surrounding this audit, which found no tax liability on the part of Ultrair.

Back in 1973, the IRS escaped from its own trap relatively unscathed because neither Congress nor the American public caught on that the real problem lay within the IRS, not the White House. The negative publicity surrounding the disclosure of Nixon's enemies list, however, left the American public with a distinct if erroneous impression that the IRS compliantly went after Nixon's enemies and cozied up to his friends. As usual, the truth turns out to be a little more complicated.

DON ALEXANDER'S WATERGATE WAR

Donald Alexander, Nixon's third IRS commissioner, inherited the IRS's Watergate hot seat. And the new commissioner's demons loomed even nearer and larger than those chasing his predecessors—

Alexander's demons were just down the hall. Alexander, who still practices tax law in Washington, recalled in 1996, "I don't think anybody would have taken the job if he had known what was coming. The hours are terrible, the pay is lousy. But on the plus side, you get a lot of abuse."

While Alexander suffered more than any modern commissioner, he admits that he pushed hard to reform the tax collection system when he arrived on the scene, perhaps too hard, expecting too much. He says, "I shouldn't have gone as fast as I did—but I wanted to accomplish certain things before I was out." Despite the pain, Alexander's reforms are perhaps the most enduring of the last generation. Change is painful. Commissioner Alexander carried that pain on his shoulders for the IRS. Alone among the recent commissioners, Alexander had the courage and strength to enact serious and lasting internal IRS reforms. He suffered the consequences.

Alexander came to the IRS with firm ideas about the proper job of the tax collector: to collect taxes, plain and simple. He did not think the IRS should be out chasing criminals for the Justice Department. "I thought the IRS should stick to tax crimes," says Alexander, which he insists irritated the overpoliticized Department of Justice no end.

"They were using IRS criminal investigation people to make the criminal cases the FBI wouldn't make and cases the DEA (Drug Enforcement Agency) was too ineffective to make," Alexander maintains. He wanted the IRS to investigate tax cases. Cheating lawyers, cheating chief executive officers, anyone cheating on taxes. The focus on helping the Department of Justice with drug cases and other special enforcement cases meant that IRS resources were drawn away from tax cases.

Alexander spent much of his tenure on tenterhooks, not knowing from one day to the next whether he would be fired. "The President took a strong dislike to me, beginning about August 9, 1973," the day Alexander publicly disbanded the Special Services Staff with a statement to the effect that the IRS had gone badly off-mission, off-track. "From that point onward," Alexander wryly recalls, "problems seemed to always come up on the ninth of the month. When I was still in office and it was the tenth of the month, my wife and I would have a glass of wine to celebrate because I had made it to double digits!"

After John Dean's revelations of the enemies list and the exposure of the Special Services Staff, the last thing the IRS needed was the additional bad publicity that arrived in early 1975. Headlines once again screamed of IRS abuses; the culprit now a dim covert operation called Operation Leprechaun.

The *Miami Herald* first broke the story with revelations of a tawdry IRS undercover operation gone astray. Operation Leprechaun was to be an IRS sting operation to gather information on prominent Miami residents. The investigation went badly awry when IRS agents started collecting data on the sex and drinking habits of taxpayers rather than sticking to their ledger books.

Congress hauled in Commissioner Alexander to explain his agents' actions. Retired IRS executive John Johnson recalls what took place. "Alexander was going to a congressional hearing on Leprechaun and asked his staff, 'Is there anything I need to know?' They said 'No, everything's fine, everything was done by the book.' But Alexander got to the hearing and they told him different—in short, he got sandbagged by his own staff."

Congress asked Alexander tough questions about the undercover operation, for which Alexander had no prepared answers. "That meant we [IRS] had lied to him," Johnson ruefully concedes. "We had jeopardized his reputation. From that day forward, Alexander was distrustful and violently anti–Criminal Investigation. It was never the same after that."

Alexander promptly suspended the Criminal Investigation Division from making payments to confidential informants, which drove IRS special agents around the bend. They pegged Alexander as a tax lawyer who knew nothing about law enforcement let alone their work. They insisted that they needed informants and had to pay them. But Alexander was bent on ensuring that the IRS do its job, not collect information about sex and drinking habits. That had nothing to do with tax administration as far as Alexander was concerned. Cutting off the funds for these covert operations was his only weapon in solving the problem.

Alexander's new guidelines also halted the IRS's routine practice of sharing information with other federal law enforcement agencies; he placed restrictions on receiving information from external sources without special permission; he withdrew IRS agents from Justice Department organized crime strike programs without special approval.

The outcry from the formerly free wheeling IRS Criminal Investigation community was fast and furious. IRS special agents leaked anonymous statements to the press, accusing Alexander of seeking to impede their work. One agent bitterly complained, "He's dismantling in a year what it has taken thirty years to put together."

Another was even more revealing and blunt: "Alexander doesn't know what it is to be a cop. My job is to put criminals away using the tax laws. Alexander is a boardroom tax lawyer who thinks that tax law is something accountants use to save companies money."

The IRS agents had grown so accustomed to freedom and latitude that Alexander feared they had forgotten their real mission: to collect taxes. The *Miami Herald,* which broke the initial stories on Operation Leprechaun, came to Alexander's defense. In an October 9, 1975, editorial, the paper noted that Alexander was "being smeared because of his efforts to put a leash on some of his own IRS investigators." The article forthrightly concluded, "Some of his field men are as skilled at bureaucratic backstabbing as they are at short-cutting investigations."

The complaints of IRS special agents were not ignored. The Justice Department, accustomed to unfettered assistance from tax investigators, appeared determined to maintain the status quo. In November 1975 the Department of Justice opened an investigation of Commissioner Alexander, apparently based on charges emanating from Alexander's enemies within the IRS. A grand jury was duly convened, and charged Alexander with halting an investigation of tax shelters in the Bahamas because one of his former clients was a target of that investigation. It took five months for Alexander to be totally exonerated by the grand jury. By that time, the White House had floated stories to the press that it was considering removing the IRS commissioner. The damage to Alexander was done, but he refused to resign, remaining steadfastly in office until Jimmy Carter became president in January 1977.

Twenty years later, Alexander still reflects on his years at the helm of the IRS. "I didn't know that I was any great civil rights person," the former commissioner says with a slight chuckle, acknowledging his still conservative political leanings. "I didn't think I was a zealot. I just don't like sting operations very much. I didn't like breaking and entering. I thought that sounded like Watergate. I found out that the IRS was doing both, mainly in Florida."

IRS'S OWN DEEP THROAT

The last lingering legacy of the IRS's murky role in Watergate involves the late president himself, whose own 1040s were questioned in June 1973 in a series of articles in the Washington Post. While reporter Nick Kotz didn't have access to Nixon's tax returns, he obtained information that independent appraiser Ralph Newman had valued Nixon's vice presidential papers for tax purposes as a charitable deduction at $570,000. This was the precise amount of the deduction Nixon had claimed on his 1969 tax return for donating his papers to the National Archives. With a deduction of this size, it was easy to conclude that President Nixon had probably paid little or no federal income tax in 1969.

In response to the popular outcry that inevitably ensued from the revelation that the President was taking advantage of a tax loophole to lessen his tax burden, the Nixon White House duly confirmed the 1969 donation of papers, but refused to comment on the estimated value of the tax deduction. On July 30, 1973, Tax Analysts, a public interest organization in Washington, D.C., called upon the much put-upon IRS Commissioner Donald Alexander to appoint a team of independent tax auditors to review Nixon's tax returns. Tax Analysts questioned the validity of the huge deduction Nixon was claiming for donating papers created while he held public office, and duly submitted its own sixteen-page analysis of Nixon's tax posture to Commissioner Alexander for review. Citing Internal Revenue Code restrictions against disclosing "tax information," the IRS declined to follow the suggestion from Tax Analysts.

In early September 1973 *Baltimore Sun* reporter Adam Clymer wrote that an analysis of available financial data led him to conclude that Nixon had probably paid no federal income tax in 1970 and 1971. The public outrage recently directed against the disclosure of a list of millionaires who in the late sixties escaped paying federal taxes because of the many gaping loopholes in the tax code was now firmly directed at the holder of the highest office in the land. The $570,000 deduction for personal papers would have been the principal offset to Nixon's $200,000 presidential salary.

While Nixon denied the stories, claiming that he most certainly had paid income taxes for every year in question, he staunchly refused to release his tax returns, or reveal the amount of tax that he did pay. He defensively pointed out that the IRS had accepted his returns as filed. With access to tax returns locked up tight, inaccessible for public or press scrutiny, we might have never known the true story hidden in President Nixon's tax returns. But thanks to a critical leak by an IRS employee who sacrificed his career to expose the reality of the Nixon 1040s, the story didn't end there.

This particular employee who, unlike the press, did have access to the information on Nixon's tax return, didn't like what he saw. Despite Nixon's public protestations that he had indeed paid his income taxes, this unsung hero of the IRS knew that the amount Nixon had actually paid was negligible, considering his sizable income. This anonymous "Deep Throat" inside the agency leaked this tidbit of information, along with the amount of tax Nixon paid in 1970 and 1971, to the *Providence Journal-Bulletin.* On October 3, 1973, the paper ran with the story. The headline said it all: "NIXON'S INCOME TAX BILL $1,670 FOR TWO YEARS."

The paper reported that Nixon had rendered unto Caesar a paltry tax payment of $1,670—for two years—or somewhat less than the amount that would be paid by a taxpayer earning around $7,000, who had only one exemption and no itemized deductions. Nixon's salary had been $200,000. The Rhode Island paper reported that Nixon received a refund of $131,503.84 for the same two years, a grand sum for the donation of documents created while in public office to a federal institution, the National Archives.

The White House was apoplectic. The IRS was embarrassed. This leak was a serious breach of taxpayer confidentiality. The IRS had no idea who provided details from Nixon's tax returns, but the reporter coyly provided a hint. He wrote, "Nixon's complete income tax forms . . . reportedly are kept sealed in a safe across the hall from the

Commissioner's office." Only someone with knowledge of how presidential 1040s are segregated from all other tax returns and stored in the Washington IRS headquarters could have sprung the leak.

The day after the initial story appeared, the *Providence Journal-Bulletin* ran a follow-up reporting that the White House refused to comment on Nixon's tax returns beyond a statement from Nixon's deputy press secretary that Nixon had again stated on the record that the IRS had accepted his returns as filed, and no change had been requested or made. The IRS declined to comment.

Two months after the IRS leak, with the story refusing to die, the *New York Times* reported that the White House had conceded there might be serious questions about Nixon's returns, with the largest issue involving the deduction for donating his vice presidential papers to the National Archives. Still refusing to release his returns, Nixon provided a copy of a letter from the IRS accepting his returns as filed, dated only eight days after they had been turned over to the IRS by his accountant.

Faced with unrelenting media pressure, Nixon finally released his 1970 and 1971 tax returns on December 8, 1973. He further agreed to allow the Joint Committee on Internal Revenue Taxation to review his returns and publicly promised to abide by their judgment. This unprecedented disclosure of the president's tax returns has now become the common and expected practice of politicians at all levels, local and national.

No one knew it at the time, because the IRS is restricted from acknowledging that any particular taxpayer is under audit scrutiny, but Nixon's December 8 announcement was a clever public relations ruse on his part. On December 7, the day before his public announcement, the IRS, still under the helmsmanship of Donald Alexander, had personally delivered to the White House a letter addressed to President and Mrs. Nixon, indicating that their tax returns were to be reopened for audit. By asking the Joint Committee on Internal Revenue Taxation to look into his returns, Nixon possibly hoped that its conclusions or influence would sway the IRS audit. Nixon's maneuver was revealed seven months later as part of the impeachment inquiry by the House Judiciary Committee just weeks before his resignation.

Meanwhile, Connecticut Congressman Lowell Weicker returned to the issue of the donation of Nixon's vice presidential papers. Weicker had learned that the IRS had not contacted either the National Archives or an independent appraiser to determine the validity of Nixon's deduction for his papers during its first review of Nixon's returns. Under normal circumstances, a deduction of this size by any other taxpayer would have been routinely questioned and verified by the IRS.

Weicker upped the ante by questioning whether Nixon's donation took place after a 1969 change in the tax laws, which would invalidate the entire deduction. The 1969 law had been passed by a Congress reacting to an irate public response to the revelation in the national media that inflated deductions had allowed a number of certified millionaires to escape the tax noose entirely. In response, among other changes, the amended law allowed the deduction of personal papers only up to the value of the paper they were printed on, virtually with one stroke of the Capitol Hill pen wiping out a much abused loophole in the Byzantine tax code.

Weicker's question on the floor of the Senate raised the heat of the debate over Nixon's deduction, since the only question so far raised had been whether the papers were truly worth the $570,000 value placed on them by Nixon's appraiser. Weicker claimed to have information indicating that Nixon's papers were physically turned over to the National Archives on April 10, 1970, long after the July 25, 1969, expiration date for the deduction.

On January 2, 1974, going against a deeply ingrained tradition, the IRS tersely revealed that it was auditing a specific taxpayer's returns: President Nixon's. The IRS released a one-paragraph statement that it was conducting the audit because of "questions raised in the press as to the relationship of the consideration of the President's tax returns by the Joint Committee on Taxation and any consideration of the returns by the IRS." An IRS spokesman further confirmed that the audit announcement was unprecedented, but that the president had authorized the IRS to disclose the audit. The acknowledgment of the audit came nearly a month after the tax collector informed Nixon that it was under way.

Three months later, with the audit complete, the IRS notified

Nixon on April 2, 1974, that he owed back taxes of $271,148.72 on his 1970 and 1971 returns, as well as a tax deficiency of $148,080.97 on his 1969 return. Since the statute of limitations had expired on his 1969 return, Nixon was not legally obligated to pay this deficiency. The IRS slapped a 5 percent negligence penalty onto the 1970 and 1971 deficiencies, adding $13,557.44 to the tax bill.

In a classic pass-the-buck response, the White House issued a statement claiming that "any errors which may have been made in the preparation of the President's tax returns were made by those to whom he delegated his responsibility for preparing his returns and were made without his knowledge and without his approval."

On April 17, 1974, Nixon paid the IRS $284,706.16 to cover the 1970 and 1971 tax deficiency, ignoring the 1969 liability. But the baying dogs of the Fourth Estate refused to let this juicy bone drop into oblivion. In June the *Baltimore Sun* pointed out, "If an ordinary taxpayer had been in Richard Nixon's shoes, his tax case would have been referred to the Department of Justice for possible criminal prosecution." Also in Nixon's case the IRS had a choice between two penalties: It could assess a civil fraud penalty, which would have been 50 percent of the tax due, or the negligence penalty of only 5 percent. The IRS chose the lesser penalty and was soundly criticized in the press for its leniency.

Nixon resigned on August 9, 1974, thus avoiding impeachment proceedings. Nixon's tax problems were prominently placed in the proposed articles of impeachment. Three months after Nixon's departure, former White House lawyer Edward L. Morgan confirmed Congressman Weicker's suspicions when he pleaded guilty to conspiring to violate the tax laws by backdating Nixon's gift of vice presidential papers in 1969.

One of the lesser known legacies of the Watergate years, as they pertain to the IRS, is the now routine practice for sitting presidents, and even for most political candidates, to open their tax returns to the public. All because an IRS employee didn't think Nixon was being forthright with the American people about his 1040.

6

"TO BETRAY YOU MUST FIRST BELONG"
The Barnard Hearings

"The IRS eats its children, you know," Don Curtis told me in his office one fine summer's day in July 1989, just ten months into my new job.

"You've got to watch your every move around here. They'll drag you along for your entire career, and then one false step—poof! You're outta here! Your support is gone. Your goals are wiped off the slate. Your career is gone. That's just the way it is." He shrugged in philosophical resignation.

"Has that happened to anyone you know of?" I inquired.

Don waited a long time before responding: "Shelley, why don't you go sneak a peek at those hearings on Capitol Hill? Even if they do give you grief for it—and I'm sure they will—it'll be a spectacle worth witnessing. It's your responsibility as our official historian to be there."

He was right. And so I went.

You couldn't say that I hadn't been warned. In an around-the-water-cooler hallway conversation with an acquaintance, I'd casually mentioned strolling over to Capitol Hill to attend the fearsome Barnard hearings, scheduled to begin any day now. This long-term IRS employee furrowed his brow and said, in all seriousness, "Shelley, I

Source of chapter title: Harold Philby, *New York Times*, December 19, 1967.

don't think that would be such a great idea. You know"—he awkwardly fumbled for words—"I don't think the agency wants all sorts of extraneous people crowding the hallways. . . ."

He didn't have to say another word. I had been warned. For the record, no one in my specific chain of command ever spoke a word to me on the subject. So I went. It *was* my professional duty.

The Barnard hearings, to be chaired by Congressman Doug Barnard of Georgia, seemed likely to be the most important congressional oversight of IRS malfeasance since the notorious King hearings of 1952. The King hearings had resulted in a wholesale reorganization of the IRS hierarchy directed by President Truman. (Former IRS Commissioner Sheldon Cohen once told me that, during his tenure under President Johnson, he kept a copy of the King hearings on his desk at all times, in plain sight, so that he'd never forget those dark days in the late forties and early fifties when the IRS—at least key elements in it—had been for sale to the highest bidder.)

Barnard's congressional investigation might easily rival the King hearings in their positive, purgative effect on the IRS. Surely the agency hierarchy would welcome any attempt to uncover and correct genuine malfeasance. But my view did not align with that of the IRS higher-ups, who derided congressional overseers as a lot of know-nothings poking their noses into subjects that should have been none of their business, threatening the very life-blood of the American tax system.

At a few minutes before nine on the morning July 25, 1989, I set off on foot for Capitol Hill. Outside the IRS building, I ran into a man from the IRS Legislative Affairs Office waiting for a cab to the hearing room a mile away. He politely invited me to hop a ride with him, an offer that I accepted, just to hear what someone "in the loop" on the around-the-clock preparations for the hearings had to say. The look on his face, one of mental and physical exhaustion, signaled that this particular guy was up to his neck in hearings. You could hear it in his voice the moment he opened his mouth, which he did reluctantly, according to the tight-lipped IRS custom.

"I just wish these hearings would go away," my informant groaned as he barked at the driver to get us to the Rayburn House

Office Building ASAP. "Please hurry," he sputtered, clearly getting ever closer to the end of his rope. In his defense, that early morning rush-hour traffic *was* murder. As we made our way across town he vaguely alluded to "the extraordinary lengths we went through to prepare for the hearings." I gathered from his resigned tone that he and his colleagues had been up in the wee hours of the night prepping their superiors to respond to innumerable obscure questions likely to be posed by limelight-seeking representatives, eager to score points against the enemy—the ever-lovin' IRS.

Once in the hearing room—Room 2247 of the Rayburn Building—we went our separate ways. He joined his crowd in the rows of chairs at the front while I deliberately sought a seat in the back. The room was a medium-size congressional hearing chamber, with enough padded seats arranged in even rows to hold about a hundred spectators. It was carpeted with the congressional seal and featured the requisite federal dark wood paneling on the walls. There were the typical imposing set of tables up in front, where the representatives sat. The young, starry-eyed, eager-beaver Capitol Hill staffers shuttled to and fro, whispering importantly and urgently in their bosses' ears, carrying white papers under their arms like aides-de-camp bearing military dispatches into a field of battle.

Though I've often wondered, I still don't know whether coincidence or convenience dictated the fact that we happened to be *between* commissioners as the hearings commenced. This left only the ever-loyal career bureaucrat, Senior Deputy Commissioner Michael Murphy, in the hot seat to fend off tough questions and play hardball for the IRS team. Murphy, who looked like your quintessential flat-footed cop from Central Casting, sat flanked in the hot seat by the outgoing commissioner, Larry Gibbs, and incoming commissioner Fred Goldberg, neither of whom could be held accountable for any horror stories likely to be revealed during the hearings. Gibbs was gone and Goldberg too fresh to accept the blame for anything.

In the chairman's seat sat Congressman Doug Barnard, a gray-haired, distinguished former Georgia banker, who had been elected to Congress on the Democratic ticket in 1976 (the Jimmy Carter election)—as he later put it to me—"as a Southern conservative, not a big business basher." Barnard was no rabble-rouser. He was certainly not the sort of man who adopts causes lightly. But during eighteen years of serving his constituents in the House before retiring home to Augusta, Georgia, Barnard went after the IRS like a true good-government reformer. What routinely went on at the IRS made this respectable Southern citizen hopping mad, in a genteel, polite Southern sort of way.

Barnard's elevation to the chairmanship of the Commerce, Consumer, and Monetary Affairs Subcommittee of the House Committee on Government Operations in 1983 provided him with a broad mandate to look into issues related to the interaction of government and the public. One of his greatest successes, he believes, was the banning of dangerous three-wheel all-terrain vehicles.

One of Barnard's first brushes with the IRS occurred when he and his staff decided to look into a chronic problem, brought to his attention by innumerable frustrated constituents, involving the IRS's ill-trained, low-paid "taxpayer service representatives," who had an unfortunate habit of giving too many wrong answers to taxpayers' questions over the agency phone lines. Rather than admit that they didn't know the right answers—assuming they knew they didn't know—they often gave out bad information. This resulted in many taxpayers being given bum steers by their own government, often resulting in headaches down the road, since the IRS amazingly can't be held responsible for errors made by its own telephone assistants. Let the taxpayer beware.

"I realized that there needed to be some legitimate oversight of the IRS," Congressman Barnard later recalled. "We found that over 50 percent of telephone answers were wrong." The result of Barnard's investigation: IRS beefed up its training for telephone assistants, while the public at large learned that it couldn't always trust what came out of the mouths of the tax assistants. Before Barnard's revelations, few taxpayers knew that if they made a mistake on their tax returns based on wrong advice from an IRS telephone assistant, they were still liable for taxes due. That didn't change, but at least the problem was now out in the open.

Over time, Barnard's subcommittee developed a reputation as just about the only place on the planet where IRS problems had a chance of receiving a serious airing and even a slight chance of being resolved. As a result, the subcommittee began hearing from IRS employees, whistle-blowers who would relate horror stories of chronic mismanagement, misconduct, and outright corruption reaching up to the highest ranks of the IRS. As the calls continued to come in, and congressional investigators looked into each allegation, a pattern began to emerge: a broad breakdown in the ability of the IRS to police itself; an appalling decline in ethical standards at the highest levels of the tax collector.

In the spring of 1988, the subcommittee staff selected some of the most serious allegations for full investigation. After nearly fourteen months of intensive interviews and research conducted by trained investigators attached to his staff, Congressman Barnard was ready to present the committee's findings to the public. The IRS, to put it mildly, was apoplectic. Despite public claims that it "welcomed" Barnard's inquiry, from what I saw inside the IRS, it considered this entire probe not only a massive waste of its precious time, an outrageous insult to its integrity, and an irresponsible smear campaign, but a dire threat to its basic mission as well.

Over the years, the IRS has developed a marvelous method of deflecting any and all criticism against it, marvelous at least in its cunning ingenuity and sheer duplicity. Any open airing of misconduct and corruption inside the IRS, the party line went, would inevitably cause the average taxpayer to lose confidence in the agency, and thus severely hinder the IRS's ability to "promote voluntary compliance," with the nation's tax laws. Thus, the theory goes, if the public doesn't have confidence in the IRS, they might stop sending their 1040s in on April 15. The IRS seems to forget that voluntary compliance is backed up by the heavy hand of IRS enforcement pavers, keeping taxpayers in check. Anything—and that meant *any-thing*—that might in any way undermine the public's remarkably high rate of voluntary compliance was to be avoided at all costs. Unearthing corruption within the organization, according to this defensive reaction, constituted a threat not simply to the IRS's oft-sullied reputation, but to the integrity of the tax system itself.

Though by snooping around the IRS I had picked up enough to realize that the place was hardly the gang of streetcorner Santa

Clauses that agency PR would have you believe, the congressman's harsh opening remarks shocked me all the same. Somehow, until that day—July 25, 1989—I hadn't quite grasped the awesome depth and breadth of the service's problems.

"The IRS," Congressman Barnard began, after gravely rapping his polished wood gavel, "has a greater impact by far on the day-to-day lives of our citizens than does any other federal agency. It is for these reasons that those vast powers must be exercised with great care, and within a system organizationally structured to prevent employee wrongdoing."

"Our investigation indicates that there are serious employee integrity problems among senior managers at the IRS," he solemnly intoned in his deep Georgia drawl. "And we strongly believe that these hearings will be a positive force within the IRS for the reform of public integrity policies, practices, procedures, and organizational structure."

Turning to two men on the panel, Congressman Barnard formally introduced the two primary investigators for the subcommittee, Richard Stana and Leonard Bernard. Stana was assigned the task of starting off the briefing to Congress, and through them, the nation, on the overriding thrust of the investigation. A tall, rangy, methodical, academic gentleman, Stana spoke in measured, complete sentences, notably devoid of inflection, rendering the sound of his words a trifle soporific, even as their import struck close to home.

"One issue of grave concern to this subcommittee," Stana carefully enunciated, "is the manner in which the IRS has responded to our investigation. We regret to say that in many ways, IRS has not been cooperative with our probe." This charge was, after all, a very serious one—a cover-up, tantamount to obstruction of justice, to suborning witnesses, to paying hush money and using intimidation to silence dissent. These were the tactics of totalitarian organizations, not of free citizens in a free society.

"On two occasions," Stana elaborated, "witnesses who had agreed to be interviewed by the subcommittee staff withdrew their agreement after being briefed by an IRS Disclosure attorney on the penalties for unauthorized disclosure, even to a Congressional subcommittee, of [confidential taxpayer information]."

To subcommittee investigators, it appeared that the IRS was intent an abusing the disclosure statute, a post-Watergate mistake on the part of Congress, to muzzle Congress! I was beginning to understand why the IRS higher-ups had so strongly discouraged attendance at these hearings. To anyone employed by the IRS, these revelations were hardly likely to raise anyone's already shaky esprit de corps.

"At this point," Stana continued, "I would like to make the subcommittee aware of a document faxed to us this morning." He paused while the import of this disclosure sank in with the crowd. "It is an IRS disclosure 'Alert'—it is the bulletin No. 1, the first one of its kind—that warns IRS employees against unlawful disclosure of tax information. This form cites two examples where current and former IRS employees were prosecuted and convicted for section 6103 disclosures."

Section 6103 is the section of the federal tax code revised by an ill-advised Congress in 1976, which, in the guise of "tightening up" the IRS from misuse of confidential taxpayer information, ended up handing the IRS the perfect tool with which to intimidate its own people and withhold information from the American people. By adopting an overly broad interpretation of that key clause, the IRS has succeeded in putting the lid on just about any disclosure of any information that it didn't want aired in public.

The individual who faxed this document to the subcommittee, Stana went on, "told me that he questioned the need for IRS to issue this alert at this time and wondered whether this was an effort of the Office of Disclosure to somehow put a lid on what is being told to the subcommittee."

Obviously, that was precisely what this preposterous one-page "Disclosure Alert" amounted to. In a characteristically lame, inept attempt to put its own more positive spin on this embarrassing revelation, IRS officials quickly produced a "chronology" of the genesis and development of this one-page document, which purported to show that the "Disclosure Alert" had been in the works for fourteen months before the committee's session and thus freed them from the charge of intimidating potential witnesses. All I can say, and I assume all who attended the hearing would have concluded, is that the IRS should be charged either with egregious incompetence for spending fourteen months to create a one-page document—or with lying.

That disclosure set the stage for Richard Stana to get methodically down to business. "Our year-long probe focused on eight specific incidents of misconduct by senior IRS officials and the adequacy of IRS's response," he related, which involved twenty-five senior management officials from ten different locations, representing all seven IRS regions. In short, the misconduct uncovered was both agency-wide and nationwide. In conclusion, Stana told the quiet room of subdued IRS executives, the results of the investigations "strongly indicate that there has been a significant erosion of ethical standards among many at the highest levels of the Service."

In his desultory manner, Stana proceeded to reel off seven main "talking points," which summarized the primary concerns of the subcommittee.

1. There has been a serious failure on the part of the IRS national office to manage employee integrity programs.

2. Our work revealed that significant numbers of integrity problems exist among senior managers of the IRS.

3. Wrongdoing by IRS senior managers is too often ignored entirely or ineptly investigated.

4. A pervasive fear exists among IRS employees that reporting the misconduct of their superiors or cooperating in an investigation of those superiors will result in retaliation against them.

5. A mind-set exists within IRS that seeks to preserve the agency's public image above all else.

6. There are inadequate checks and balances on IRS criminal investigative activities.

7. When IRS refuses to take aggressive disciplinary action against the misconduct of a senior official when first

uncovered, that refusal often leads to subsequent misconduct of a more serious nature.

To sum up: Barnard's subcommittee turned up not only an inordinate number of truly bad apples, but also a number of tolerant IRS
employees who, after detecting wrongdoers, permitted them to
remain and infect the rest. The IRS defiantly turned on some of
those who dared to blow the whistle, bringing the would-be whistle-
blowers up on charges—while treating the blatant abusers of the
public trust with seeming deference.

The case with which Barnard subcommittee investigator Leonard
Bernard led off involved a complex dispute between two archrivals
in the fiercely competitive blue-jeans industry: Jordache and Guess
Jeans. The gist of Bernard's complaint was that Ronald Saranow,
head of the IRS's Criminal Investigation Division in the Los Angeles
District office for more than a decade—the largest such unit in the
nation—had, according to a probe originally mounted by *Forbes*
magazine, improperly instigated a criminal investigation of
Jordache's reputed tax liabilities, which nearly killed Jordache's business.

Early in the morning of January 28, 1986, fifty IRS and U.S.
Customs agents had burst into Jordache's New York headquarters,
and after two days of ransacking the place for evidence of tax evasion, carted off in excess of 2 million documents. But after three and
a half years, no grand jury had ever indicted anyone at Jordache.
Saranow—who had once been investigated by the agency for trying
to help out a boyhood buddy connected to organized crime—saw
the Marciano brothers, who owned Guess, on more than twenty
occasions between April 1985 and December 1986, fourteen of
which were considered social contacts—weddings, parties, and din-
ners, for example. According to a report compiled by investigators
working on behalf of Congressman Barnard's House subcommittee,
a senior IRS staffer informed the subcommittee that Saranow had
told him that he had discussed taking a job with Guess at a six-figure salary.

In later sworn testimony to the IRS itself, Saranow conceded that
at a lunch with the Marciano brothers on March 26, 1986, he had

been offered a job that would have provided him with salary, company car, and bonus. During the period that Saranow was reported to have been negotiating his cushy position with Guess, he happened to be urging the New York office of the IRS Criminal Investigation Division to stage a raid on Jordache. At the time, the two companies were involved in a bitter contractual dispute valued in the hundreds of millions of dollars.

Leonard Bernard's conclusion was perfectly straightforward: in exchange for the offer of a job with Guess, Ron Saranow, "used his reputation as one of the most powerful Criminal Investigation Division chiefs in the country to encourage two criminal investigations against the 'enemies' of informants under circumstances involving serious improprieties and possible illegal conduct." But what disturbed Bernard and Barnard's subcommittee even more was the IRS's typically lame response to these sordid revelations. In response to "serious questions" being raised about Saranow's conduct both within and outside the IRS, the service had initiated, according to Bernard's report, "what can only be described as untimely and inept internal investigations." The ultimate culprit, in Doug Barnard's eyes, was "the IRS's institutional mindset that disclosure of serious wrongdoing by its senior managers would be an unacceptable black mark on its public image."

A second case revolved around a high Washington-based IRS official, Anthony V. Langone, who between 1986 and 1988 had been head of the IRS's Criminal Investigation Division, the IRS's top criminal investigator at the time. Langone may have been a top-notch investigator, but he was also a confirmed junket junkie who routinely arranged official trips around the country by routing flights from, for example, Seattle to Washington, D.C., by way of Atlanta. Atlanta happened to be where a close female friend lived. This time subcommittee investigator Richard Stana presented the case. Stana reported that there had been "little apparent business reason" for Anthony V. Langone to be constantly flying in and out of Atlanta on circuitous routes around the country—certainly not eighteen different business reasons. Nine trips were later exposed as purely personal vacations, for which the IRS picked up the tab.

On September 9, 1986, Langone's secretary informed the head of the IRS's Inspection Division about this possible abuse of executive travel privileges. But the head of the Inspection Division didn't even bother to examine Langone's travel vouchers before deciding to take no action whatsoever on the matter. Two months later, a senior technical adviser in the Criminal Investigation Division once again brought the Langone travel matter to the attention of the Inspection Division. Once again, the Inspection Division did nothing at all about it. On a third occasion, an anonymous caller from the IRS Atlanta office alleged that Langone's girlfriend worked in the service center there and that she and Langone used federal telephone lines to call each other. Finally, two weeks after this call, the assistant commissioner for inspection, the number two man in the office, "consulted" with the second most senior official in the IRS—Senior Deputy Commissioner Michael Murphy, the man now holding the ball for the agency—about how to handle this delicate matter.

To avoid the embarrassment of a formal investigation, they handled it discreetly by tipping their hand to Langone that he was under suspicion. On July 1, 1987, the acting associate commissioner for IRS operations, Langone's immediate supervisor, was deputized to discuss with Langone his dubious travel arrangements. Langone firmly denied any impropriety whatsoever.

Not only was the matter dropped, but Langone became, if possible, even more brazen despite being warned of surveillance. On Saturday, February 13, 1988, he traveled to San Juan, Puerto Rico, as a leg of an official round trip between Washington, D.C., and L.A. He racked up an additional $294 for airfare to make the San Juan stopover "as a result of his extended travel itinerary," in the dry words of Richard Stana's report, which noted without further comment that Anthony Langone's female friend just coincidentally happened to be "on official travel in Puerto Rico at the same time."

Shortly thereafter, Anthony Langone retired from the IRS to set up as a private eye with offices in Dallas and Los Angeles, having failed to reimburse the government for an estimated $2,000 in personal travel racked up at the taxpayers' expense. Guess who his partner in the new venture was? Ron Saranow—the former friend of Guess Jeans, whose six-figure-salary job had failed to pan out, presumably as a result of the congressional attention to his alleged conflict of interest.

Even more disconcerting for someone still working for the IRS, the secretary who originally brought the charges against Langone to the appropriate authorities steadfastly refused to discuss her reasons for backing away from testifying with investigators for the subcommittee. Since I know who this woman is and that she still works for the IRS, I can safely say that her abrupt decision to reconsider backing up her charge of corruption with public testimony looked pretty fishy, particularly in light of the personal "Disclosure Alert" to which she was likely exposed.

In contrast to the careers of other IRS employees who had the courage to testify before the Barnard subcommittee, this employee's career rocketed upward rather than careening downward. No longer a secretary, this woman today holds an important position in the Criminal Investigation Division. The IRS definitely knows how to reward loyalty to the organization.

In yet a third case, criminal investigators used a seized speed boat to conduct surveillance of some suspected drug traffickers on the Great Lakes and started joyriding in it. They had stayed overnight on an island because they claimed that a storm had blown up, preventing them from crossing choppy seas to their home port; but another agent alleged they were too drunk to return.

These cases demonstrated both ludicrous and serious instances of official misconduct. And they confirmed my worst suspicions about the agency. My sole brush with iffy ethical conduct to date had involved the case of the missing records. The destruction of documents—that is, government property—is a serious federal offense, but I had no idea the IRS was capable of the shenanigans exposed by Congressman Barnard. In short, what I was witnessing at lower levels seemed symptomatic of a broader decay in ethical standards, further compounded by lax oversight at the top of the heap.

Over the next three days of testimony, a succession of my colleagues stood up and testified against their superiors. What could possess these otherwise ordinary people to risk their jobs and their livelihoods to blow the whistle on their superiors? Sure, in a few isolated cases, personal animosity or simple resentment at unjust, unfair, or unkind treatment might have prompted them to go public. But no matter how strenuously the IRS mucky-mucks sought to silence these statements, the cases that the subcommittee had chosen to present publicly were well grounded in fact.

About halfway through the first morning's session, the congressmen decided to take a break. A sizable group of IRS employees—the spin-control squad—took a powder and began milling furiously around the lobby. I threw caution to the wind and joined them, hoping to hear something worth noting. Recognizing one fellow, I asked him what he thought of the morning's testimony in a feeble attempt to make conversation.

"What did you think of it?" he answered my question with a question.

Deliberately seeking to remain noncommittal, I shrugged and said, "Interesting."

"*Interesting?*" He gulped. "I'd call it disgusting." When I failed to respond, he plunged on, "Don't you realize that these people might be getting off on being in the limelight today, but tomorrow, they'll be gone, and we'll still be here! Don't they realize their careers are *over?* Finished. Done with. Over and out." Apparently pleased with that felicitous turn of phrase, he winked at me cordially, even conspiratorially, as we parted ways—in more ways than one. My God, I thought, he thinks that I'm one of *them*—meaning the IRS loyalists manning the halls—instead of one of *them*—I gazed sympathetically at the empty seats where the whistle-blowers had gathered, like a mutual support group. During the break, they were nowhere to be seen.

There was an obvious downside to testifying—losing your job, and still having to cope with your mortgage and your kids' growing food bill. But what about the upside? Frankly, I couldn't see one, not in any tangible sense. Just the knowledge that you were doing the right thing. Sometimes that's enough.

Such was certainly the case with former IRS Criminal Investigation special agent William Duncan, who served in the IRS district office in Little Rock, Arkansas, as a specialist in tracking down money laundering. He had been assigned to a critical case involving alleged money laundering and narcotic smuggling on the part of one Adler Barriman, also known as Barry, Seal. Duncan served as the IRS chief witness before a grand jury probe into these illicit activities in the western district of Arkansas. Problems with gathering evidence hindered the investigation. Ultimately the House Judiciary Subcommittee on Crime began asking why indictments were not forthcoming.

Duncan was summoned to Capitol Hill to testify about the problems he encountered during his investigation. One of the most troubling pieces of information Duncan came across was an allegation that Barry Seal had succeeded in bribing an unnamed high-level government official, a piece of important intelligence Duncan picked up during a February 1988 telephone conversation with an Arkansas State Police investigator also working on the case.

Duncan was scheduled to testify under oath before the House Judiciary Subcommittee on February 26, 1988. Because of the sensitivity of his testimony, and to ensure he did not inadvertently disclose confidential tax information, Duncan later told Congressman Barnard's committee that he attended a series of meetings with IRS disclosure attorney Mary Ann Curtin in early January which concluded the day before his scheduled testimony. During a February 25 briefing, Duncan said, Curtin advised him that if the alleged bribe came up during his questioning by the congressional panel, he should simply respond, "I have no information." Under no circumstances was Duncan to bring up this sensitive topic on his own. Duncan testified that he was perplexed, believing that if the subcommittee asked him about the bribe, the most appropriate response would be to say that he had received a phone call and provide the context of the conversation. He certainly had no intention of introducing the matter on his own.

But Duncan said Curtin told him that what he got over the telephone was not "information" per se, but unsubstantiated hearsay. Therefore, he should tell the subcommittee he "had no information." But Duncan believed he *did* have information. Though as evidence it might not have stood up in court, it was still information. Furthermore, Duncan knew that the Arkansas State Police investigator had already been asked about the bribe by the committee, and so he anticipated questions during his testimony.

Duncan felt strongly that to tell a congressional subcommittee, "I have no information" if he were asked a specific question about the alleged bribe would be tantamount to perjury, and, he testified, he told Curtin that, in all good conscience, he could not perjure himself.

Duncan told Barnard's subcommittee that Curtin answered that the IRS simply could not have information about a bribe to this government official splashed on the front page of the *Washington Post* and, even more damagingly, attributed to an IRS agent. In response to Curtin's rationale for advising Duncan to adopt this posture, Duncan's supervisor Paul Whitmore, who sat in on this meeting, was said to have asked Curtin how it would look in the papers "if an IRS special agent lied to Congress." Whitmore had been chief of the Criminal Investigation Division of the Little Rock IRS office from 1982 through 1988, when he took charge of training for all IRS special agents at a facility in Georgia. Meanwhile, Duncan testified that Bryan Slone, an assistant to the commissioner, had, according to Curtin, said, "Well, Bill is just going to have to get the big picture."

Duncan would later refer to this entire episode as "like being in the Twilight Zone." Curtin and her boss, IRS attorney Peter Filpi, later denied that the meetings with him ever took place. A month before he was scheduled to testify before Congress at the Barnard hearings, Duncan resigned in protest and anguish from the IRS. Whitmore would later corroborate Duncan's story about receiving direct pressure from the IRS Disclosure attorneys to suppress information in testimony before Barnard's subcommittee.

The IRS's bland, nonresponsive response to these startling revelations was revealing, to say the least. At the end of three days of listening to sordid tales of misconduct among the ranks of IRS executives, Senior Deputy Commissioner Murphy finally got his moment in the spotlight. If he thought he could bask in the warmth of public attention, he ended up getting roasted instead.

Senior Deputy Commissioner Michael Murphy:

> Mr. Chairman, I would like to point out that based on my knowledge of the three hundred executives as an executive team in IRS I would put their integrity, their approach to their jobs up against any institution, and anybody, and any corporation . . . I could sit here and tell you

about all the honors that we have received in the quality area but I would rather just say to you that we truly are committed to providing quality customer services to the people we serve.

Hip hip, hooray!

But our Mr. Murphy wasn't through yet. Determined to zing home the message and win one for the Gipper, Murphy prattled on, oblivious to the negative impression he was making.

Preparing for and watching this hearing these last few days permitted me to review the time I spent in this organization. I have three pictures on my wall in my office—actually four—one from Commissioner Gibbs, giving me the highest award he can give, one from Treasury Secretary Brady giving me a Presidential Rank Award, one from Treasury Secretary Baker giving me the Presidential Rank Award, and last but not least, one from President Reagan giving me that Presidential Rank Award.

There was a long, pregnant pause in the hearing room. It was difficult to tell just what Barnard was thinking at that moment. What happened next ended up on the evening news.

Congressman Barnard wound up slowly. He began calmly. The anger underscoring his words only gradually surfaced, under a veneer of Southern politeness.

Mr. Murphy, I am just amazed. You are one of the most loquacious fellows I have ever known. I cannot believe that you would come before this committee today and gloss over as you so eloquently have done, twelve months of our subcommittee's investigation. I just cannot imagine that.

Slowly, Barnard began to pick up emotional speed. "All you have done is repeat everything that we have said and at the same time, depict that career attitude of the IRS that 'We can do no wrong.'"

Congressman Barnard's typically polite fist came down with a hard slam on the podium. With a voice tense with emotion and shaking his finger at Murphy, Barnard scolded:

The IRS world that you describe is a world where whistle-blowers are systematically punished and where wrongdoers are applauded. That is a world I don't recognize, not from our investigations. It's like the Land of Oz and you are the Wizard. It's not a real world that you describe today.

The hearing room had fallen silent. Until that emotional outbreak, the atmosphere had been surprisingly cordial. I glanced around to see how the IRS employees around me were reacting. They weren't. They sat silently, staring blankly.

Barnard's voice suddenly became tinged with a hint of melancholy resignation as he sadly concluded:

The real world is where employees throughout your agency are afraid to come forward to report wrongdoing or to cooperate in investigations of their superiors because of fear of retaliation. The real world of the IRS is where if you are not a team player, you are off the team.

7

A BAG OF MEAT
IRS Secret History, Volume IV

Any employee who has information indicating that another employee has engaged in any criminal conduct or violated any of the rules of these Standards of Conduct shall promptly convey such information to the Inspector General or to the appropriate internal affairs office ... of the Internal Revenue Service.

—Standards of Conduct, the Department of Treasury

After a brief lunch break on day two of his hearings, Congress-man Doug Barnard introduced three IRS employees from the heartland of America. The Chicago Three, I dubbed them. This trio of middle-aged, middle-class white men sitting on the panel wearing their Sunday best looked like your average midlevel government bureaucrats, nothing more and nothing less. Based on personal appearance, one would have been hard-pressed to identify any of these men as whistle-blowers, stool pigeons, or rat finks. But Stan Welli, George Ecola, and Ronald Koperniak had become three of the most hated men in the IRS—ostracized, threatened, intimidated, ridiculed, and held up to censure, scorn, and sanction by outraged and threatened superiors. All because they had dared to question the ethical conduct of their immediate superior in Chicago.

And, when their superior's superior did nothing to address their complaint, the three had insisted upon taking their allegations all the way to the top. Until, at long last, they actually got results: They found themselves targets of harassment, threats, transfers, demotions, and potential as well as actual downgrades in pay and performance ratings. The story of the Chicago Three, as told here, is based on testimony before Congressman Barnard's subcommittee, testimony before the Merit Systems Protection Board, Office of Special Counsel, and interviews.

Born in the heartland of America, in a small Kansas town, Stan Welli went to work for the IRS in St. Paul, Minnesota, after graduating from the University of Kansas in 1962. Buoyed by President Kennedy's youthful exuberance and sworn commitment to public service, Stan couldn't have been happier about his new job. "Government employment was achieving new respectability because of Kennedy's efforts," Stan recalled thirty years later. He could find nothing to be ashamed of in working for newly appointed Commissioner Mortimer Caplin's "new IRS." It would take a quarter century of loyal service for Stan Welli to become disgusted with his career-long employer.

Not long after embarking on his new career, Stan was summoned to IRS headquarters in Washington to attend a training class in basic internal auditing techniques—"boot camp" for internal auditors. "The responsibility of IRS's Inspection Service," Stan would later testify before Congress, "is to provide auditing and investigative oversight of the IRS." In layman's terms, the Inspection Service, composed of two distinct departments, Internal Audit and Internal Security, serves as the IRS's department of internal affairs. An internal auditor's job consists of sniffing out corruption, malfeasance, misconduct, or mismanagement inside the organization, everywhere and anywhere that such behavior may be detected. Internal auditors are expected to be purer than Caesar's wife. At least, that was Stan Welli's understanding.

For Welli, being in the nation's capital during the flare-up of the Cuban missile crisis in October 1962 made him feel almost a part of history. "We felt as if nuclear war might break out at any moment," Stan recalls, reliving the brief frisson when Nikita Khrushchev pounded his shoe on the UN podium to hammer home his famous threat, "We will bury you!" At each class break, Stan and his fellow classmate George Ecola would dash out to the newsstands outside the IRS building to catch up on the latest news flash out of Washington. A mile away, the President and his aides were meeting in secret session, thrashing out strategies and scenarios of how best to meet the looming Soviet threat.

As the crisis subsided, Stan was sent home to St. Paul, a freshly minted internal auditor earning an annual salary of $4,345. As the years passed and his career progressed along the standard upward path, Stan was transferred, first to Kansas City, back to St. Paul, then to Chicago. In Chicago, as luck would have it, Stan found himself reunited with his old buddy George Ecola, from Calumet, Michigan, in the Upper Michigan Peninsula. George spoke fluent Finnish, pronounced English with a flat, North Woods accent, and "was a fitness nut," Stan fondly recalls, "always running marathons."

Ron Koperniak—Stan describes him as "a tall, sandy-haired, handsome dude with a fantastic wife and four kids," rounded out the threesome of internal auditors responsible for overseeing the integrity and efficiency of the IRS throughout the Midwest Region, a nine-state swath of the Great Plains stretching from Illinois and Wisconsin in the east to Montana in the west. As Stan Welli would later testify before Congress, in pursuit of that mission he and his colleagues were routinely granted "access . . . to all tax, investigative, personnel and administrative information possessed by the Service." This access denoted the highly sensitive nature of their jobs.

Stan, Ron, and George made a good team. They got along inside and outside the office. George's two children were close to the same age as Stan's two daughters; Ron had four children of his own. Occasionally the families would socialize together, but more often the office camaraderie consisted of a casual drink after work with the boys.

Everything ran smoothly in the Chicago office until early 1979, when the three men learned they would be getting a new boss: Frank Santella, a fellow graduate of Stan and George's 1962 Internal Audit training class. Santella had developed a solid reputation in the Internal Audit community as a manager who supported his subordinates in building their careers.

By all accounts—including an official report recently released by the federal Merit Systems Protection Board—Santella was "well liked, outgoing, talkative about his family and personal matters, jovial, even flamboyant." Not to mention, Stan Welli adds appreciatively, "Frank was a great guy to party with."

Unfortunately, Santella's sterling character had a tragic Achilles heel: He fancied himself a man about town, a man of the world, a man who knew his way around the big city. To Welli, Santella epitomized "your stereotypical Italian stallion, a Frankie Avalon/Fabian type, a guy with a big ego, a compulsive talker." Upon deeper reflection, Stan Welli calls Santella "the sort of guy you used to see on *American Bandstand* who's always looking at the camera while he's dancing."

The story begins well over a decade ago, when, one day toward the end of 1983, Santella dropped by for a friendly chat with the three men. Without embarrassment, he alluded to a phone call he'd taken a day or two before from Leonard Altimari, an aide to Chicago-area congressman Frank Annunzio.

"He got my name by flipping through an IRS phone book," Santella exclaimed, according to Stan's later testimony. "He just kept flipping through until he came to the first good Italian name he saw."

"What did he want?" Stan asked hesitantly.

"He needed help with some tax questions," Santella casually explained, as in: "Hey, what's the diff?"

"Santella obviously considered this a funny story," Stan would later recall. "But personally, I wasn't so sure. Whether Frank grasped it or not, our job was to keep the IRS *clean*. I mean, squeaky clean. This didn't sound like something Santella should get involved with. Our hackles went up right away."

That Frank Santella would consider discussing a personal "tax situation" with a private citizen, especially a Congressional staffer, was truly beyond the pale. Santella's job as assistant regional inspector for the Midwest Region did not—repeat, *not*—include giving tax help to *anyone,* with or without a good Italian name. He was supposed to manage IRS internal audits. He had no brief to deal with the public.

Stan, Ron, and George liked Frank Santella. As an official report on the matter would later put it, they were thankful that "Santella supported the Audit Managers and encouraged them to seek appointments to higher-level positions in the IRS." Of all three men, Ron Koperniak, whose office was right next to Frank's, enjoyed the closest relationship to Santella. Santella would later confirm that over the years, Koperniak and he became "good friends."

The personal bonds made it all the harder for Stan, Ron, and George to think the worst of their friend and boss. For the time being, at least, Stan and the gang figured they'd give the guy a break, knowing that he had a tendency to puff himself up, to play around as if he was some sort of smooth-talking Italian street hustler, a cross between Al Pacino and George Raft. "Santella always tried to put on this movie star aura," Stan recalls. "He thought he was hot stuff."

But Santella's questionable conduct didn't stop there. Before long, the three auditors would later testify, he was gleefully regaling Ron, Stan, and George with glamorous tales of late-night glory, all too often featuring mysterious and disreputable acquaintances. Santella was not in the slightest bit ashamed to admit that he had become a habitué of a notorious hangout for organized crime figures in Milwaukee. He regaled his office mates with stories of staying up until all hours singing, chatting, and being plied with drinks on the house by the restaurant's manager, who happened to top a local FBI list of area organized crime figures. The manager was, as an official federal report later put it, "associated with illegal bookmaking in the Milwaukee area."

Frank's colleagues didn't find what they were hearing quite so amusing. Even after Santella's acceptance of free theater and political fund-raiser tickets, Stan, Ron, and George gave their boss and buddy the benefit of the doubt. Aware of Santella's tendency to grandstand and name-drop, to themselves they hoped that Santella was merely engrossed in some private yet harmless fantasy.

Stan tried to quietly and privately warn Santella that he was walking on thin ice. But Santella refused to listen. When Stan's colleague George Ecola made a fumbling attempt to talk to Santella about his association with the Milwaukee mobster, Santella just scoffed at their concern. Their concerns only intensified when, through the office grapevine, they learned that Santella had bypassed them and called in the Kansas City audit staff to look into Altimari's "tax question." Altimari, it seemed, owed the IRS roughly $400,000 in unpaid employment taxes.

Protecting the organization, particularly in light of subsequent events, was foremost in their minds when at long last the three men decided that Santella had to be stopped before he got them all into trouble. On May 17, 1984, some six months after Santella first bragged of taking the phone call from Altimari, George Ecola asked for and was granted a confidential meeting with Joe Jech, Santella's immediate superior as regional inspector for the Midwest Region.

During Ecola's private meeting with Jech, a former cop from Cicero, Illinois (where Al Capone holed up when Chicago got too hot), Ecola clarified that he spoke not just for himself but also for Ron and Stan. He told Jech that Santella had, by his own admission, accepted free theater tickets from Altimari, and had used the weight of his office to help his friend resolve a vexing "tax situation."

Making matters even worse for himself, Santella had earlier tried to borrow money from George Ecola, his subordinate, to help pay for a $2,000 deposit to his Individual Retirement Account. He had apparently failed to deposit all of the funds in his account before the April 15 Tax Day deadline. George had decided against loaning Santella the money, because he knew it was against IRS rules for a supervisor to request a loan from a subordinate. But Santella simply hit another employee up for the loan. For employees of the IRS to get into tax trouble is supposedly considered unacceptable behavior. For the assistant regional inspector of the Midwest Region, the IRS second-highest cop on the beat in the region, to fudge on his income tax deductions was unthinkable, if not unbelievable. But there it was. And it was hard to ignore.

According to Ecola, Jech did "express some concern" about these disconcerting disclosures. But at the same time, he seemed more interested in seeking to minimize their significance. At one point, Ecola says Jech asked him: "What's wrong with accepting gifts from friends?"

Jech, for his part, would later admit in testimony before the Merit Systems Protection Board that hearing these allegations of misconduct put him in "a difficult position." He and Santella were close friends. Jech chose to handle the situation with utmost delicacy.

"If he crosses the line again," Joe promised George, he would confront Santella personally. But George Ecola was far from satisfied. Particularly, as he later testified, after Jech remarked that he didn't want to report these disclosures to IRS headquarters, as required by IRS rules.

Within days of Ecola's "confidential" meeting with Joe Jech, the old easygoing atmosphere in the office became tense, awkward, and uneasy. The friendly banter ended. The tension eased for a few months when Santella was sent to another city on detail.

It resumed shortly thereafter, with Santella's return in mid-1984. Since Santella continued to give his colleagues the cold shoulder, they guessed that Joe Jech had told Santella of his meeting with George Ecola—a blatant violation of federal rules designed to protect whistle-blowers from fear of retaliation, not to mention retaliation itself.

In September 1984 Stan Welli was summoned to Santella's office for his annual performance review. Leaning ominously across his big GS–15 desk, Stan later told federal investigators that Santella whispered, "I know you guys ratted to Jech on me."

Stan sat speechless, waiting for Santella to continue. "I figured you sent George as the messenger because you're too tough and Ron is too mild." Apparently, Santella knew that all three of the audit managers had been involved. According to Stan's testimony, Santella threatened, "None of you can ever hope to move up in this organization."

Ecola testified that Santella not only issued similar threats to him during his annual performance review, he dared to lower his performance rating, costing Ecola a substantial reduction in pay. Deeply upset by this latest turn of events, George Ecola decided to confront Jech with his belief that Jech's conduct not only dismissed their allegations as trivial, but exposed his staff to blatant retaliation.

George later recalled that Jech said, "I know all about your lower performance rating," when George protested at their subsequent meeting. "I can't believe it has anything to do with your allegations."

Denying that he had told Santella about their allegations, Jech turned on Ecola. He had been "disappointed," he insisted, that Ecola had not more strongly supported him when he tried to promote Santella's secretary into a management position. Nor had George supported Jech's futile attempt to close one of the region's field offices. Still, without explanation, Jech reversed Santella's decision to reduce George's annual review a few weeks later. He awarded George Ecola a higher performance rating, and a cash award for excellent performance. To put that award into perspective, Jech simultaneously awarded his pal Santella with an outstanding performance report, a higher level of reward than Ecola received, along with a substantial cash award. Santella was just what the IRS considered an outstanding employee. I suppose he was, in a manner of speaking.

On an early spring day in 1985, Stan was surprised to find Bob Kozal, one of his Kansas City–based supervisory auditors, sitting in Frank Santella's office. To Stan's knowledge, an audit supervisor from Kansas City would have had no business being in Chicago at all. As Kozal's supervisor, Stan should in any case have been advised of his travel plans. With Ron in tow, Stan walked into Santella's office. Santella waved them away: "Give us five minutes, guys." Santella closed his office door the moment they exited.

What really incensed Stan was Santella's bypassing him to call on the Kansas City office, which was under his jurisdiction. By rights, Santella should have checked with him before engaging a K.C. agent to work for Chicago. Later that same afternoon, after a long lunch, Kozal showed up in George Ecola's office. Kozal "started blabbering," Ecola would later recall, about "Frank's political friend." Kozal confided to George that he had brought information about Altimari's corporations to Chicago from Kansas City, and that he suspected Altimari's web of corporations to be engaged in a scheme in which a corporate taxpayer files an Employment Tax Return but fails to pay the tax, quarter after quarter.

Kozal clarified that he had advised Santella of his misgivings about Altimari and his corporations. Ecola would later testify that he understood it to be "an escalating process and nobody's collecting anything. It's the type of situation where we would be looking for fraud."

But, instead of looking out for fraud, Santella appeared to be looking out for a friend. According to testimony, two days later, just after lunch on April 3, 1985, Santella mentioned to Ron Koperniak that he was meeting Leonard Altimari to discuss his "tax problem." The next morning, the testimony continued, Santella dropped by George's office and proceeded to regale him and Koperniak with a riveting tale of an afternoon cruising around the mean streets of the Windy City.

After a swank lunch at the Como Inn, and presumably a frank and free discussion of Altimari's myriad tax problems, Altimari had escorted his friend Santella to a wholesale meat shop on Chicago's West Side, the Chicago Three later testified. It was closed, but Altimari knocked on the doors and windows until the owner let them in. Altimari then strolled over to a huge walk-in freezer and personally filled a large shopping bag with six prime steaks, ten pounds of ground beef, and a few pounds of cheese, and presented it to Santella.

Ecola and Koperniak were stunned. Ecola would later testify that for him, the bag of meat was the last straw. A high-level IRS employee—their boss—accepts a bag of free meat and cheese from a private businessman after discussing his suspicious tax situation over lunch. Not good. Ironically, as Stan would testify, the trio wasn't even trying to gather evidence against Santella—he kept openly bragging about his exploits.

Again, the three audit managers decided to speak with their senior manager about their boss. On April 18, 1985, nearly a year after George first "ratted" on Santella to Joe Jech, George and Ron decided to give proper channels a second shot. This time they included all the gory details: Kozal's meeting with Santella, Kozal's admission that he was working on Altimari's tax problems, the bag of meat given to Santella by Altimari—the works. Joe Jech seemed remarkably unperturbed.

"I think," Ron and George recalled Jech telling them, repeating his concerns of their meeting a year before, "that we should handle this matter locally."

Ecola and Koperniak rebutted, "Joe, we tried handling it locally last year."

This time around, George and Ron swore to Jech's face that, if he didn't do anything, they and Stan would go over his head, to Assistant Commissioner for Inspection Robert Rebein at the IRS headquarters in Washington.

"Frank has a lot of friends." Joe Jech shrugged, loosely conveying his primary concern: that their formerly friendly Chicago office would become a snake pit if the three betrayed their boss to headquarters.

"Besides, guys, where will it get you?" Jech asked rhetorically, according to Stan. "Maybe five days' suspension for Frank, at most."

Despite a combined total of sixty years working for the IRS, Stan, George, and Ron were perplexed. Five days' suspension for consorting with, advising, and accepting gratuities from someone with a potentially serious tax problem? Five days' suspension for the assistant regional inspector of the Midwest Region, one of the IRS's top cops in the area? Later that day, Stan also had a heart-to-heart with Joe Jech, complete with written memos detailing Santella's links to Altimari.

"Don't worry, Stan," Joe Jech assured Stan. "I'll talk to Frank. I'll handle it myself."

To see that Jech followed through this time around, Stan, George, and Ron advised Jech that they would forward their complaint to the chief inspector of the IRS. Once again, Jech implored them to keep the problem at home. But, according to George, when Jech realized that their minds were made up, he backed off and asked to be informed when their complaint was on its way. He at first said he didn't want to see it or read it, but later asked to read it.

Over the weekend at George Ecola's home, the three men composed their referral to Chief IRS Inspector Robert Rebein in Washington. It featured a full disclosure package accusing Santella of associating with Altimari and the mobbed-up restaurant manager, his receipt of gifts and gratuities from them, and a laundry list of minor problems and transgressions chiefly relating to Santella's escalating personal financial predicament. All three signed the letter; all for one, one for all.

On Monday, April 22, 1985, they mailed the package. Little did they know what lay ahead. Years later, testifying before Congress, Stan Welli would compare their experience to "being hit by a ton of bricks."

Four days after mailing their letter, word came down from Washington that the national office was investigating Frank Santella. There was general relief all around—at least outside Santella's spacious office. By May 3 investigators had interviewed all three audit managers; on May 8 Santella himself got the third degree. Through this questioning, Santella learned of the precise nature of his colleagues' disclosures.

With the onset of the investigation, the once happy-go-lucky office atmosphere rapidly turned from chilly to arctic. Santella went about his business but scrupulously avoided personal contact with his three former friends. According to the later official report, "Santella became withdrawn and stayed in his office; communications were via buckslip; contacts between him and Ecola became 'very strained.'"

One day, in mid-June 1985, Ron Koperniak decided to visit Santella's office because, as he later put it, "I just wanted to talk to him." Koperniak felt bad about having to "rat" on Santella, to make damaging disclosures against a former friend. For the first time, Ron recalled, Santella talked openly about the investigation. He complained that the investigation had hurt him and his family, that some of the allegations were "really petty." Point-blank, he asked why Koperniak had signed the disclosure.

At one point, Koperniak would later testify, Santella finally leveled with his old friend. "Didn't you guys realize when you go for the king you have to go for the kill? You guys didn't get the kill. You guys thought you were going to be heroes, and you're not. Didn't you realize your careers around here would be over?"

Ron Koperniak stood in bewildered silence, not knowing quite what to say. Maybe Santella was right. Unfortunately for them, and for America, Santella was right. On June 17, the IRS completed its investigation of Santella, confirming most of the major allegations raised by the staff auditors. The Report of Investigation (ROI) was duly sent on to the Department of Treasury for official review. On July 12 the department's assistant inspector general for investigations, William J. Schaeffer, returned the ROI to Robert Rebein.

"This investigation shows," Mr. Schaeffer wrote in his transmittal letter, "that Mr. Santella associates with individuals reported to be involved with organized crime; that he accepted gratuities from individuals for whom he provided tax research assistance; that he had his staff research tax information of friends, associates, and his son. [And] that Mr. Santella did not timely pay his 1983 real estate tax; filed false tax returns for the 1983 and 1984 tax years, and that he made an unauthorized disclosure of tax information."

From the look of it, the case against Santella was open-and-shut. But that would not be taking the Byzantine, labyrinthine ways of the IRS into account. Schaeffer tersely concluded his letter to Rebein: "Please advise within 45 days of any action taken as a result of this investigation." Taxpayers should hope that the top of the IRS Internal Audit Division would purge the likes of Frank Santella, considering the strength of the evidence against him. But Jech feebly proposed that Santella be suspended for twenty-one days without pay "for failing to fully comply with requirements for meeting your personal tax obligations ... for improperly [disclosing] tax return information ... for accepting gratuities from an outside source ... and for [misusing] your official position by directing other Internal Revenue Service employees to access certain tax accounts and provide information to you even though you had no official reason to request such information."

A few days later, without explanation, Chief of Inspection Robert Rebein issued a final decision sustaining all the charges against Santella except the second—"improperly disclosing tax information"—but, contrary to the thrust of the report, reduced Santella's suspension from twenty-one days to twelve. Rebein also administered an "oral reprimand" to Jech for failing to refer Stan, George, and Ron's original allegations to the director of Internal Security a year earlier.

Santella quickly pounced on his first victim: George Ecola. During Ecola's annual performance review, Ecola remembers Santella telling him that his performance had been only "fully satisfactory," two levels of performance below the previous year. Ecola testified that when he protested, Santella replied: "Hey, I'm on the cuff for six months, so you're on the cuff for six months."

George asked him what that meant. Santella exploded, "I'm not getting an award because of the investigation and you're not getting an award for the same reason!" George testified.

According to Ecola, the two men scarcely discussed his work; they mostly discussed the investigation. He told Ecola that Ecola's career "was over," that he was "not promotable" and that none of the regional inspectors (who were all, Santella claimed, his friends) would ever accept Ecola as an assistant regional inspector, like himself. Ecola had not received such a low performance rating since joining the IRS in 1962.

Ecola was stupefied. He and his staff had been involved in five Nationally Coordinated Audits (NCAs) that year, of which Ecola had personally directed all operations since September 1985. One of these NCAs had generated revenues to the federal government of $69 million and had been the subject of a glowing letter of commendation from the director of the Internal Audit Division at IRS headquarters. Another audit managed by Ecola had generated revenues in excess of $100 million. Ecola had been personally responsible for a third of his entire division's revenues for 1985. Yet here was Santella downgrading his performance rating to a mediocre "fully satisfactory."

Next, during *his* annual performance review, Welli testified, Santella launched into a lengthy discussion of how deeply the internal investigation had hurt him personally. At one point, off the cuff, he remarked that Welli and his fellow audit managers had "destroyed their credibility by throwing in everything but the kitchen sink."

Welli said that Santella proclaimed himself "stronger than ever," said that he could have "beat the suspension if I'd chosen to go outside the IRS." As far as he was concerned there was no longer any basis of friendship between him and the audit managers.

Welli testified that Santella ominously observed, "If I turned in my boss, I'd be looking for another job." To the three men, it appeared that Frank Santella was obviously doing all he could to drive Stan and his fellow audit managers out of the IRS altogether. What particularly puzzled them was the role of Joe Jech in all this— this was, after all, the guy who, upon first meeting Stan, had complained to him about how hard it had been to be "the one honest cop in Cicero, Illinois." Stan wondered, Had the IRS corrupted Joe Jech?

Under later questioning by lawyers conducting an Office of

Special Counsel hearing, Santella grudgingly admitted that he had felt "hurt" by the audit managers' action because he had "put a lot of trust in the three audit managers and I did a lot for them, and then they turned around and accused me in the—I felt the wrong way, in the wrong fashion."

Pressed to elaborate on this point, Santella alluded to his disappointment that his three accusers had gone "and fired their missile off to Washington without sitting down and discussing it and getting to their major concerns . . . I wasn't concerned about the investigation," Santella boasted, "because I knew I didn't do anything improper."

IRS criminal investigator Norman Schweber, who had reason to discuss the matter with Santella on several occasions during this period, would later testify that Santella had complained bitterly to him that "after all he had done for the careers of the Audit Managers . . . they turned around and bit the hand that fed them." In another conversation, Santella called George, Stan, and Ron "snakes."

During this tense standoff, the three men were treated to a series of sneak previews of how their actions were likely to be viewed throughout the Internal Audit hierarchy. Internal Audit is a notoriously closed group within the IRS, like a private club or a secret society, and acts accordingly when one of its members is attacked, particularly when one of its members on an executive level is attacked from within the community, by one of his subordinates. By turning in one of their own and rejecting the habits of subservience expected to rule between manager and executive, Stan, George, and Ron had alienated themselves from the club. And they were going to pay for that big-time.

Later that summer, in August 1985, the three auditors attended a seminar in "effective writing" at the IRS Atlanta Service Center. Stan recounts the amazing turn of events. During a break in the class, Paul Kearns, a regional inspector from Dallas, entered the room in the company of regional inspector Ben Redmond, who had already snubbed Ecola during a visit to St. Louis. While Redmond escorted his own staff auditor out of the room, Paul Kearns (whom Welli describes as "looking like Tip O'Neill, but not as fat") walked up to two auditors from IRS headquarters and deliberately raised his voice: "In my region, we know how to handle whores like those three in the back there."

Then, turning to face the three Chicago auditors, Kearns issued a chilling threat: "The organization will get you, you whores!"

"Never in my life have I been as angry as I was after that insult," Stan recalls a decade later. "We took a lot of deep breaths. We left, went outside and paced back and forth in the parking lot. But ultimately, we bit our tongues." Upon returning to Chicago, Ron called IRS Chief Inspector Robert Rebein's assistant, Derle Rudd, in Washington to report this disgraceful incident. While Rudd voiced dismay at the situation, nothing concrete ever came of his concern. Paul Kearns retired the following year, leaving the IRS after a grand farewell celebration. Today, with apologies to Franklin Delano Roosevelt, Stan calls August 8, 1985, the day that an IRS executive called him and his co-workers a whore, "the day that will live in infamy."

In an apparent effort to contain this intradepartmental dispute, Chief of Inspection Robert Rebein flew to Chicago to meet with Stan and George, hoping to cast oil on the stormy waters of Lake Michigan. Rebein informed the three auditors that Santella would remain in Chicago, that he would not be transferred out of the office, and that if things didn't take a quick turn for the better, "I'll come back here and move you elsewhere."

Rebein was not about to disturb Santella, who was clearly steeped in hierarchy. Instead, he let the three staff auditors try to make amends with their boss. At least Rebein admitted, "You guys did the right thing." That didn't matter, though, as Stan recalls, Rebein sadly reflected: "the whole country is against you."

Now that's support from the top. By early November, Santella was back in the saddle in Chicago. At one meeting, Santella told his former friend Ron Koperniak that, just weeks before his suspension began, he traveled to a conference for top-level IRS inspection personnel, despite the findings against him. During that conference, some of the IRS regional inspectors took up a collection to reimburse Santella for his lost pay during his twelve-day unpaid suspension. He gloated over the total of $1,500 (it was later revealed to be closer to $850) that his fellow IRS cops gave him just before he returned home to begin his suspension. Point made: The auditors' club was staunchly behind Santella, and against the Chicago Three. Santella taunted Ron to tell "his friends" Stan and George about the collection.

Not until journalist David Burnham asked the IRS to confirm the collection for Santella did the IRS concede knowledge of it. Though the law prohibits private individuals from contributing to the salary of a public official, the IRS never disciplined any of the IRS employees who donated to Santella's collection plate.

Remarkably, despite confirmation of all the charges against him but one, Santella moved quickly to regain his lost ground. Life at the agency for George, Stan, and Ron slipped into rapid yet inexorable decline. After lowering performance ratings for both George and Ron, Santella awarded a "distinguished" performance rating and a cash award to Bob Kozal, the Kansas City audit supervisor who had helped out with Leonard Altimari's "tax problem."

At last, Santella's attention turned to Ron Koperniak. During a meeting, Koperniak testified that Santella haughtily informed him that he planned to report him to IRS authorities for helping Frank's secretary track down the status of her tax refund. Koperniak recalls that he had expressly informed Santella about his intention to help his secretary earlier in the year, to which Santella had replied casually, "Okay." Santella followed through on his word, however, lodging an allegation of misconduct against Ron.

After that, the war-torn Chicago office quieted down. The Bears won the 1986 Super Bowl. Stan recalls, "I lived for my weekends, where there was real comfort at home. I had my daughter Susan living with me. Little did we know that there was more afoot."

In the spring of 1986 IRS headquarters began looking into the muddled organizational structure of Internal Audit throughout the country. A report on that evaluation issued in early August recommended increasing audit staff in most IRS offices, and specifically recommended increasing staffing in the Chicago office from forty-five to sixty-six. A second recommendation was to standardize staff auditor positions in all regional offices.

There were to be three audit managers in each regional office. Some regions, including the Chicago office, had two audit managers and one operations manager, though the positions were considered interchangeable. In the Chicago office, Ron, George, and Stan rotated among the three positions. Barely a month after release of the headquarters report, Joseph Jech forwarded a separate, private proposal to Washington to reorganize only the Midwest Region Internal Audit Office. The memo, apparently prepared by Santella, recommended eliminating the position of the operations manager altogether. Jech suggested replacing this position with a lower-level "staff assistant" and transferring one of the three positions in Chicago to either Kansas City or St. Louis. The impact of Jech's proposal would be to reduce the status of all three of his staff auditors.

Despite the fact that Jech's proposal flew full in the face of the recommendations from the IRS national office, the new Chief Inspector, John Rankin, acting on the advice of two subordinates (who reputedly were close to Santella) approved this one-of-a-kind reorganization plan. On November 17, 1986 Santella called George, Stan, and Ron separately into his office to inform each of them of their sorry fates.

George was to be transferred to Kansas City. Stan was told he would lose a pay grade and be reclassified as a staff assistant. Ron, "the quiet one," was to stay put. Stan immediately protested his proposed reclassification and downgrading to a "staff assistant," a bizarre demotion considering that he had held a variety of management positions at the IRS for sixteen years. Santella and Jech suggested only one other option: early retirement.

But Stan was just forty-nine. He had two children to put through college, including Susan and a second daughter, who continued to live with his ex-wife. Under the circumstances, retirement wasn't a viable option. Besides, until the mid-eighties, he had enjoyed his IRS work.

George Ecola hadn't the slightest desire to leave Chicago. His children were in high school; he saw no reason to disrupt his family with an unwanted move. Ecola strenuously protested to Santella and Jech that the transfer was retaliatory and suggested that they let Stan transfer to Kansas City, since Stan wouldn't have minded moving closer to his childhood home, particularly if he retained his current rank and pay. Insisting that Ecola was "best qualified" for the Kansas

City job, Jech and Santella made it clear: If he didn't relocate to Kansas City, then he "might end up in a lower position, like Stan."

The very next day, Stan informed Ron of his plans to fight the reorganization. He was convinced that his proposed reduction in grade constituted blatant retaliation for bringing charges against Santella. But peacemaker Ron, the one with the most to lose, with years before he was eligible for retirement, feared opening up old wounds. Ron volunteered to move to Kansas City so that Stan could keep his job and George could stay in Chicago. Ron later admitted that he made his offer not because he really wanted to move, but because he couldn't stand any more tension in the office.

Jech and Santella continued to toy with their frightened mid-level employees. The day after the news of the reorganization, Santella insisted that whichever auditor agreed to make the move to Kansas City would have to report to the new job by January 1, 1987—only five weeks away.

But when Ron Koperniak informed Santella that he was prepared to move to Kansas City, Santella and Jech backed off a bit. All of a sudden, whoever decided to make the move could wait until spring to do it. But, Santella insisted, if Ron ended up refusing the transfer but was selected anyway, he would have to report by January 31. Afraid that this timing might lead to a mandatory move sooner than he could possibly prepare for, Ron and his wife left for Kansas City in early December, to have a look at their new, more peaceful city.

But after Ron returned to Chicago from the exploratory trip, he found that another plan had suddenly emerged during his absence. While Ron was away, Jech informed Stan and George that two of their subordinates in Chicago would be raised to a higher level. But the plan to downgrade Stan Welli remained in full force. This move was the last straw for Ron Koperniak, the would-be peacemaker. After that last devious twist, Ron insists, he "didn't trust anything they were telling me anymore."

In the midst of these Machiavellian machinations, Ron recalls that Santella had the nerve to tell him that moving to Kansas City would "help him rebuild his reputation." *His* reputation! "If it hadn't been for your misconduct," Koperniak erupted, "I wouldn't have to rebuild my reputation!"

To which, Ron testified, Santella responded, "You had a choice, Ron—you should have listened to Joe."

By "listening to Joe," Koperniak understood Santella to mean that he should have heeded Joe Jech's warning, "Frank has friends," and his forecast that the Chicago office would turn "into a snake pit" if they pressed their claim.

Over his strenuous objections, Ron was ordered to Kansas City but resolved to stand firm against the pressure. He refused to go, even agreeing a take a downgrade in rank to a nonsupervisory position rather than abandon his principles. He had been in his position for eleven years. As far as Ron was concerned, the whole scheme stank to high heaven. As Ron Koperniak would later testify before Congress:

> At best, the information used to support the reorganization proposal was sketchy and full of generalities. It contained no cost-benefit analysis, no specifics as to how the management of the operations would be more effective or more economical. Most incredible was that only our region was being reorganized, even though two other Inspection regions had smaller staffs, had Service Centers located in their communities (as opposed to 500 miles away) and had no other post of duty. The only definite thing about the reorganization plan was that it would remove Stan Welli from management and Ecola or me, if we decided not to relocate.

In March 1987 Stan Welli filed a formal grievance against Frank Santella, claiming that he was being retaliated against through his impending removal from a management position. Ron also filed a grievance protesting the reorganization's impact on his career. Later that month, Stan Welli and George Ecola met with IRS Chief Inspector John Rankin in Chicago, the man who had approved the ill-advised reorganization plan in the first place. "He seemed shell-shocked after our meeting," Stan would later recall. "We were convinced he'd do the right thing." But to their astonishment, Rankin returned home to Washington and, according to Welli, "helped launch one of the biggest cover-ups in IRS history."

The IRS Internal Security office, in conjunction with the Treasury

Inspector General, in due course commenced a formal "evaluation" of Stan Welli's grievance and charges of retaliatory behavior. Remarkably, the office quickly issued a "letter of clearance" to Frank Santella, claiming that they had found "no evidence of retaliation." After rendering this peculiar decision, the Treasury Inspector General's office freely admitted that it had rendered the ruling even though it had failed to locate a key piece of evidence—a 1985 affidavit prepared by George Ecola documenting Jech's knowledge of Santella's earlier misconduct.

Stan interpreted Rankin's ruling on his grievance as predicated on a concerted and doubtless deliberate attempt to narrow the scope of the investigation to only those events that occurred during the calendar year 1985. Of the seven witnesses to the alleged retaliation Welli had provided in his grievance filing, the Internal Security inspector assigned to the case was supplied with only three names. Even more telling, the inspector was ordered not to interview Stan, George, or Ron—the primary complainants and witnesses. Instead, the investigation focused on Welli's factual analysis of the reorganization, by which he hoped to prove it pure fiction, a retaliatory as opposed to a management tool.

Nonplussed by Rankin's adverse ruling, Stan Welli took his protest one rung higher up the ladder. His case was duly assigned to IRS grievance examiner Herbert Roth, an independent reviewer with no ties to the Inspection community or the Chicago office. After a four-month investigation, Roth readily concurred with Stan that the reorganization of the Midwest Internal Audit office had been a blatant reprisal against Welli and the others for whistle-blowing. Open and shut, right?

Wrong. Stan Welli's Sisyphean grievance, unfortunately, did not stop there. According to the Byzantine customs of federal procedure, Stan's grievance wended its way on up to IRS Senior Deputy Commissioner Mike Murphy, the "top top cop," who would later dither and blather so ineffectually at Congressman Barnard's IRS hearings, going on and on about all the plaques and awards and merit badges he had received from Presidents Reagan and Bush.

While awaiting what he expected to be a final rubber stamp of approval on his grievance package from Michael Murphy, Stan took the precaution of filing an additional complaint with the Office of Special Counsel, the government agency that exists to protect federal employees from wrongful personnel actions.

Unknown to Stan, Senior Deputy Commissioner Michael Murphy was evidently growing concerned about the possibility of Santella's case "going public," possibly during the upcoming Barnard hearings, creating an embarrassment for the agency. Murphy accordingly sat on Roth's report for four months, during which time Murphy offered Stan a dubious "deal" to settle his grievance. In February 1988, Robert Hilgen, Murphy's assistant, approached Stan's attorney with a "settlement offer."

The deal was simple: If Stan withdrew his grievance and complaint with the Office of Special Counsel and agreed never to raise the issue again in any other forum, the IRS would pay Stan $15,000. This offer coincidentally equaled roughly the amount of Stan's legal fees at the time. The proposed agreement further stipulated that Stan could never reveal the settlement amount, and that the $15,000 would be disguised as a cash "award" for having the courage to report wrongdoing by his superior.

This was no reward, Stan felt. This was hush money. "I was overwhelmed with a feeling of revulsion," Stan says today. "It was shameless, arrogant, and deceitful." The settlement offer, especially its silence clauses, simply reflected the IRS's compulsion to "do just about anything to keep a lid on things," Stan believes. Most disheartening of all, the settlement offer undermined any remaining confidence or trust Stan still had in Mike Murphy, the highest-ranking Civil Service employee in the IRS. "This effort to buy my silence erased all hope that anyone in management would do the right thing."

Jettisoning whatever trust and confidence he had ever placed in the IRS hierarchy and turning to the legislative branch of government, Welli fired off a letter detailing the entire sordid saga to Illinois Senator Paul Simon and six other members of Congress. A few days later, on March 14, 1988, after formally turning down Mike Murphy's settlement offer, Stan Welli received Murphy's final ruling on his grievance.

Remarkably, Murphy had reversed Herbert Roth's decision favoring Stan, claiming that he had found insufficient evidence to prove that Stan had suffered retaliation. Most discouraging, on a set of notes detailing the settlement offer and Stan's rejection of it, Murphy had penned in the word "MISTAKE" in block capital letters. Just as Joe Jech's dismal prophecies about the reaction of the IRS hierarchy to the original allegations had come true, Mike Murphy's little mash note was to haunt Stan Welli for years to come. Mike Murphy was stonewalling him.

A few weeks later, on April 8, Santella called Stan to his office to give him his annual performance rating. For the first time in his twenty-five years of government service, Stan received a "minimally successful" rating. Santella insisted that his reason for the low rating was simply poor "human relations," a function of Stan's failure to spend "enough time with him to adequately manage the internal audit program."

Now *that* was rich, Stan thought. Santella expected Stan to spend "quality time" with the very man who was making his life hell on earth.

In the meantime, Stan appealed Murphy's decision all the way to the top, to IRS Commissioner Larry Gibbs, the final authority on all disputed grievances. In late April, the commissioner's office agreed to settle both Stan's and Ron's grievances by restoring both men to their previous positions and salary levels. Chief Inspector Ted Kern flew to Chicago to settle the grievances in person with the two auditors. The IRS also reversed—quietly—the Midwest Internal Audit reorganization overall. Jech was transferred to work in the IRS headquarters Inspection office. Despite the oral reprimand from Robert Rebein for failing to report the initial allegation of misconduct by Santella, Jech was still promoted to the prestigious job of assistant director of internal security, the second highest position responsible for investigating allegations of wrongdoing by IRS employees!

After a brief stint in Washington, Frank Santella declined a proposed transfer to IRS headquarters and quietly left the IRS, to assume a new position with the Railroad Retirement Board Inspector General's office based in Chicago. There he helped oversee a $7 billion benefits program. According to the transcripts of the

Office of Special Counsel investigation of Stan Welli's complaint, when an IRS inspector asked Santella if he resented reassignment to Washington after the investigation against him, Santella forthrightly replied, "Why would I fight to remain working with those three scumbags? I tried to befriend [those guys] but all they did was fuck me."

Despite the positive ruling on Welli's grievance, the efforts of senior IRS officials to discredit him went on. Ted Kern, the new chief inspector and a longtime associate of Mike Murphy—by then Joseph Jech's boss—asked the Treasury Inspector General to investigate Stan on a charge of unauthorized disclosure of tax information, according to clearance documents released to Stan years later. Although found to have no merit, the original allegation, curiously enough, stemmed from charges leveled against Stan from one of his Chicago office employees, who soon left the IRS to join Santella at the Railroad Retirement Board.

Stan recalls that the investigator on the case came across like a complete novice, advising him of his constitutional rights and fumbling the words as if pronouncing them for the first time. At first, Welli wondered why the Treasury IG would have chosen to assign such an obviously rank beginner to such an obviously sensitive case. But then it dawned on him: She was likely to be more pliable than a more experienced agent might have been. Stan later learned that her immediate supervisor "had almost nothing to do with the investigation."

On April 27, 1989, IRS served Stan with a letter of reprimand alleging a conflict of interest involving a review of bankruptcy cases recently transferred into his jurisdiction. Stan's disciplinary action, such as it was, coincidentally preceded his scheduled appearance before Congressman Barnard's hearings by only a few weeks. The letter of reprimand would hang over Stan's head for more than two years and would not be removed until Stan sent a letter directly to the Secretary of the Treasury, Nicholas Brady.

After his 1989 congressional testimony, in which Congressman Barnard's investigators clearly concluded that retaliation had occurred against the Chicago Three, Stan Welli detailed the various ways that IRS Chief Inspection personnel attempted to trivialize and undermine the true significance of the Barnard hearings. During a meeting at Stan's office in June 1989, Kern disparagingly remarked: "They [the committee] must have spent $1 million on this investigation, and they came up with so little." During a second meeting at their office in November 1991, Stan recalls that Kern implied that the subcommittee hearings and Barnard's entire probe were "politically motivated."

At an employee awards dinner held in conjunction with an Internal Audit seminar in late October 1989, none other than good old Mike Murphy was the keynote speaker.

"I don't want to retire simply because I happened to be the Senior Deputy Commissioner at the time of the Barnard hearings," Mike Murphy quipped. "I began with the IRS thirty years ago, which is when Stan Welli first began picking on me."

What must have irked Mike Murphy most was that, at the Barnard hearings, Frank Santella's acceptance of the free bag of meat probably received by far the most prominent press attention. The three whistle-blowers even shared a rare lighthearted moment when they made late-night television.

"I hear that the IRS is now accepting gratuities," Jay Leno joked, shortly after their testimony. "I'm not sure if they want to take 15 or 20 percent of your income."

Testifying before Congress, before the nation, and before the world was no joke for Stan, George, and Ron. They had risked their livelihoods and careers to seek justice, and they were forced to listen in frank amazement as newly appointed IRS Commissioner Fred Goldberg responded with the same old platitudes about whistle-blowers: that they should be rewarded, not punished. But none of the Chicago Three ever heard any words of support from him. Not a thank you and definitely no reward.

If anything, it was quite the reverse. Through a March 1989 office newsletter, Stan learned that the IRS had awarded Mike Murphy with a meritorious plaque for "exemplary conduct which sets the standard for ethics and integrity for all IRS employees."

In the meantime, Stan's 1987 grievance with the Office of Special Counsel wended its way through the legal thicket. On May 31, 1990, three years after he filed his complaint, the Office of Special Counsel filed a four-count "Complaint for Disciplinary Action" against Jech and Santella for retaliation against Stan and George. The next day, Joe Jech retired from the IRS.

On March 3, 1992, administrative law judge Edward J. Reidy issued a ruling on Stan's complaint, finding Santella and Jech guilty of taking reprisals against Stan. Because Jech was already retired, the most severe punishment available was a $1,000 fine. Judge Reidy fined him $750. Santella was ordered reduced in grade from the executive rank he now held to a nonsupervisory GS–13 level, a drop of three pay grades. Even though they were found guilty, the IRS paid Jech and Santella's attorney fees—to the tune of a whopping $262,000—even as Stan's private attorney's fees remained unreimbursed.

But Stan Welli's woes were far from over. Two and a half years after Judge Reidy ruled that Stan had suffered retaliation for whistle-blowing (but after he testified again in a second round of hearings before Congressman Barnard's subcommittee), the Office of Special Counsel vacated Judge Reidy's decision. The entire case was sent back to the drawing board under the scrutiny of a new judge, since Judge Reidy had retired.

The Office of Special Counsel maintained that it had tossed aside Judge Reidy's decision more than two years after the case was over because, in the interim, a number of court cases had shifted the burden of proof required for proving retaliation cases. The standard to prove retaliation had shifted from what lawyers called the "contributing factor" test to the "significant factor" test. This meant that the Office of Special Counsel prosecutors now had to prove that Stan's whistle-blowing was a "significant" rather than merely a "contributing" factor in his lowered performance rating and transfer to an inferior position.

Despite strenuous protests from the Office of Special Counsel prosecutors that this new requirement imposed an "impossible burden of proof" on their side, a newly appointed administrative law judge, Paul G. Streb, vacated Judge Reidy's entire decision on November 13, 1995. Judge Streb found that the one-of-a-kind reorganization hatched by Jech and Santella was not retaliatory, supported by evidence provided by former chief inspectors Robert

Rebein and John Rankin, who, as Stan claims "were the very people who conspired to cover up this situation in the first place."

With both sides of the case given one more opportunity to present their arguments following Judge Streb's reversal of Judge Reidy's favorable ruling, Stan's case remained unresolved thirteen years after he first raised his charges against Frank Santella. Stan retired in 1996 with thirty-four years of federal service without final resolution of the problems prompted by Santella's outrageous behavior.

Was it worth it? Stan replies: "Well, we couldn't have lived with ourselves had we not done something. We have the satisfaction of knowing we did the right thing. Although by now," he admits, after thirteen long years, "I'd have to say it's a somewhat Pyrrhic victory.".

With a wry smile, Stan picks up a photocopy of an amateurish-looking mimeographed newsletter called *The Inspection Connection*—a newsletter circulated internally to employees of the IRS Inspection Division. On the second page, right-hand column, he points to a crude cartoon of a man on a pedestal marked "ARI/IA"—IRS lingo for assistant regional inspector/Internal Audit, and Frank Santella's position in August 1987, the date of the newsletter.

Under the pedestal, a paragraph reads:

Did you ever cheat a little on your income tax?

When the boss is away, do you leave the office early?

Did you ever pass off someone else's work as your own?

Have you ever covered up mistakes, exaggerated insurance claims, poured cheap Scotch into a Chivas bottle?

Even such seemingly innocent indiscretions can eventually take a toll on our integrity.

So, next time you're flirting with a weak moment, remember the words of Thomas Macaulay: "The measure of a man's real character is what he would do if he knew he never would be found out."

In light of his experiences at the hands of this particular ARI/IA, Stan Welli finds these remarks just a bit disingenuous.

8

CODE OF SILENCE

Many times 6103 was used as a moat to hide information from us, as opposed to permitting us to get to the actual wrongdoing, which typically did not involve taxpayer information at all.

—Congressman Douglas Barnard of Georgia

I'd never seen Doug Barnard so outraged as when the IRS tried to stonewall him on the Jordache jeans case. As he harshly lamented from his perch on the panel in one of the high points of the June 1989 hearings, perhaps the most egregious, flagrant case of high-level official misconduct he had uncovered during his subcommittee's fourteen-month-long investigation involved the IRS's dubious intervention in a commercial dispute between the Marciano brothers, owners of Guess Jeans, and the Nakash brothers, owners of Jordache jeans.

Acting on questionable information provided by the Marciano brothers, fifty IRS agents and other law enforcement officials raided the Manhattan corporate headquarters and New Jersey warehouse of Jordache jeans on the morning of January 26, 1986. During that well-coordinated search-and-seizure operation, some 2 million documents were confiscated by the authorities—voluminous enough, said Congressman Barnard, "to fill two large-size packing cartons."

There was something fishy about the whole operation. According to Congressional investigators who testified before Barnard's committee, not long after the Jordache jeans company was subjected to this image-tarnishing tax probe, Ron Saranow, IRS chief of Criminal Investigation in Los Angeles—the prime mover behind the raid—claimed to various co-workers that he had been offered a cushy job by the Marciano brothers with Guess Jeans, complete with a six-figure salary and a company car.

Had the alleged job offer been an attempt to influence the IRS and damage the corporate image of Jordache jeans, the Marcianos' commercial rival? The bitterly feuding Nakash and Marciano brothers had at one point thought well enough of each other to go into a fifty-fifty partnership on a joint venture jeans outfit called Gasoline. But after a nasty contractual dispute rumored to involve some $100 million in profits, the Marcianos decided to play hardball with their former partners, and apparently resolved to use the IRS as their weapons of warfare. The Los Angeles–based Marcianos contacted IRS officials with the claim that they could document that both Gasoline and Jordache jeans had been operated by the Nakashes as vehicles to further a scheme designed to defraud U.S. Customs officials and the Internal Revenue Service.

There wasn't much substance behind the Marcianos' allegation, certainly not enough red meat to lead to any indictment or charges against Jordache jeans. When the suspicious circumstances surrounding Ron Saranow's role in the whole dubious affair came to light, Congressman Barnard began asking awkward questions. To wit: Had the "former CID [Chief of Inspection Division] been improperly induced to initiate a tax fraud investigation of Jordache?"

In his own probe of loose cannons inside the IRS, Congressman Barnard sought a waiver of the "tax confidentiality provisions of Internal Revenue Code 6103," enabling his subcommittee to analyze "the quality of the information provided the Service by the informants in the case"—the Marciano brothers. The IRS, as is its wont, threw up its favorite all-purpose smokescreen, claiming that the Section 6103 confidentiality clauses protected the confidentiality of all tax information, including the key documents in the case. A wily Barnard succeeded in neutralizing this legal threat by obtaining "tax disclosure authorization" from Jordache jeans permitting his sub-committee to sneak a peek at the documents.

The IRS proceeded to launch favorite weapon number two against the ongoing probe: Congressman Barnard couldn't see the records, IRS maintained, because a criminal investigation by the Justice Department was in progress, and a public congressional inquiry might queer the pitch. But Barnard obtained a waiver from the Justice Department permitting him to look at the documents. Round one to Congress.

At that juncture, one might have imagined that IRS would throw in the towel. But that would be vastly underestimating the IRS's great power and need to control access to information it deems unworthy of disclosure—because it might embarrass the agency. As an irate Barnard publicly announced to his panel and to the public, "On June 20, 1989"—five days before the hearings—the Justice Department notified him that while "they were attempting to facilitate our subcommittee access to these documents, the IRS was being vague concerning their whereabouts." By the next day, that vagueness had congealed into a stone wall of embarrassing dimensions: the documents, in fact, "could not be located in any IRS office."

Now, wasn't that curious? Adding insult to injury, later the same day, the subcommittee was notified by the Justice Department that all the documents had been destroyed by the IRS criminal investigator assigned to the case. My ears pricked up. The destruction of documents pertaining to sensitive subjects was an issue close to my heart. Could the IRS have simply ordered the documents destroyed to keep them out of Barnard's hands? If so, it would have been in blatant violation not only of federal law, but of proper criminal investigative procedure as well as a clearcut obstruction of justice. Congressman Barnard furiously concluded his debriefing on the whole blue jeans fiasco by calling for the Public Integrity Section of the Justice Department to undertake an investigation into this document destruction immediately, "to determine if a criminal investigation is warranted." In closing, he reminded us that the destruction of federal property had occurred without special agent Steve Levy—the IRS employee who finally owned up to deep-sixing the documents—even bothering to inform anyone at the U.S. attorney's office what he was up to.

Just as all this was coming to a head, the IRS spin-control team deployed on Capitol Hill continued to assure a skeptical public that the Saranow-Jordache-Levy scandal was, just like so many other egregious cases of official misconduct recently uncovered, an "isolated incident." But a matter of months later, in mid-1989, the IRS once again was caught red-handed trashing and losing sensitive documents. *Las Vegas Sun* investigative reporter Jeff German revealed a covert IRS undercover operation gone wrong called Operation Layoff—a screwy scheme involving the establishment of an illegal bookmaking operation in Las Vegas in the hope of uncovering similar operations. Unfortunately, unbeknownst to the IRS, the FBI had been engaged in a similar covert effort in the Las Vegas area, which caused the FBI and the IRS to become, shall we say, unproductively entangled in each other's nets. When congressional investigators sought to trace the ill-fated background behind Operation Layoff, all evidence pertaining to the covert operation had mysteriously vanished. As Nevada congressman James Bilbray sorely lamented: "Records were destroyed. They were gone. They said they can't find them. They were either shredded or somebody took them out of the IRS facilities."

"Under the law doesn't anybody have responsibility for these documents?" Congressman Albert Bustamante of Texas asked rhetorically from the House floor. "Money and documents were lost, yet nobody has been brought before either the Inspector General, a court of law, or any other type of judicial service" to remedy the situation.

"What are they hiding?" Nevada congressman Richard Bryan pressed on. "Where there is reluctance to make a full disclosure . . . it certainly does invite your suspicion. What is out there? What is it that they know that they are not sharing?"

Of course, the real answer was and is: We'll never know. And the IRS would like to keep it that way.

6103: THE SILENCER

Chapter 61 of the Internal Revenue Code contains several quite interesting—if obscurely written—provisions. Under the chapter title "Information and Returns," Subchapter A is subtitled: "Returns and Records." It reads, in part: "Every person liable for any tax imposed by this title, or for the collection thereof, shall keep such records, render such statements, make such returns, and comply with such rules and regulations as the Secretary may from time to time prescribe." The law clearly states that you—the taxpayer—are fully accountable for maintaining all records necessary for fulfilling your "tax liabilities" under federal law.

Some ninety pages later on in the tax code, under the vague title "Miscellaneous Provisions," we find a section numbered 6103, of Subchapter 6, of Chapter 61, of Subtitle B, entitled "Confidentiality and Disclosure of Returns and Return Information." Buried between Section 6102 ("Computations on Returns or Other Documents") and Section 6104 ("Publicity of Information Required by Certain Exempt Organizations and Certain Trusts") IRC Section 6103 is the IRS's ultimate defensive weapon. I call it the IRS's Strategic Defense Initiative.

It's 1976: the immediate post-Watergate years. In the wake of all the nasty publicity surrounding Nixon's enemies list, and Paul Wright's covert Special Services Staff, the overwhelming concern of both the public and Congress with regard to the IRS was to prevent unauthorized disclosure of, or politicized access to, confidential tax returns. As Senator Floyd Haskell, then chairman of the Senate Subcommittee on the Administration of the Internal Revenue Code, maintained: "The Constitution of the United States never specifically mentions the word 'privacy.' However, the Constitution is replete with explicit protections of citizenry, their homes, and their personal possessions, and as Justice Brandeis once said, 'The right to be left alone is a constitutional privilege.'"

Following the significant abuses of the system during the Nixon administration, protection of personal privacy quickly became the paramount public issue. As Senator Haskell pointed out: "It is alleged . . . that tax returns have . . . shown up in the files of private detective agencies, of insurance adjusters, and on one occasion, county records." Senator Bob Dole of Kansas reinforced Senator

Haskell's rhetoric by praising President Gerald Ford for signing an executive order specifying that citizens' tax returns could be reviewed only upon written authorization by the President himself. No more would run-of-the-mill White House officials be routinely allowed to snoop around in ordinary citizens' tax returns in the hope of making political hay.

Still, as far as the newly converted civil libertarians in Congress were concerned, President Ford's executive order did not go nearly far enough to tighten up access to tax returns in the campaign to reestablish severely eroded public trust in American institutions damaged by the revelations of Watergate. Liberal senator Lowell Weicker of Connecticut captured the mood of the country when he chided his colleagues for failing to act more decisively to stop the IRS from abusing its privileges as the most powerful government agency in the land.

Waving at a tall pile of papers he had amassed detailing flagrant IRS abuses, Weicker proclaimed: "The stacks of paper [before me are] the substance of a two-year public record of wrongdoing connected with the IRS. The air between us is the substance of the legislative response to that record. . . . Insofar as the mess can be cleaned up legislatively," he urged his fellow senators, "let's get on with it. Please, before any more horror stories surface, let's have one concrete, positive act by the Congress which can be interpreted as work rather than politics."

And so, in the spring of 1976, the United States Congress amended Section 6103 of the Internal Revenue Code, placing the most severe restrictions on access to citizens' tax returns in the history of American taxation. Senator Lloyd Bentsen of Texas proclaimed that a preliminary version of the legislation sponsored by him would:

1. Impose strict limitations on who is allowed access to confidential tax information as a means of reassuring American taxpayers of the privacy of their tax returns.

2. Insulate the IRS from partisan political pressure by requiring that all requests for tax information be submitted in writing along with reasons detailing the purpose and intended use of that information.

3. Impose criminal penalties against any official, however high, who misused or tried to misuse confidential tax information.

What a grand, high-minded concept. Who could possibly oppose an effort to protect taxpayers? Opposition would be akin to asking small children to begin smoking. But little did senators Bentsen, Weicker, Haskell, or any of their esteemed colleagues in Congress know how the IRS would twist and distort their high-minded legislative initiative so that it would in due course become a tool to deprive the very body that passed the legislation of the information it needed to oversee the inner workings of the IRS. Little did they know that the very legislation they passed, to such vast relief and fanfare from civil libertarians nationwide, would end up shielding the IRS from public scrutiny.

In retrospect, the problem with the newly amended Section 6103 was straightforward: The broadness of the statute permitted the IRS hierarchy to wield 6103 as a blunt weapon to intimidate its own employees from blowing the whistle on official misconduct. As the IRS self-servingly construes it, Section 6103 gives it the right to forbid the release or disclosure of any and all information relating to itself—period.

This excruciating Catch-22 is of course strictly of congressional creation, and only the Congress in its wisdom can undo it. The great irony is that, to the IRS's credit, the privacy of your tax return is quite well protected by the system in place. The IRS understands the importance of protecting your 1040. Unfortunately, it extends that protection to itself as well as taxpayers, which is not what Congress intended in 1976.

Congressional hearings several years ago pounded on a few IRS employees for "browsing" in tax files, but that episode was dramatically overblown compared with far more serious internal IRS abuses, which did not see the light of public disclosure because the service used Section 6103 to invoke blanket protection of nearly every piece of paper generated by or received by its employees.

Here's how it works. Let's suppose that you would like some information from the IRS on the Watergate-era Special Services Staff. Under the law, as an American citizen and taxpayer paying the bills for your country, you have a right to information about what the government does with your money. You have a right to know about the activities, the goals, the strategies of the IRS's Special Services Staff, just as you have a right to know about how the Defense Department planned for World War II or how the Social Security Administration was funded. It's your right. It's the law. You submit a Freedom of Information Act request to the IRS outlining the information you would like access to. You sit back and wait for a reply. Eventually, you receive a letter from the IRS thanking you for your interest, but regretfully declining your request for information because the information is protected by IRC Section 6103.

The tricky part is that though you might argue that information relating to the sordid history of the Special Services Staff can hardly be considered "tax information," the IRS's basic, unmovable stance is that all information relating to the enforcement of the tax laws is, for all intents and purposes—its purposes—"tax information."

What is supposed to happen is that the IRS should evaluate all available records—we already know that's not a big job since the IRS has destroyed almost everything—and, if they do find actual, legitimate information that is tax-specific to an individual or organization, they are to redact it—black it out—and send on the document, complete with deletions. That's what the FBI does; that's what the CIA does. The IRS just says No.

As amended by Congress in 1976, Section 6103 defines "tax returns" as "any tax return or information, declaration of estimated tax, or claim for refund." These "public records," it states, "shall be open to inspection only upon order of the President and under rules and regulations prescribed by the statute." It goes on to define "return information" as including a taxpayer's "identity, as well as the nature, source, or amount of his income, payments, receipts, deductions, exemptions—or any other data, received by, recorded by, prepared by, furnished to, or collected by the Secretary [of the Treasury] with respect to a return or with respect to the determination of the existence, or possible existence, of tax liability." In short, everything but the kitchen sink. The IRS, for its own benefit, has further broadened this blanket protection of "tax information" to cover information not remotely connected to any individual's tax return or tax case.

In its eagerness to shield itself from public scrutiny, the IRS typically neglects to mention that Section 6103 explicitly stipulates that such restrictions do not apply to "data in a form which cannot be associated with, or otherwise directly or indirectly identify a particular taxpayer." Furthermore, a host of exemptions to this supposedly impermeable statute have left loopholes in the law big enough to drive a truck through. Exceptions apply to agencies charged with enforcing child support laws and student loan provisions. The Department of Justice, under certain circumstances, may inspect returns in the course of federal criminal investigations. A few congressional committees have open access to tax returns, and even the General Accounting Office may examine returns. The only people who can never on any account be made privy to "tax information" would appear to be reform-minded congressmen, academics, and journalists bent on exposing the IRS's shortcomings.

One government agency not explicitly permitted to examine tax returns by the law, but implicitly granted carte blanche to do so, curiously enough, is the National Archives. Nothing in the federal law says that the Archives can look at taxpayer information. But nothing says the archivists can't, either. Without exception, the IRS has interpreted 6103 as prohibiting the National Archives from examining its files, or from interfering with the IRS's routine practice of discarding and destroying its internal records. Yet the Federal Records Act, quite to the contrary, explicitly states that the National Archives is the only federal agency with the power to authorize the destruction of federal records. So when the IRS destroys records without explicit approval from the Archives, it is breaking the law. Pretty simple. Very scary. The National Archives reviews highly classified Defense Department files, even FBI files, CIA files, and top secret NSA files, on a routine basis. But not IRS files.

When pressed on this point, otherwise reasonable IRS employees explain that the IRS could never release information to the National Archives because "tax returns would end up being handed out to tourists strolling along Pennsylvania Avenue." Ridiculous. To my knowledge, no leak of national security information from the National Archives has ever been reported. For twenty years, in the face of enormous pressure for public access, the Archives has kept a tight lid on countless hours of unreleased Nixon Oval Office tapes. A number of senior archivists listened to the tapes years ago, and none of that information ever filtered out into the media. The Archives' record of protecting information remains impeccable, which is more than can be said of the IRS.

Despite the facts, IRS routinely claims that it can't trust the Archives to keep mum about IRS secrets. It routinely deploys 6103 as an excuse to keep IRS internal documents out of the hands of the Archives. But, ironically, nearly all the IRS-related material retained at the National Archives facility in College Park, Maryland, is tax information, including tax ledger books, lists of taxpayers, microfilm reels with tax data. What isn't there, historically speaking, is of far greater significance: internal documents that might shed light on how the IRS operates, how it makes decisions and mistakes.

Moreover, the National Archives operates the nine vast ware-houses across the country that store the mountain of 1040s and 1099s. When the IRS needs to look at your 1040 from three years ago (in pursuit, let's say, of a question raised during an audit), an Archives employee, not an IRS employee, pulls the physical file. Doesn't that Archives employee have to double-check the face of the return to pull the right one? How can Archives employees have no right or access to "confidential tax information" even though the IRS uses them to manage all the sacrosanct IRS files? A journalist who covers the IRS calls this the "Reverse Playboy Philosophy"—you can touch, but you can't look.

One curious fallout of the 6103 post-Watergate amendment is that material the IRS made freely available before 1976 is now out of public bounds. In 1969 author Hank Messick completed a book called *Secret File: Inside the Confidential Files of the Intelligence Division of the IRS*. As Messick explained in the book's preface, the pre-1976 IRS granted him unprecedented access to the "secret files" of the Intelligence Division—the part of the IRS that tracked down Al Capone and other tax cheats and is known today as Criminal Investigation. Had Hank Messick decided to write the same book ten years later, he never would have been granted the same access.

In 1976 author Frank Spiering published his contribution to the scintillating Al Capone saga, *The Man Who Got Capone*—completing his manuscript just under the secrecy wire. Based on extensive access provided by the IRS Intelligence Division to Capone's Case Jacket SI–7085–F, the book could never have been written had Spiering been unable to get his hands on this juicy IRS file. Historians can only hope that the IRS hasn't shredded Al Capone's case jacket. I do know that the IRS couldn't locate all the materials that had been provided to Messick and Spiering when I asked about them in the early 1990s.

Some ten years ago, Professor James Calder, who teaches criminal justice at the University of Texas in San Antonio, decided to write a book about federal crime policy in the thirties, when the IRS was not only quite active but successful in tracking down criminals and enforcing the nation's first gun control laws. At the time, the Bureau of Alcohol, Tobacco, and Firearms was a division incongruously located within the IRS. But when Professor Calder came calling on the IRS in the 1980s in search of Al Capone's Case Jacket SI–7085–F, the IRS cited IRC Section 6103 restrictions in turning his request down flat.

Having already read Messick's and Spiering's books, Calder knew perfectly well that the IRS had previously granted authors access to the same material he was seeking. But like any good researcher, he wanted to see the original documents for himself. Under the new and improved code of silence, Calder's prime sources had suddenly become official secrets. Calder challenged the IRS's decision all the way to the district court level, which remarkably ruled that Calder had "failed to demonstrate that there was a history of access to the files," despite the fact that Calder had presented to the court detailed evidence of published works based on the now secret files.

In my official capacity as IRS historian, I was often asked to field questions about Al Capone's extensive cat-and-mouse game with the IRS, a struggle in which the IRS ultimately triumphed. One might imagine that the IRS, even in its paranoia, would not object to being glorified in the press. One of the most popular IRS recruiting posters features a close-up of Al Capone's mug, under the tagline: "Only the IRS could get Al Capone." But when I checked with IRS attorneys about how to answer these questions in light of the 6103 issue, they advised me that I would be violating the law if I even told someone *that Al Capone went to prison for failure to file his tax returns.*

"But that's common knowledge!" I would protest. "It's in books. It's out there. It's in the public domain! It's even disclosed by your own recruiting poster!"

But as far as the IRS Disclosure attorneys were concerned, their hands were tied. How convenient. Any discussion, no matter how basic or how banal, of anything involving taxes, including internal IRS operations, was strictly off-limits. They told me to refer such questions to Messick's and Spiering's books. Surely this was not the intent of Senator Lloyd Bentsen and his colleagues when they promised the public that access to confidential tax returns would be kept from politically prying eyes.

The very title of the office of "Disclosure Litigation" is dismayingly adversarial, presuming litigation, not resolution of routine information requests. As one IRS Disclosure attorney patiently explained to me: "Our job is to say no. When we say no, we make our client—the IRS—happy, because the IRS doesn't want to disclose information. Not only that, by saying no we keep ourselves busy. If we said yes, the IRS might not need us anymore." As the same worldly-wise attorney cynically concludes: "Our tortured interpretation of the tax law keeps us in the loop."

Most disturbing to members of Congress is that they have become the number one victims of their own high-minded intentions. When pledging to reform the IRS in 1989, Congressman Barnard ran up against wily IRS Disclosure attorneys, who, in his own words, employed "an excessively broad definition of 6103 in advising [IRS] witnesses." And that was putting it mildly.

As Representative Albert G. Bustamante of Texas lamented:

> Sixteen years ago, during the Watergate affair, we learned that the professionalism of the IRS was compromised by an Imperial Presidency. Congress, in the aftermath [of those abuses,] enacted safeguards that protect the taxpayers from the unauthorized disclosure of taxpayer information. It is ironic that the very reforms Congress enacted were used by the IRS to impede the investigation of this subcommittee.

Senator Lloyd Bentsen first proposed tightening up 6103 because "rampant revelations of IRS abuse have contributed to the current loss of public confidence in the government." He observed, "The Federal tax system has been successful only because it enjoys wide voluntary support." But the end result of the highly touted 1976 legislation has been a marked decline in respect for the very agency that the legislation was intended to strengthen and reform. Why should American taxpayers voluntarily comply with the tax code when the agency they entrust with highly sensitive personal information routinely refuses to comply with federal law? Why should taxpayers save records when the IRS won't?

Furious about this lack of accountability, California congressman Matthew Martinez threatened: "I have a great idea for a new TV series. It will be called 'The Untouchables.' Only it won't be about Prohibition days. It will be about the IRS today. Because if the public becomes irate enough, they're not going to remain untouchable much longer."

IT WASN'T ALWAYS THIS WAY

On the confidentiality issue: Congress first passed an income tax in 1862, to help pay for the Civil War. This first income tax wasn't rejected because it applied only to the top 3 percent of wealthiest citizens of a then-fractured Union. This original "soak the rich" tax law stipulated that anyone could inspect the information gathered by the tax collector. Between 1864 and 1870, newspapers routinely published lists of taxpayers and what they paid. Congress believed that recalcitrant taxpayers might be detected through full public disclosure of names of compliant taxpayers. While this practice ended in 1870, IRS lists remained open for public inspection in local tax offices until the Civil War income tax expired the following year.

During Reconstruction, this income tax vanished from the federal scene. When it staged a brief comeback in 1894, Congress belatedly took the issue of privacy into account by creating stiff penalties for anyone who revealed information from tax returns. But that provision never went into effect, because the Supreme Court declared the 1894 income tax itself unconstitutional. In a move that foreshadows today's proceedings, the commissioner of Internal Revenue ordered that all records from the Civil War income tax be destroyed. That's why if you look in the nineteenth-century IRS collection in the National Archives, you'll find loads of assessment lists from the dizzying variety of excise taxes, but virtually nothing about our first income tax. Of course, one hundred years ago, there was no National Archives charged with the responsibility of approving or disapproving the destruction of government records.

When the income tax was again revived in 1913—still only affecting the very wealthy—tax return information became subject to tight restrictions. Only the President could make tax returns available to anyone outside Internal Revenue. These limits loosened somewhat in 1918, when World War I ended, and Congress directed the commissioner to make a list of the names and addresses of everyone who filed a return available to the public. Just names and addresses. No tax information. Six years later, Congress added the amount each taxpayer paid to this public listing. But just two years after that, under fire from civil libertarians among its constituents, Congress reversed itself again, eliminating the amount of tax paid from the list. Congress further restricted access to "tax information" to a handful of congressional committees.

In 1934 a new law required taxpayers to fill out a small pink slip to send to the tax collector, attached to their tax return. The pink slip listed the taxpayer's name, address, income, amount of tax paid, credits, and deductions. IRS employees pulled the pink slips from the tax return and filed them for public inspection in the tax collector's office. You couldn't look at your neighbor's 1040, but you could find out his income, how many deductions he claimed, and how much tax he paid by looking at his pink slip.

The pink slip era was cut short in 1936 with the conviction of Bruno Richard Hauptmann for kidnapping the infant of Charles and Anne Morrow Lindbergh, raising fresh concerns—particularly among the wealthy—that disclosing high income or great wealth left them vulnerable to crimes of abduction and extortion. Congress, eager to assuage potential campaign contributors, hastily rescinded the pink slip provision in the next revenue bill to come up for a vote. You could still get a list of the names and addresses of all taxpayers from the IRS, but the financial information was now unavailable.

In 1966, Congress decreed that tax collectors no longer had to make the list of taxpayer names and addresses available to the public. If you wanted to know whether your neighbor filed a tax return, you could no longer visit your local tax office to see for yourself, but you could call the IRS office for the information.

Remarkably, that public inspection provision—a cheap way of keeping the citizenry honest—remained on the books until 1976. Since Watergate, the IRS has refused to confirm whether your neighbor actually exists, let alone whether this neighbor filed a tax return.

Over the following decades, the IRS has learned only one lesson from every congressional investigation into its frequently abusive behavior: Information, particularly information that might portray the IRS negatively, should never leave IRS headquarters at any cost. IRS officials play out this tired mantra time and again.

To restore accountability within the IRS, Congress alone can undo this ill-advised provision of 6103. To date, I've detected precious little enthusiasm inside the IRS for revising what benefits only those who have something to hide.

Of course, congressional aggressiveness in policing the IRS has had a distinctly mixed record, in part because the IRS has time and again proven itself quite adept at retaliating against its enemies on Capitol Hill. In the early fifties, Tennessee representative Estes Kefauver sought a presidential executive order granting his committee the right to examine income tax returns and related materials from IRS internal files to further its exploration of corrupt links between organized crime and politicians. Without such access, Kefauver and his investigators persuasively argued, their efforts would be stymied by corrupt politicians eager to protect their own skins. That admirable effort, combined with the 1951 King hearings into official corruption at the IRS, was the last time the House Ways and Means Committee exercised any meaningful congressional oversight over IRS operations, according to former tax commissioner Sheldon Cohen. In recent decades, under the tight grip of future felon Congressman Dan Rostenkowski, Ways and Means not only did little to reform the IRS, but actually took concrete steps to inhibit genuine probes like that of Congressman Barnard. The Joint Committee on Internal Revenue Taxation, the other congressional committee charged with oversight of Internal Revenue affairs, has had a dismal record with regard to reforming the IRS.

"If you can come up with four times in the last forty years when the Joint Committee has written a report on the administration of the internal revenue laws, I'd be amazed," Sheldon Cohen charges. Even a former commissioner takes Congress to task for not meaningfully policing the most powerful government agency in the land.

You wouldn't imagine congressmen and senators fearing retaliation from the all-powerful tax service. But some elected officials who dared to look too closely at IRS internal operations have found themselves at the other end of an audit, or subject to innuendo, leaks, and other forms of harassment, just as Stan Welli did as an IRS employee.

As far back as the Roaring Twenties, Michigan senator James Couzens launched an investigation into rampant corruption at the IRS, at a time when Prohibition ensured that an extraordinary crime wave—remember Al Capone—had gone largely unchecked, and high-level malfeasance was common. The IRS quickly got in its licks. Couzens's headline-making maneuver was to target William Boyce Thompson, a New York millionaire and prominent fundraiser for the Republican National Committee. After Couzens dared to charge that Thompson—a personal friend of Treasury secretary Andrew W. Mellon—had saved half a million in excise taxes when the IRS issued him a favorable ruling despite his inability to document the questionable deduction, the IRS made a preemptive strike. On March 27, 1925, David H. Blair, the commissioner of Internal Revenue himself, hand-delivered a letter to Couzens—as he left the Senate floor—accusing him of owing nearly $11 million in back taxes. Though Couzens was ultimately vindicated—the feds ended up paying him close to $1 million for his overpayment of back taxes—his reputation was sufficiently damaged. Everyone forgot Commissioner Blair, the man who bared his teeth on Capitol Hill, as just another government bureaucrat fulfilling his duty. Everyone remembered Senator Couzens as the guy who had trouble with the tax man.

Fast-forward forty years, to the Swinging Sixties. Missouri senator Edward V. Long launched an unwelcome and ill-advised (in light of subsequent events) investigation into the IRS's long-standing practice of controversial investigative techniques. Wiretaps. Bugs. Illegal searches and seizures. Senator Long held a dramatic series of hearings. But rather than audit Long publicly, some higher-up at the IRS leaked news apparently to the Justice Department, which in turn leaked the information to a reporter for *Life* magazine, that Long enjoyed uncomfortably close ties to notorious Teamsters president Jimmy Hoffa, who was closely connected to organized crime. According to these unsubstantiated rumors, the Teamsters Union hierarchy itself inspired Long's investigation, which insinuated that Senator Long was in a gangster's pocket. The hearings, this anonymous source at the IRS alleged, were actually a ploy to obstruct the service's ongoing effort to crack down on organized crime. When Long faced reelection the following year, he lost his Senate seat.

In the mid-seventies, New Mexico senator Joseph Montoya rashly decided to urge his constituents to contact him about their tax problems. He even announced bold plans to hold his own series of hearings on IRS responsiveness to taxpayers. Then *Washington Post* reporter Bob Woodward published a front-page story in October 1975 alleging that IRS Commissioner Donald Alexander had personally halted an audit of Montoya. How strange that the IRS had sought to audit one of its most dangerous critics! The primary source for Bob Woodward's article was clearly a leak from some "Deep Throat" within the IRS.

Woodward's story hit the stands just as Alexander had come under attack from IRS special agents for cutting off access to funds for shadowy underworld informants and severely restricting IRS undercover operations in general. So what presumably began as an audit to punish Montoya for presuming to scrutinize the IRS was distorted into an accusation of IRS favoritism in halting an audit.

When Congressman Doug Barnard risked the IRS gauntlet, Congressman Dan Rostenkowski's powerful House Ways and Means Committee refused him access to tax data necessary for his investigations. The IRS no doubt enjoyed that presumably unso-licited "cooperation" from congressional power seats. One staff member who worked for the Barnard subcommittee blamed the denial of 6103 access on "intra-Congressional rivalry." Richard Stana, an investigator for Barnard's subcommittee, insisted that "a subcommittee charged by the House rules with IRS oversight responsibility to be denied access to the records it needs to do its work" is highly irregular. "Everyone strongly supports the need to safeguard the confidentiality of tax information. But the broad impact of Section 6103, as utilized by the IRS, has served to shield the Service from efficient Government Operations Committee over-sight, a consequence we believe Congress never intended."

Congressman Barnard plunged ahead, uncovering a remarkable number of cases of unethical behavior by high-ranking IRS officials across the country. In 1992, after wrapping up nearly four years of tireless investigation of abuses by the IRS, he retired to Georgia, satis-fied that he had at least done what he could to expose the more shameful and shadowy IRS practices. But he remains upset to this day about the shabby way that Dan Rostenkowski and the Ways and Means Committee treated him. "They thought they were the only oversight committee with IRS jurisdiction," he recalls. "They simply did not want to give us access to confidential information. We fought this tooth and nail. We were full members of Congress, but we were considered poor stepchildren to Ways and Means. Their attitude toward us was, 'We'll stub that into the ground like a cigarette.'" Doug Barnard refused to be stubbed, or snubbed. Dan Rostenkowski went to jail.

9

THE MYSTERY OF HISTORY

Those who cannot remember the past are condemned to repeat it.

—*George Santayana*

The one issue raised at the Barnard hearings that fell into my per-sonal bailiwick was the service's chronic compulsion to eradicate its identity by destroying and discarding critical internal documents. Until the third week of July 1989, I had viewed this matter from a purely professional standpoint: How could I ever hope to write a comprehensive survey of the IRS with hardly any primary sources?

But after Barnard, I got the bigger picture: By routinely destroying documents, the agency was avoiding public accountability. When the special agent assigned to the Jordache case chucked the relevant documents without checking with the D.A.'s office first and when the records of Operation Layoff (not to mention countless other lesser-known scandals) disappeared, the goal had obviously been to erase a paper trail. By fostering an environment in which employees can routinely and blithely trash documents with impunity, the IRS was holding itself above the law. As far as I was concerned, that had to stop.

That the agency dared to pay lip service in its *Internal Revenue Manual* to complying with standard government procedure in this regard only made its position more hypocritical. If I could change anything at the IRS, I might hope to change that, perhaps even influence the internal operations of this federal agency.

I left Capitol Hill newly energized to tackle the records issue head on, but admitted that, after just one year in office, I lacked authority to prevail against a deeply entrenched status quo. Perhaps I could do more by boosting morale, providing a context for accomplishing a common task, and imparting some sense of historical purpose as a group—a cultural turnaround, if you will.

For some reason, I found myself thinking about the Boston Tea Party and the Whiskey Rebellion, the latter of which posed President Washington's first real internal threat to his regime. I thought of today's tax protesters, who style themselves "sovereign citizens," above the law and immune to the obligation to pay taxes. We are a nation of tax protesters, although—as is so often repeated by IRS hacks—our level of voluntary compliance with the tax laws is truly the envy of the industrialized world.

Since the IRS gets more than its fair share of abuse for the innumerable faults and flaws in our unfair, loophole-ridden tax system, agency higher-ups have historically seized upon this manifest unfairness as a blanket excuse for dismissing all criticism of it as an attack on the tax system. In a late 1996 appearance before a congressional commission investigating IRS administration of the tax laws, Commissioner Margaret Milner Richardson performed masterfully in the IRS tradition of deflecting blame for faulty administration onto Congress for faulty tax laws. When asked about citizens' responses at a public session to air IRS issues, the commissioner waved away complaints about the IRS by claiming that "no one has ever liked the tax collector." She chuckled as she recalled that some citizens had complained about unfair property taxes—a state issue— to her. See, she seemed to be saying, they'll blame us for anything and nothing is our fault.

Yes, when people knock the IRS, they are often really expressing resentment toward an outdated tax code drastically needing an overhaul—by the elected members of Congress, who created it in the first place. But you can't blame the system when the IRS seizes a Boy Scout Troop's bank account, due to a preventable computer malfunction. Or say that it's Congress's fault when an overzealous IRS agent arranges the seizure of a twelve-year-old Virginia boy's savings account to satisfy a tax debt incurred by his parents—when the payment has already been mailed.

So, I pondered, what should I put in a truly accurate, comprehensive history program for this eight-hundred-pound gorilla? Since morale was now an issue, I resolved to strike first at the barren walls whose emptiness had seemed so appalling a year before. What would be more appropriate for a media display than an exhibit of official portraits of all the commissioners of Internal Revenue? In the course of researching the personal histories of the commissioners, I imagined I'd dredge up some intriguing material about the evolution of the IRS itself.

Conversing with public affairs specialist Mary Francis Kirwin, I learned of her access to a collection of vintage photographs, purportedly the commissioners' official portrait gallery. As she led me into a dank, dusty storage room on the first floor, where the old photos had been unceremoniously stacked helter-skelter in a corner, Mary Francis made a point of warning me that this collection was by no means complete. These were not, I should point out, portraits in oils, but standard-issue eight-by-ten black-and-white prints in plain-Jane wooden frames. The IRS is not a cabinet-level agency, which means that the government won't sponsor fancy oil paintings.

"I can't vouch for the accuracy of these pictures," Mary Francis said tentatively, clearly not wanting to be the source of idle rumor or innuendo. She told me that a former commissioner had handed the hapless task of dredging up pictures of the commissioners to a certain long-since-retired IRS employee, so that the commissioner might proudly display an impressive row of his predecessors outside the door to his suite. In the absence of records and documentation, hallway gossip disseminated all information about the past in our massive organization, as a form of primitive tribal lore. This employee had become frustrated when he couldn't easily locate the commissioners' official portraits. He thought that, since nineteenth- and early-twentieth-century gentleman all looked pretty much alike anyway, why not just head out to the nearest junk shop off Dupont Circle and round up some old photos of guys with white hair, beards, and side whiskers? The result of this conceptual breakthrough lay at our feet, in a pile of dust—precisely where it belonged.

Starting from scratch, I confirmed that many photos indeed did not match the names indicated on the brass plaques. I learned quite a bit about those characters as I tracked down their photos.

William Orton (the commissioner with the shortest tenure in office) served for four months in 1865, before going on to become chairman of Western Union. Fortunately, Western Union had kept a formal portrait of him in its corporate archives—thank God for American free enterprise.

Guy T. Helvering, the longest-tenured IRS commissioner, served under President Franklin D. Roosevelt for more than a decade, from June 6, 1933, to October 8, 1943. Helvering was the complacent Kansan who, as broadcaster David Brinkley relates in his recent memoirs, presided over a tax investigation of a close friend of the President's, who was duly ordered to cough up $20,000 in fines, interest, and penalties, or face the consequences. When old FDR got wind of the news, he got Mr. Helvering on the hotline, and in no uncertain terms informed the commissioner that the amount was too high. "Cut it to three thousand," the president barked, in the hearing of some members of the Washington press corps, including Brinkley. Mr. Helvering apparently did what he was told. As Brinkley wryly observes, "Nobody seemed to think it was news or even very interesting." Playing political games with the tax service is old hat.

An even more curious tall tale about Helvering was that his body remains buried somewhere deep inside the thick walls of 1111 Constitution Avenue. I determined that Helvering had indeed died in Washington in 1946, while attending a gala Fourth of July festivity celebrating our victory in the Second World War. But as far as I know, his final resting place is not 1111 Constitution Avenue.

The final resting place of Commissioner Edward Rollins of New Hampshire can be found on the campus of Dartmouth College. After being appointed by President Andrew Johnson in 1865 (on the heels of Commissioner Orton's move to Western Union), Rollins donated a handsome sum of money to Dartmouth, his alma mater, to construct a chapel on its New Hampshire campus. Poor Mr.

Rollins attended the dedication ceremony in his honor and suffered the misfortune of passing away shortly after the service. Needless to say, Rollins's own was the first funeral ever conducted at Rollins Chapel.

Unfortunately for his position in the IRS rogues' gallery, Ed Rollins did not die before prosecutors got a chance to file criminal charges against him on numerous counts of tax evasion, bribery, corruption, and blackmail. But all the charges were dropped when a key witness was arrested for perjury. Commissioner Joseph D. Nunan Jr. of New York (who followed Guy Helvering into office in March 1944) was not nearly so fortunate in his nasty scrape with the law. After serving with remarkably little distinction from March 1944 until June 1947, Commissioner Nunan was tried and convicted on charges of—you guessed it—tax evasion, and spent an embarrassing year in federal prison. As you may have gathered, the mid-forties were hardly the IRS's ethical glory years: Nunan's successor, George J. Shoeneman of Rhode Island, appointed by President Truman in July 1947, was accused of failing to pay taxes on income of $176,000, but was never indicted.

I slapped a picture of jailbird Nunan up on the wall in any event, with his relevant dates of service, provoking a bitter protest from none other than Chief of Inspection Teddy Kern, the newest incumbent of the position which administered a slap on the wrist to Frank Santella for consorting with organized crime figures, retaliating against whistle-blowers, and fudging on his own taxes. That I would enshrine a portrait of Nunan on an IRS wall was, Teddy Kern claimed, "glorifying a criminal and a despicable act."

"How could you glorify that crook?" Kern upbraided me, "I'd like to take a big black paintbrush and paint bars across Mr. Nunan's face so everyone will know that he spent time behind bars."

I had half a mind to ask why the IRS proved so willing to stand by and let boorish Frank Santella ride roughshod over Stan Welli, Ron Koperniak, and George Ecola. Instead, I remarked, "Maybe that's why they call it a rogues' gallery."

I tried to explain to Teddy Kern, the man responsible for the ethical behavior of the IRS, that we could not afford to forget our past, to submerge painful memories, and pretend that they never happened.

"We can learn from our history," I told Kern, "and perhaps we can avoid repeating such mistakes." Kern appeared unconvinced.

I heard through the grapevine that my putting up portraits of the commissioners also displeased Senior Deputy Commissioner Mike Murphy, because I was glorifying "a group of white men." Perhaps Murphy appreciated President Bush's appointment of Shirley Peterson as IRS commissioner in February 1992, and President Clinton's appointment of Margaret Richardson the following year, adding a bit of diversity to the photo display.

Another fatuous stab at PC posturing occurred in the mid-seventies, during the christening of the newly renovated auditorium on the top floor of IRS headquarters. In a contest to name the auditorium, some lucky employee won a cruise to nowhere for suggesting the Honorable George Boutwell of Massachusetts, the first commissioner of Internal Revenue, as the perfect candidate for enshrinement. Boutwell had been appointed by President Lincoln in 1862 to collect the first income tax, imposed on our wealthiest citizens to help defray the costs of the Civil War. In due course, a plaque appeared on the wall beside the door, proudly proclaiming the all-new Boutwell Auditorium.

A year or so after the contest, a group of irate women inside the IRS protested the memorializing of George Boutwell, whom they labeled a "male chauvinist pig," based on an unsubstantiated rumor that, at some point in his long, distinguished career in public office, he fired all the women who worked for him.

Other stories about Boutwell were far more compelling. As an early anti-slavery advocate, as the Massachusetts representative to the 1861 Peace Convention in Washington, D.C., Boutwell delivered one of the most rousing orations on abolition at the convention, denouncing the moral evil of slavery in such eloquent terms that he brought tears to the eyes of the delegates. At the founding of the Emancipation League in 1861, a year and a half before Lincoln's Emancipation Proclamation, Boutwell delivered yet another passionate speech in support of what was then known as Negro suffrage—giving freed slaves the right to vote. Boutwell was not only a prominent abolitionist and a distinguished governor of Massachusetts, he was a coauthor of the Fifteenth Amendment, which provided for black suffrage after the Civil War.

Today, the former Boutwell Auditorium shamefully has no name. It's just "the Auditorium." It would be very PC in the nineties for the IRS to restore Boutwell's name to the auditorium.

TAXATION IN THE UNITED STATES

As I dug deeper into the history of taxation in America, I began to appreciate why the tax agency harbors such a deep-seated sense of shame regarding its own mission. Though the agency likes to pride itself on a high level of "voluntary compliance," "voluntary compliance" is hardly a term I would use to describe the behavior of most Americans when paying their taxes—more like "under protest" or "under fear of IRS enforcement paver." After all, the rousing rallying cry during the War for Independence was "No taxation without representation!"

Colonial and Revolutionary Era

During the harsh winter of 1764, the financially hard-pressed American colonists first received notice of Parliament's intent to impose a stamp tax on American trade goods. Soon thereafter, the mercantile British taxed molasses, sugar, and other articles imported into the colonies, to defray debts incurred during the Hundred Years War—fought between the French and the British—at a fearsome cost in men, money, and arms on North American soil.

In the first act of public opposition to the new taxes, Samuel Adams stood before a Boston town meeting and stoutly declared, "Our greatest apprehension is that these proceedings may be preparation to new taxes; for, if our trade may be taxed, why not our lands? Why not the products of our lands and every thing that we possess or use?"

Our American history of armed guerrilla warfare as a form of tax protest began in October 1765 with the Stamp Act Congress, the first convention of the distressed colonies to oppose British policies. When British revenue agents sought to enforce the stamp tax, irate colonists threatened them with bodily harm. For a time, Parliament backed off and finally repealed the hated Stamp Act in March 1766; but it maintained its right to tax American colonies, though no colonists were eligible for election to Parliament.

A year later, to compensate for revenues lost by the repeal of the Stamp Act, Parliament imposed heavy new excise taxes on lead, glass, paper, painters' supplies, and tea imported into the colonies. Against mounting opposition, in the early 1770s, Parliament rescinded all but the tax on tea.

To Parliament, it represented the preservation of what Britain considered an inalienable right to impose taxes, and its fiscal will, upon its unruly colonies. To colonial revolutionaries, the tea tax symbolized ongoing foreign oppression, the last straw in a despised system of unjust extortion—a direct threat to personal and national liberty.

These mounting frustrations climaxed in December 1773, when members of the Sons of Liberty, disguised as Indians, boarded ships of the East India Company and dumped more than three hundred crates of tea into Boston Harbor. The infamous Boston Tea Party prompted Parliament to enact even more punitive measures against the rebellious colonists, thus sealing their spirit of armed opposition to foreign domination and unwanted taxation.

Nine months later, delegates from all thirteen colonies from Maine to Virginia convened the first Continental Congress, paving the path to the defiant Declaration of Independence of July 4, 1776. The following year the Continental Congress adopted the Articles of Confederation, which proved pretty tentative in seeking authority for the central government to raise money through taxation. Congress could spend money and take on debts, but had no means of raising funds to pay its mounting bills.

Federalist Era

No government, however spiritually endowed, can operate without money from somewhere. The need for revenue to pay off Revolutionary War debts to support the new centralized government was the main reason that the colonists replaced the now obsolete Articles of Confederation with the Constitution. At the postwar Constitutional Convention of 1787 in Philadelphia, heated debate focused on the minimal power of central taxation for which the Articles of Confederation provided. Article 1, Section VIII of the Constitution holds that "Congress shall have power to lay and collect taxes, duties, imposts, and excises, to pay the debts and provide for the common defense and general welfare of the United States; but all duties, imposts, and excises shall be uniform throughout the United States." Ironically, in 1789 (the year of the Constitution's ratification) Benjamin Franklin wrote to a friend, "Nothing is certain in life but death and taxes."

In 1790 newly appointed Secretary of the Treasury Alexander Hamilton proposed an excise tax on whiskey as America's first "internal" tax. "External" taxes, mainly tariffs and duties on imports, were popular with the public, but fell heavily on regions and industries dependent on foreign imports. Those on the new country's newly opened western frontier—then the Allegheny Mountains of western Pennsylvania down into the North Carolina Appalachians—considered Hamilton, a New York fiscal conservative and friend of large, efficient industries, the sworn enemy of the common man.

In this wild West, the popular response to Hamilton's whiskey tax was fierce enough to frighten the most fervent Federalist. Desperately cash-poor frontier farmers used whiskey as currency for barter. Converting grain into whiskey was the most efficient way to transport produce to distant markets, given the lamentable state of the roads at the time. A wealthy Pennsylvania lawyer named David Bradford helped organize an armed protest. On September 11, 1791, sixteen men dressed in women's clothing—cross-dressing was a favorite habit of these early tax protesters—assaulted an excise collector named Robert Johnson in Washington County, in western Pennsylvania.

They cut off Johnson's hair, tarred and feathered him, stole his horse, and abandoned him in the forest. Despite their disguises, Robert Johnson recognized two of the "women" and obtained warrants for their arrest. Rather than risk his own neck by serving the papers, the local deputy marshal hired an illiterate cattle drover named John Connor to do his dirty work for him. Connor was set upon by an angry mob, whipped, tarred, feathered, robbed of his horse and money, and left tied to a tree for five hours.

What most aroused the ire and indignation of the Whiskey Rebels was a sense that this new tax was manifestly "unfair"; an attempt on the part of urban elites to balance the budget on their backs, as the primary producers of whiskey. When tax man John Neville rented working space in the home of Pennsylvania army officer William Faulkner, an armed mob dressed as Indians—deliberately copying the patriotic hosts of the Boston Tea Party—broke down the door to Faulkner's home, rampaged through the residence, and shot bullets into the ceiling of every room.

General John Neville, a boyhood friend of President Washington, was sixty years old when he agreed to serve as inspector for revenue for the southwestern region of Pennsylvania, the red-hot center of tax revolt country. When Neville tried to serve process for tax evasion on a popular farmer named William Miller, about one hundred men rode to Neville's elaborate home, known as "the finest house in the West," and threatened to burn it to the ground, with all the tax ledgers inside. Neville fired on the protesters, killing William Miller's nephew Oliver, in an act of desperate assertion of central authority prophetic of the recent fiasco at Ruby Ridge. Neville's murder of Oliver Miller—even if it was in self-defense—only fanned the flames of protest higher.

In a concerted assault on the Neville residence mounted by the self-styled Mingo Congregation Militia (a direct predecessor of our contemporary right-wing militias), Neville was driven out of town and his fine house burned to the ground. In the wake of that victory, lawyer David Bradford, proclaiming himself "Brigadier General Bradford," attempted to take the federal Fort Pitt by force.

Though that skirmish ended in a bumbling standoff, President Washington decided to nip this fast-spreading revolt in the bud. He marched on rebellious Pennsylvania at the head of his own militia, numbering in excess of twelve thousand troops—an army substantially larger than any force he had commanded during the entire War of Independence. This overwhelming authority succeeded in dispersing the enemy and in rounding up a ragtag bag of tax protesters who were forcibly marched all the way to Philadelphia on foot, with orders having been issued to the militia to behead any rebel who attempted escape. After being double-timed through the city as virtual prisoners of war, the tax rebels were tried, though only two were convicted—convictions later overturned when the two were discovered to have been not competent to stand trial. Most of the protesters were ultimately pardoned for their offenses after they signed an oath of allegiance to the government.

Nineteenth Century

With the Whiskey Rebellion suppressed, the ruling Federalist Party in Washington felt free to pile on tax after tax, including direct taxes on houses, land, and slaves between the ages of twelve and fifty. It even passed a "stamp tax" strikingly similar to the one that sparked the first colonial uprising. But the Federalists, egged on by Secretary of the Treasury Alexander Hamilton (a fierce proponent of centralized fiscal power and founder of the first central bank), ended up hoisting themselves on their own petards. In the election of 1800 the Jeffersonian Democrats voted the too-tax-happy team out of the White House mainly on the strength of candidate Jefferson's solemn vow to cut taxes. Sound familiar? As liberal economist John Kenneth Galbraith once remarked, eighteenth-century Americans objected to taxation without representation, but they objected nearly as much to taxation *with* representation. No matter what the year, 1796, 1896, or 1996, announcing massive tax cuts "across the board" is always popular with the people.

For nearly a century, until the Civil War, the federal government ran a nice surplus on tariffs alone, without levying direct taxes on its citizens. Steep tariffs on imports sheltered budding domestic industries from foreign competition. Few people objected to high tariffs, though some regions of the country—particularly the South and West—that relied on foreign imports felt unfairly burdened.

As the nation industrialized throughout the first half of the nineteenth century, this system of steep tariffs was ultimately understood as promoting the interests of northern manufacturers at the expense of southern agriculturalists. Whatever the true merits of this argument, resistance to high tariffs became a southern rallying cry in 1828, when silver-tongued southern politicians thunderously denounced a new steep import tax as the "Tariff of Abominations." The Nullification

Crisis that quickly ensued threatened the integrity of the union itself, and foreshadowed the coming Civil War.

As the Civil War tore the country in two through the battlefields of Virginia, Pennsylvania, and Maryland, the cost of combat rapidly skyrocketed to over $1 million a day for the Union side alone. Of the estimated $4.2 billion cost of the war to the Union, some $3 billion was raised through the sale of government bonds; $450 million through the printing of currency not backed by gold; and another $750 million through an innovation—the first American tax on income.

Along with the Gatling gun—the ancestor of today's machine gun—combat photography, and abolition of slavery, our present-day income tax is one of the lasting legacies of the Civil War. In 1862, in the heat of the conflict, President Lincoln established the Bureau of Internal Revenue, the direct predecessor of today's IRS. The first income tax was not nearly as odious as the welter of excise taxes that Lincoln's administration slapped on nearly everything that could move or be exchanged for money—including legal documents; ferry, railroad, steamboat, and toll bridge receipts; and even advertising, however primitive at the time. The tax on income, by contrast, was shockingly progressive, exempting the first $600 in income, and taxing income between $600 and $10,000 at the comfortable rate of 3 percent. Incomes above $10,000—enjoyed by only a handful of our most fortunate citizens—were taxed at a rate of 5 percent.

Though the income tax affected only the rich, the elaborate system George Boutwell devised to collect this new mountain of excise taxes touched nearly everyone on the Union side of the Mason-Dixon line. By early 1863 the Bureau of Internal Revenue was firmly entrenched as a strong arm of the central American government, employing an army of four thousand tax assessors and collectors. Assessors, who compiled lists of citizens and estimated the amount of tax owed were paid between $3 and $5 a day, plus $1 for every one hundred names submitted in lists to the tax collectors. Collectors were paid a flat commission of 4 percent on all money they collected up to $100,000, and 2 percent above that.

A system of paying collectors a flat commission for revenue raised inevitably led to widespread abuse and corruption. Only three years after the establishment of the Bureau of Internal Revenue, a dismayed Congress appointed a Special Revenue Commission charged with "reforming" the scandal-ridden bureau. When, after the war, as many Congressmen called for the extinction of the income tax, the corruption of its collectors was frequently cited as a major reason for its demise.

An 1869 editorial in the *New York Tribune* denounced the income tax as "the most odious, vexatious, inquisitorial, and unequal of all our taxes." In 1871 Commissioner John W. Douglass of Pennsylvania (a noted antitax state) wrote to the House Ways and Means Committee deriding the income tax as "most obnoxious to the genius of our people." He most strenuously objected that it "exposed the private financial affairs of private citizens to the snooping eyes of the government," was "not productive of great revenue," and was "inquisitorial."

The following year, the income tax was repealed. But the revocation didn't make the new Internal Revenue Service any more popular with the vast majority of American citizens. Commissioner Green Raum of Illinois (appointed by President Grant) lamented in an 1877 annual report that his revenue officers "found themselves unsupported in execution of the laws by a healthy state of public opinion. Many citizens," he claimed, "not guilty of violating the law themselves, are in strong sympathy with those who do violate it."

Commissioner Raum spoke from painful experience: In North Carolina, when federal revenue agents shut down several illegal distilling and tobacco operations, local judges issued more than fifty warrants to arrest federal officers on trumped-up violations of state laws. Rising violence against tax collectors even led the IRS to appeal to the U.S. Army for help. The Army provided military personnel with horses and carbines to accompany IRS agents into the field.

In the absence of an income tax, Congress had to become ever more creative in cooking up methods of extracting hard-earned income from a reluctant citizenry. In 1886 Congress passed the first tax generally understood to have a "regulatory"—as opposed to a "revenue-based"—purpose. A regulatory tax, like the tax on cigarettes or spirits, aims to raise money while manipulating moral behavior or material. In 1886 the fearsome substance considered obnoxious to the future of the republic was not demon rum or marijuana, but oleomargarine.

At Napoleon's request, French chemists had concocted margarine as the spread that wouldn't go rancid overnight in hot weather. Dairy farmers denounced margarine as a direct threat to their livelihoods, and thus to the healthy, wholesome American way of life. Though the oleo tax raised over $1 million in revenues in its first year, its regulatory effect proved nearly nil: Margarine enjoyed such a boom market in the United States that gross sales receipts doubled in five years.

Attacks on revenue agents decreased toward the end of the century, but the adversarial relationship between taxpayer and collector by no measure improved. A poem by John Kendrick Bangs published in *Harper's Weekly* in 1895 reflected the negative public mood—at least on the part of the affluent—toward the reimposition of an income tax on fat cats "with stocks."

The Income Tax

What is the size of your income? Give us the figures, pray;
And don't you be modest about it, for shyness won't do today.
All you who've been ostentatious, and living beyond your means,
Go down to the tax-assessor and invite him behind the scenes.
Where is your cash invested? Open your coffers wide.
The Bogie-man of the Treasury is standing at your side.
He's noted your yacht and your horses; he's noticed the way you sup;
And he's going to be mighty careful how you foot your columns up.
He's been on the roof at the opera, and has envied you down in your box;
And he's always wanted a chance like this to whack at the man with
*   stocks.*
He's stood by the café window and watched you lunching within,
And he has a pretty good notion of the size of your pile of tin.
He's thought you were going it lively, were traveling much on your
*   shape,*
But now he is going to prove it, backed up by square miles of red tape;
And you who've been ostentatious must tell the whole truth to-day.
You've got to admit you're a fraud, sir, or you've got to step up and pay.
So tell us the size of your income; account for each little red cent.

This terrible cad, the collector, knows pretty well what you have spent;
And if you think to escape him by making it small you will fail,
And end, if you try to deceive him, in a small private box at the jail.

By the Gilded Age of the 1890s, as the great steel and railroad monopolies of Andrew Carnegie and Cornelius Vanderbilt threatened to strangle the nation's booming economy—while sprouting mansions of Brobdingnagian proportions in Newport and Saratoga—populists saw a soak-the-rich income tax as the ideal way to redistribute wealth from the grossly rich to the pathetically poor.

The reputation of Democrats as the "tax and spend" party was further enhanced during the financial Panic of 1893, when Democrat Grover Cleveland in the White House and Democratic majorities in both House and Senate threatened to join forces to push through a new income tax. The new tax would strike only the really rich: that 1 percent of the population with household incomes over $4,000. William Jennings Bryan, the passionate populist from Nebraska, was the most ardent proponent of the new income tax in the House. But Congressman Bourke Cochran of New York, a fellow Democrat (whose wealthy constituency in baronial palaces along Manhattan's Fifth Avenue would pay the brunt of the tax), insisted that the new tax was far from necessary and represented "class warfare" at its most malign.

In the short term, Bryan's faction won, overwhelmingly passing the 1894 Wilson Tariff Act, a bill Grover Cleveland grudgingly allowed into law without signing it. But a group of wealthy tax resisters succeeded in taking their suit against the income tax to the Supreme Court, which ruled the income tax unconstitutional in 1895, on the grounds that it was a "direct" tax not equally apportioned among the population, as duly prescribed by the Constitution.

Early Twentieth Century

The twentieth century brought new notions of an income tax as the most efficient means to keep capitalists and monopolists from amassing what Theodore Roosevelt (a Republican and scion of great wealth himself) denounced in 1906 as "fortunes swollen beyond all healthy limits." A sharp financial panic in the following year, with its attendant poverty, swung the political pendulum back toward imposing a wealth-balancing tax on the unhealthily wealthy.

In 1909 Congress passed a proposed constitutional amendment supporting an income tax, still chiefly to soak the rich. As Kentucky congressman Ollie James entreated his peers from the House floor: "Who is prepared to defend as just a system of taxation that requires a hod carrier, who for eight long hours each day wends his way to the dizzy heights of a lofty building with his load of mortar or brick, to pay as much to support this great Republic as John D. Rockefeller, whose fortune is so great that it staggers the imagination to contemplate it?"

But ardent conservatives like Senator Nelson Aldrich of Rhode Island (whose daughter had married John D. Rockefeller Jr.) were not impressed by the populist rhetoric of Ollie James and his ilk. Aldrich and his cronies in Congress, in a blatantly protectionist move, pressed for ever higher trade tariffs instead of an income tax. Conservative Republican President William Howard Taft sought a Solomonic compromise by permitting the passage of a 2 percent tax on the income of corporations. Since fewer than 10 percent of the population then owned common stock, the tax arguably soaked the rich again. To the delight of Progressives, the corporate income tax was deemed constitutional by the Supreme Court—being judged not a "direct" tax, but a form of excise or "indirect" tax. With the plutocrats on the run, Progressives in Congress pushed through the proposed Sixteenth Amendment in February 1913, amending the Constitution to permit a "direct" income tax.

On October 3, 1913, following the ratification of the new amendment by the states, President Woodrow Wilson signed into law the first personal income tax bill since the Civil War. But news of Wilson's refusal to accept an honorary membership in the Chevy Chase Country Club, and the outbreak of hostilities between Turkey and Bulgaria, Serbia, and Greece—the first battles of World War I—overshadowed one of the most significant pieces of domestic legislation in American history.

The first income tax law of the American century was only fourteen pages long, but it contained enough exceptions and exemptions, loopholes, and inconsistencies to keep top-notch accountants capably employed until the next century. It featured an exemption for income below $3,000 and a marital deduction of $1,000—an obvious act of social engineering to support marriage and family. Nevertheless, at the rates stipulated, only about 1 percent of the U.S. population had to pay the new tax. In 1914, taxpayers filed 357,598 tax forms, labelled 1040s in those days because the number represented a sequence of federal forms used since the mid-nineteenth century. This molehill of 1040s—compared to today's mountain—grew only modestly to 500,000 by 1916. Still, the federal government's deficit leaped in the same year to well over $175 million.

The mounting deficit was directly tied—once again—to war. World War I raging in Europe had severely cut into imports, causing tariff revenues to plummet. The one way out of this hole was greater income taxation, which the Wilson administration reluctantly chose to do. Within three years, rates had doubled, to a not exactly confiscatory 4 percent of income. But once America declared war on Germany and began mobilizing for war, the income exemption formerly set at $3,000 was slashed to $1,000, thereby pulling in millions more taxpayers. On top of the new base rates, a complex system of surcharges sent marginal rates soaring into the stratosphere, in some cases running as high as 77 percent of income.

Not surprisingly, federal revenues rocketed from $800 million in 1916 to $3.7 billion two years later. Money flowing into Washington endangered the government's long-standing fiscal restraint. By 1920, seven years after the reintroduction of the income tax as a soak-the-rich tax, the number of income tax forms filed by American citizens had jumped to 5.5 million, representing roughly 13 percent of the work force. By the dawn of the Roaring Twenties the income tax had become the federal government's main source of revenue.

The income tax still remained strikingly progressive: The 1 percent of Americans pulling in household incomes above $20,000 paid around 70 percent of the total tax bill. The rich, who a decade before had paid hardly any taxes at all, were now, to their chagrin, shouldering the lion's share of the burden.

But once marginal rates soared to the 70-percent level, the rich began aggressively sheltering income in tax-exempt state and local municipal bonds while furtively shifting assets into personal holding companies taxed at the lower corporate rate. The result was that revenues relative to the gross national product dropped even as rates soared. Angry plutocrats not only stopped paying their fair share in taxes but mobilized enough ardent opponents of high taxes among the growing middle and upper-middle classes to swing the election of 1920 to the Republicans. As the Roaring Twenties began, Warren Harding, champion of personal wealth, sailed to the White House on a platform proclaiming a "return to normalcy." For "return to normalcy" read: no more scalping the wealthy.

With no war, the Progressives could do little to fend off the rollback, while a period of rising prosperity at least suggested that the rising tide would raise all boats. Tax rates were lowered. Overseeing this counterrevolution was Warren Harding's secretary of the Treasury, Andrew W. Mellon, one of the richest men in the country.

During his twelve years in public office, Mellon grew so politically potent that liberals joked nervously about the three presidents serving under him. In today's ongoing debate on the value of supply-side economics, Mellon could be counted among the earliest practitioners of what George Bush once denounced as "voodoo economics." Mellon was first and foremost a banker, not a politician, and in his capacity as a man of business proposed to run the U.S. Treasury on "business lines." Having keenly observed that railroad freight rates were traditionally set at a level known as "what the traffic will bear," Mellon sharply cut tax rates three times in ten years. As a result, overall revenues in fact rose. Of course, this favored state of affairs occurred during a period of unprecedented prosperity and of rampant speculation on the stock market, raising nearly everyone's prosperity.

Until Black Friday 1929. The country plunged deep into the Depression. Herbert Hoover, a wealthy engineer and entrepreneur and no great fan of the common man, pressed Andrew Mellon to boost tax rates in a desperate attempt to plug a growing deficit. The results were predictable. The economy's already escalating collapse turned into a total freefall. Franklin Delano Roosevelt swept into office proclaiming that Americans had nothing to fear but fear itself—that he would give them a New Deal.

FDR's New Deal attacked "economic royalists" and cranked up tax rates, reaching a level not seen since Woodrow Wilson's day. An ever more complex tax code evolved to snare the wealth of the plutocrats and efficiently divert funds to the federal coffers. But as author John Steele Gordon has written, precisely the opposite occurred. "Sailing as a guest on a Vanderbilt yacht one day, Franklin Roosevelt was astonished to learn that many rich men were incorporating their yachts to escape taxation. A New York financier was overheard in a Paris bar proudly proclaiming: 'My fortune is in the Bahamas and is going to stay there as long as that bastard remains in the White House.'"

Once again, the rich had kept busy diverting their money into low-tax and nontax financial instruments, located both inside and outside the country. Only a world war could jump-start the economy, the staggering cost of which would have bankrupted the nation if the New Dealers hadn't learned John Maynard Keynes's lessons of deficit spending. The wartime government desperately needed ready cash to pay for guns and butter.

WARTIME TAXES: FROM CLASS TAX TO MASS TAX

"Pay as you go" became the new motto and mantra of the hard-pressed Bureau of Internal Revenue. In simpler times, citizens could pay their income taxes to the feds in quarterly installments throughout the following year. But the installment plan left the government holding too much debt and taxpayers faced with hefty tax bills they were unable to pay. Beardsley Ruml, a member of the Federal Reserve Board in New York and chairman of R.H. Macy & Co., devised what he called a "pay as you go" plan. Employers were obliged to withhold tax payments from workers' weekly paychecks, which meant that workers never even saw or held the money they earned before it was shipped off to Washington. Broadcaster David Brinkley contends that passage of the Current Tax Payment Act of 1943, "combined with wartime tax rates that eventually reached 92 percent in the top bracket, turned Washington into a money machine, an ATM."

During wartime, citizens will bear impossible burdens if they believe the fate of the nation is at stake. By 1941, as combat costs skyrocketed, the IRS was collecting over $7 billion annually in tax revenue, an amount already three times higher than the amount collected a decade earlier. By 1945 tax revenues had swollen to $45 billion, an almost unbelievable jump in merely four years. Well over 50 million Americans were now paying their dues involuntarily.

Postwar Era

But once the war was over and peace was declared, what possible excuse did the government have to keep funneling so much of its citizens' money into its coffers? According to David Brinkley—who heard it straight from Truman veep Alben Barkley—Truman held an informal meeting with key members of Congress "to decide what to do about the Niagaras of money the withholding tax was pumping into Washington."

Congressmen quietly insisted that they "wanted to keep the money coming in for a while." During the war, the public grew used to paying high taxes; in peacetime, they wanted results at home. "Now we want the roads and bridges and hospitals," the congressmen said, "and we want our names on them."

The devilishly complex tax code developed to pay for World War II not only shifted what had been a "class" tax into a "mass" tax, it ushered in a new era of fiscal complication, with subtle deductions for medical expenses, investors' expenses, charitable contributions, and other opportunities for dodges and loopholes. With high marginal rates still in effect, the rich predictably took their business elsewhere, moving money into tax-free bonds and other sheltered or tax-preferred investments. Of course, the higher the tax rate, the more valuable the deduction. As economic historian John Steele Gordon maintains, "An income tax system featuring high marginal rates and generous deductions is, not to put too fine a point on it, a welfare program for the rich, and a generous one at that."

The new financial tap soon turned into a welfare program for corrupt tax officials, appointed by local politicians through an archaic system in place since the Civil War. So-called collectors of Internal Revenue received their lucrative appointments in return for managing the election of their senators or representatives, or contributing heavily to their campaign.

The King hearings of 1950–51, launched by California congressman Cecil King, uncovered rampant corruption among Internal Revenue employees, who were charged with bribery, misuse of public office, and innumerable other ethical lapses. In contrast to the nonresponse to Congressman Doug Barnard's 1990s revelations of ethical misconduct at the highest reaches of the IRS, public outrage permitted Harry Truman to massively overhaul the tax agency, with a stroke of the presidential pen transforming the Bureau of Internal Revenue from one of the most politicized federal agencies into one of the least. After Congress voted overwhelmingly to approve the President's proposed changes in January 1952, the agency retained just one political appointee—the commissioner—while every other influential position was filled by career civil servants.

On the downside, the massive reorganization effected by Truman, establishing a three-tier executive structure of district offices, regional offices, and a national office, would in time harden into the monolithic, moribund, virtually unreformable IRS that looms over America today. In 1955, in an ineffectual public relations ploy, the Bureau of Internal Revenue was renamed the Internal Revenue Service to emphasize its providing a service to the public. But, because the new "service" was so massively decentralized, employees in the field could largely ignore policies adopted by successive commissioners—the only IRS employee truly accountable to the public.

BACK TO THE PAST IN THE PRESENT

I had my gallery of commissioners' portraits up on the walls for only a brief period when I received a phone call from the newly appointed assistant to the senior deputy commissioner, Mike Killfoil, an IRS executive serving as an executive officer (glorified go-fer) to Mike Murphy. We and the IRS had just entered the nineties, and there was a mood floating around the halls of 1111 Constitution Avenue that perhaps can best be described as mini-perestroika, a warming trend possibly traceable to the end of the Cold War.

Mike Killfoil considered himself a make-things-happen, can-do kind of guy. When he stumbled upon a safe in his office containing the tax returns of most if not all the twentieth-century American

Presidents, he called me in for a brief consultation as to how best to dispose of them—not in the sense of "discard," but rather of "appropriately place." Killfoil explained that he had asked his secretary to conduct a complete inventory of the contents of this safe, which contained presidential tax returns dating back to 1913—the first year of the income tax in this century. With that accomplished, Killfoil's question to me was: Should they be sent to the National Archives?

He asked me to research the question from a legal and policy standpoint, and get back to him ASAP. I was impressed by his asking the right questions, rather than preserving the "yours is not to question why, yours is but to do or die" attitude that congeals into a simple "That's how it's always been done, that's how it is to be done." Killfoil was actually wondering whether there might not be some better way.

Glancing over the material in question, I could easily see in physical form how the size and the complexity of the income tax code grew over the decades. The first tax returns—filed by President Wilson—were more slender than those filed by Kennedy, Johnson, Nixon, Ford, Reagan, and Bush. Wilson's 1040 was short, without the abundance of attachments that junk up modern 1040s, at most two to three pages in length. By the Truman-Eisenhower years, the forms had become as fat as the bureaucracy.

Due to 6103 regulations, I cannot detail the contents of those tax returns. I can note, to my dismay, that the signature blocks on nearly all the returns had been torn off—where the president had set down his autograph. When I brought this vandalism to the attention of Mike Killfoil's secretary, she shook her head sadly and mumbled something about "souvenir hunting" by former members of the commissioner's office. So much for stewardship of historical records and documents. No trained archivist or historian would ever have permitted those tax forms to be defiled. Still, the question remained: Could these valuable documents be turned over to the National Archives, where they would presumably be better taken care of than in the IRS commissioner's office?

"Talk to Disclosure Litigation," Mike Killfoil advised. The junior attorney at Disclosure Litigation assigned to ponder this problem didn't ponder—she pounced.

"That's 6103 information. It cannot be handed to the National Archives." Case closed.

I didn't even broach the fact that the National Archives already manages such tax information, all of our 1099s and 1040s. Instead, I reported to Killfoil that I had just stumbled over Internal Revenue Code 6103. It occurred to me, though, that the presidential libraries were managed by the National Archives, and might be the appropriate resting place for the national chief executive officers' assembled 1040s. With Killfoil's blessing, I took a flyer and called the director of the Herbert Hoover Library in West Branch, Iowa, and asked him if he'd be interested in obtaining a complete collection of Hoover 1040s.

The director of the library, thinking fast on his feet, offered to do just about anything to ensure the confidentiality of the returns. He observed that while many scholars had expressed great interest in delving into Hoover's business interests, there was a surprising dearth of material available on his commercial affairs. The tax returns would be immeasurably helpful in directing scholars toward various aspects of Hoover's prepresidential career. The bottom line: "They might shed a tremendous light on the history of the Hoover presidency."

Armed with this ammunition, I fired off a memo (cc to Mike Killfoil) informing the workers at Disclosure Litigation of the great interest among the community of presidential scholars in obtaining even the most restricted access to presidential tax information. Employing a classic bureaucratic defense tactic, the recipient of my memo responded quickly with a nonresponse: She would get back to me.

She never did.

Pre-1913 tax returns for the presidents do not exist because, with the brief exception of the Civil War period, citizens weren't required to file tax returns. President Lincoln must have filed a 1040, but it was lost in the massive destruction of tax returns directed by John W. Douglass of Pennsylvania, commissioner during the Grant administration. Douglass so despised the income tax that abolishing this "inquisitorial" government invasion of privacy became his personal mission. Today, in the regrettably incomplete IRS collection in the National Archives, there resides a lone tax refund letter from commissioner of Internal Revenue to Lincoln's estate, indicating that

Lincoln overpaid his income tax for the year in question. But under the current law, the IRS contends that permitting public access even to this innocuous document would constitute an illegal disclosure of tax information.

HISTORY IS BUNK

Not long after being stonewalled on the presidential tax return issue—the documents presumably still sit, safe and sound (if sadly shorn of their valuable signatures) in that same four-drawer safe in the commissioner's office—I took a call from the director of an IRS management training program; she asked whether I'd like to review some material for the IRS's short course on IRS history.

"The class is boring, nobody listens, everyone just sits and stares at the floor," this woman said, hoping that I might lighten up her deadly dull, perfunctory hour. After skimming through her material—a boring rehash of tired old jargon and vague statements about "purpose"—I concluded that even this short course needed such massive revision that I might as well rewrite it for her from scratch. I called her and volunteered my services as teacher. I could use the program as a platform to advance my credo that history mattered, that it provided context for the present, and that preserving the artifacts of the day could be the best possible gift for future generations of leaders and citizens.

The class was a gas. It went over so well that I was soon being asked to deliver a similar talk to newly hired attorneys, and to other groups of new IRS hires. I had actually achieved my tenure-long dream of helping to enlighten IRS employees about the long, sometimes proud, sometimes not-so-proud history of the IRS. I took a strong line on the issue of being ashamed of what we do and went into some depth—as I have done in this chapter and throughout much of this book—to demonstrate that, while there's reason to be contrite, there's also reason to be proud of the system's efforts. Without taxes, America would have no National Parks, no National Institutes of Health, no interstate highway system. Of course, I could have added, "no bloated defense budget, no unavailing welfare program, no Golden Fleece Awards from Senator Proxmire."

I'd show my students the IRS's mission statement:

> The purpose of the Internal Revenue Service is to collect the proper amount of tax revenue at the least cost; to serve the public by continually improving the quality of our products and services; and to perform in a manner warranting the highest degree of public confidence in our integrity, efficiency, and fairness.

That was it. But that was enough. My immediate supervisor, Bob Johnson, dashed off a detailed memo to Mike Killfoil in enthusiastic support of my latest proposal to establish formally an Office of History and Archival Services at the IRS.

This proposal was my attempt to raise awareness of IRS document management in such a way as to ensure compliance with federal law while accounting for the IRS's unique role as a repository of highly sensitive, private information, access to which had been strictly controlled by an act of Congress. As Bob Johnson wrote to Mike Killfoil:

> The IRS decision to create an internal history program a year ago is very much in line with similar activities in both the federal and corporate worlds. Organizations as diverse as the GAO, Anheuser-Busch, NSA, Wells Fargo Bank, and the FAA have established historical programs. Although our initiative resulted in the first professional historical position in the Department of the Treasury, the Comptroller of the Currency has recently established a similar position as well.

So far, so good. But the real core of the proposal concentrated on the document management issue, as I understood it, and attempted to place my "historical function" squarely in the context of a management crisis—a crisis exacerbated by IRS's obliviousness to it.

> Using knowledge of past activities to develop insight into future planning is hardly an idea that can be faulted, yet many organizations feel it is not practical to take the time to sift through dusty records in search of items of historical significance. The solution to this dilemma is to establish an internal historical function staffed by professionals trained in the identification and interpretation of historical records. . . .

The benefits to be derived from an established and supported historical function are many, including improving employee morale through promoting an awareness of the heritage of the IRS and pride in being associated with a government agency with a long and successful history; improving taxpayer relations through informational materials briefly explaining the historical foundations of our tax system.

It took some time, but it wasn't long before I was unofficially informed that my proposal had been met with a very positive response at the "highest levels" of the organization—which I assumed meant Mike Killfoil.

Then I learned that Mike Killfoil was being transferred from his glorified gofer status in the national office to become the director of a suborganization in the headquarters known with the bizarre name of Facilities and Information Management Support—two seemingly unconnected areas mindlessly lumped together in what was known as FIMS for short. Just when I had given up hope, Mike Killfoil invited me to follow him to his new assignment. After surviving the agony of HRT, I was about to become part of a new team: FIMS. Once again, I found myself in a suborganization that had nothing to do with performing my duties as the official IRS historian. But at least this time I would have a sympathetic boss. Maybe Killfoil could shepherd my proposal through, after all.

Mike Killfoil didn't last long as head of FIMS. Within a few months, he took another step up the ladder, transferring from the Beltway madness to a district directorship in the real world. Mike Killfoil's replacement as head of FIMS was a friendly fellow, Bob Brazzil, who also pledged to support my fledgling history-cum-records-management program. But soon Bob Brazzil was packing for Chicago. I remained in Washington, forced to reeducate a stream of IRS senior executives—who were playing a seemingly endless game of musical chairs as they bounced among various executive positions quickly enough to ensure that no one could ever be held accountable for anything—about the viability of the "historical function" as a bona fide management tool.

Bob Brazzil's replacement, Jim Casimir, an IRS lifer awaiting retirement, was rumored to have been transferred to this unlofty position from the important job of IRS Director of Appeals due to some mysterious ethical mishap. Casimir was stuck in a holding pattern atop FIMS for what everyone knew to be a brief tenure—and he proved to be my undoing.

From our first meeting, I knew that Casimir thought my history program was bunk. With his abrupt and often rude brush-offs, he often made me feel like bunk. While biding my time, I put together a small exhibit on the Whiskey Rebellion, using material I'd gathered on a field trip through the relevant sites, with a few maps and photos in an old banged-up display case in the dreary lobby of 1111 Constitution Avenue. Quite a few people passing by stopped to see it and praised it as a welcome diversion while waiting for the elevators. The last time I checked, the exhibition was still there, a few feet from where IRS internal security threatened to arrest me for trespassing a few years later.

ENVIRONMENTAL DISASTER

It was Thursday, October 13, 1994, and David Junkins, chief of headquarters operations for the IRS, decided it was high time to clean up the basement storage area that had not been given a good going-over for decades. Dave Junkins was large, bearded, and jovial—the sort of guy you could easily see playing Santa Claus at the office party. But Junkins wasn't laughing on that October day, because the basement was a godawful mess. He was new to his job, and he wanted a clean slate, as far as the underground storage facility was concerned. There were ancient boxes of outdated envelopes and stationery to be discarded. There were old pieces of broken office furniture to be thrown out. And, as he set off on his cleaning jag, someone noticed a mysterious steel box sitting in the corner of the basement. No one knew or remembered what the devil it was.

Dave Junkins instructed his cleanup crew to get the box out, along with the rest of the garbage. The movers dutifully rolled their dollies up to the box, which was about four feet square and made of thick, shiny welded steel. They tried to lift it so it would glide down to the elevator. It wouldn't budge. It must have weighed a ton. The guys called for help to lift the mysterious box. Somehow, with reinforcements, they managed to hoist it onto the dolly, and began pushing it down the hall to the elevator.

At some point, the box slipped off the dolly and landed on one of its welded side edges. The seal on one side wall cracked; out spilled a thick, shimmering liquid, which quickly began spreading a silvery sheen across the concrete floor. The workers didn't know what to do. Some guys ran to find rags to mop up the mess. The thick liquid pooled as it leaked from the cracked weld. At last, one of the men decided to report the spill to Dave Junkins. They needed instructions on what to do next.

The manager arrived a few minutes later and deduced that this wasn't just any old liquid. It was liquid mercury—a pretty dangerous substance to have running all over the floor. The drains in the floor probably flowed into the Washington, D.C., sewer system. The IRS didn't need to be spilling hazardous waste into the public sewer system.

The manager quickly located a company that specialized in emergency response to hazardous spills. A crew soon arrived in the IRS basement to clean up the mess, outfitted in protective gear to protect them from skin contact with the mercury. The drains were blocked to contain whatever mercury hadn't already flowed down them. The parking garage used by IRS executives adjacent to the area where the spill had occurred was declared off-limits for the duration. Car owners were shooed away from the area with little explanation and told to find another route home.

After containing the spill, the IRS launched into an internal damage-control effort to contain information about the spill. Despite the environmental health hazards of liquid mercury, the IRS felt no compulsion to inform workers in the building about the event. It wasn't until word leaked, so to speak, to the employees' union that the IRS sent word over the telephone voice message system that a spill had occurred. Just as when low-level radiation is released from many nuclear plants, an executive decision had been made: What you don't know can't hurt you.

When I heard about the spill, something didn't make sense. As I knew, the IRS had never used mercury to hunt down tax dodgers. I tracked down Dave Junkins, whom I'd known since my first days at the agency, to ask him what he knew about the source of the box. He'd always been jovial and friendly with me. But when I asked him if he knew what the box was, he brushed me off in a brusque manner.

"It doesn't matter," he said. "The mercury's gone. It's cleaned up. All the mercury that was still in the box was disposed of properly, I can assure you."

I hastened to reassure him that I hadn't any intention of questioning his judgment; I was just curious. What was a big welded steel box of liquid mercury doing in the basement of IRS headquarters? My innate historian's curiosity was once again to become the bane of the IRS.

With a troubled look, Dave Junkins pointed sheepishly at the loading dock. The box was still there, waiting to be picked up for what Junkins promised me was "proper disposal."

I took a look. The box was bigger than I'd expected. Its sides were constructed of hollow-walled steel about an inch and a half thick. Each side wall had been filled with liquid mercury. That's why, I supposed, the box weighed so much. Still, why was it in the basement of IRS headquarters?

I tried again, "I'd like to know where that box came from."

Dave Junkins looked at me as if I were nuts. Crazy or not, I made a few phone calls. No one could or would tell me anything about mercury use at the IRS. But then I recalled an old IRS agent I'd met a few months before who'd been a regular font of knowledge about the headquarters building. When I called him, he thought a moment: The mercury might have been used as some sort of testing device by the Alcohol, Tobacco, and Firearms laboratory, which had been located in the IRS headquarters building until 1972, when Commissioner Randolph Thrower resigned rather than place G. Gordon Liddy or Jack Caulfield in key ATF jobs.

He suggested that I contact the current ATF laboratory, a modern facility in the Washington, D.C., suburb of Rockville, Maryland. I dialed the number, explained who I was, and began describing the box. Once I mentioned the liquid mercury, I had only completed about half a sentence when the man on the other end of the line stopped me and asked me to go through it again, this time in detail.

After I repeated the scene, he paused before revealing that he had built the box. He was very upset about the mercury spill. "It should never have happened," he said. "I can't believe it was still there."

He explained in detail to me that when ATF moved from the IRS building after gaining its independence in 1972, he had completed all the necessary paperwork to have the mercury-filled box removed. That had been twenty-two years before, and that was the last time he'd seen the box, or even thought about it.

"We used the box to analyze paint and other substances using nuclear bombardment," he explained. "Let's say the ATF recovered a paint chip from a crime scene, it could be analyzed for type, make, manufacturer, and so on, by placing it inside the box and bombarding it with neutrons. The hollow walls were filled with mercury to contain the nuclear particles."

When the ATF moved in 1972, it purchased more modern equipment for its new laboratory and made arrangements to dispose of everything from the old lab. The person responsible for removing the box must have just left it there, figuring that it was too hard to move and that no one would care anyway. Perhaps the same man who substituted pictures of any old guys with white beards and muttonchops for the commissioners' portraits or the secretary who ripped the presidential signatures off those old 1040s.

I stopped by Junkins's office to inform him of my discovery. My "research" had taken fifteen minutes. I gently reminded Junkins that perhaps if he had called upon me for help before attempting to remove unidentified objects from the IRS, the hazardous spill might have been prevented. Just as former Commissioner Donald Alexander claimed that he never considered himself a zealot for civil liberties, I never saw my job as a platform for promoting environmental awareness. But, by default, by ignoring its problems and its history, the IRS had pushed me into environmental advocacy. The clean-up operation cost the IRS nearly $175,000. That would have covered my salary for several years.

"I don't care what was in the box or why it was there," Junkins told me. "All I care about is that the box is getting taken out of here."

"History is bunk," Henry Ford said. At the IRS at least, he was right.

10

DO THE RIGHT THING?
IRS Secret History, Volume V

While my response to the Barnard hearings had been to try and ramp up a history/archival program that might help plug the ever-widening IRS records management gap, the IRS's institutional response to the ethical and moral challenges presented was decidedly more pro forma. Of the twenty-five high-level executives investigated by Barnard's subcommittee, the IRS punished only one miscreant: Frank Santella.

The IRS spent most of its energy defending itself from external attack, rather than plucking the bad apples from its higher limbs. In a futile attempt to take the sting out of Barnard's invective, the IRS lined up an impressive array of current and former commissioners—outgoing Commissioner Larry Gibbs, incoming Commissioner Fred Goldberg, and Senior Deputy Commissioner Michael Murphy. While Murphy did most of the talking, all three sought to convey shock, regret, and surprise at the appropriate moments during witness testimony. Former D.C. tax attorney Fred Goldberg, the incoming commissioner, whom the Senate had confirmed a few weeks before, registered his intention to address and redress (not to mention window-dress) the legion of moral, ethical, and management woes currently afflicting the IRS. Outgoing Commissioner Gibbs, who had conveniently jumped ship four months before, could no longer be held accountable for his actions, or inactions, as a private citizen. His appearance at the hearings was a publicity coup for the IRS in deflecting criticism.

On October 4, 1990, Barnard's subcommittee issued a scathing report taking the IRS to task for "extensive misuse of enforcement powers," a display of unbridled power only compounded by a "pattern of improper and possibly unlawful conduct by a significant number of senior IRS employees." The IRS internal police function (Inspection) badly needed serious retooling. Not only had Inspection repeatedly failed in its duty to investigate or appropriately punish those few miscreants whom it had actually detected, but it had seen fit to unleash the awesome powers at its disposal only against whistle-blowers while letting the real creeps and bad guys get off, for the most part, scot-free.

The Barnard report concluded ominously—from the IRS's point of view—with a brief reminder that a one-day "follow-up" hearing was scheduled for mid-1992. This left the besieged IRS brass with just a few short years to get its ethical act together. Given the depth and strength of the institutional bias against change, three years was not a long time.

Over the next three years, I observed the IRS hierarchy's scurrying to make a good show by the July 1992 deadline. What evolved in the corridors of the 1111 Constitution Avenue after the Barnard hearings was a model of illusion and deception, moral smoke and ethical mirrors. You could hardly step down one of those dingy halls without some self-appointed moral authority mouthing off about the "ethical ramifications" of this or that issue.

The one concrete promise incoming Commissioner Goldberg had made to Congressman Barnard—and to the nation—in response to the hearings was that he would personally see to the enrichment of the IRS's woefully inadequate "ethics program." When a memo landed in my in box calling for volunteers to teach the one-day mandatory ethics classes recently revised by a high-priced "ethics consultant," I stepped forward as a candidate. I didn't consider myself any great moralist but did have some teaching experience.

When I sauntered to my new supervisor's office with memo in hand, my supervisor—the third or fourth in as many years—swiveled uncomfortably in his high-backed chair, shoved a few pieces of paper around on his desk, and finally formulated a credible excuse for turning me down.

"Shelley," he broke it to me gently. "I think they're looking for 'management officials.'"

After nearly four years of slipping and sliding like a greased hockey puck all over the organizational chart, I hadn't the faintest idea of what a "management official" was, or, for that matter, did. To the IRS the term seemed to connote a manager of supervisory rank below an "executive" but above a mere "manager." As a GM–14, I was a "manager," but apparently not a "management official." Better leave the morality and ethical ramifications to the experts, of which there seemed to be hundreds crawling to and from the woodwork in those days.

When my turn came to attend the mandatory one-day "ethics training course" in the training center in the basement of IRS headquarters, I arrived eager and ready to drink in all that the IRS had learned about ethics since the painful 1989 testimony of the likes of Stan Welli and his co-workers. I had a hunch that the soothing sea of soft pastel colors in which the training center was painted had been installed at the behest of the "ethics consultants," according to currently fashionable theories of workplace environment positively "impacting" employee behavior and morale.

At the head of the ethics classroom was Tony, the records manager who'd kindly debriefed me on the decades-old dispute between the IRS and the National Archives during my first weeks on the job.

The relentless pressure in the IRS to be a "team player" had been one of the key elements of the IRS culture that Douglas Barnard had gone out of his way to denounce. "If you're not a team player, you're off the team." The method of selecting teachers for the ethics course had nothing to do with teaching ability or moral fiber and everything to do with rewarding loyalty to the organization. All that hokum about wanting "management officials" to teach the course had of course been a total crock. Tony was a notch below me in the Civil Service rankings, and no more a "management official" than I was. But he was a team player.

As Tony eagerly launched into a prepackaged spiel, I had to hand it to him: He was smooth as silk in his assigned role as moral instructor. About as slick and superficial as the fancy workbook (prepared at God-only-knows what cost to the long-suffering taxpayer) that he distributed to launch the upcoming Socratic seminar. Beneath the inspiring title on the cover, *All Employee Ethics Awareness Workshop*, the key word "Ethics" had been boldly printed above the words "Principles and Practices." The examples of sticky "workplace situations" contained in the workbook were about as far removed from the real world of the IRS as Mars is from Alpha Centauri. None, for example, came close to the reality that Stan Welli faced when forced to confront Frank Santella.

Do you report *YOUR* supervisor to *HIS* supervisor if you have reason to believe that he is openly consorting with an organized crime figure, particularly if he is bragging about it to *YOUR* face? What if the same man, your boss, has also been fudging on his income taxes? What if *HIS* supervisor tells you that he doesn't want to report this matter to headquarters because it might "turn the office into a snake pit"?

What if, when *HE* refuses to perform his ethical duty, *YOU* go above his head and do it for *HIM*? What if *YOU* are then forced to suffer the consequences for doing *HIS* duty, nearly forced to resign, mocked by your colleagues, and hauled up on trivial charges after turning down an offer of settlement money from the highest-ranking civil service job-holder in the organization, who proceeds to use *YOU* as the butt of a sick joke at an after-dinner speech at an employee convention?

Sad to say, the examples of moral dilemmas cited in the book were less threatening to our moral/ethical status quo. One of my favorites was Optional Case Study #2:

I'm a manager with a value in my life—smoking. I have a private office and under current regulations, I can declare my office a smoking area. I can do it and smoke my head off. Is it ethical?

The eccentric punctuation and style is, of course, theirs.

Well, what do *YOU* think? As our workbook went on to bafflingly declare, "This little case study should yield the stake-holder concept and the core of the ethical decision-making mode, i.e., my right to smoke vs. fairness and caring/respect for others."

More than forty years ago, George Orwell made the point in a famous essay that totalitarian governments deliberately distort and debase language itself as a means of deceiving their own citizens. At the IRS, the language employed—I should say deployed—to address "touchy" subjects all too often veered into linguistic thickets the most experienced literary deconstructivist would have been hard pressed to untangle. Take the phrase, "I'm a manager with a value in my life." Couldn't they have written, "I like to smoke"? As for "the stake-holder concept" and "the core of the ethical decision-making model," the less said the better.

> The Ethical Compass Logo featured on the title page of this report has been developed for all ethics-related materials published by the Service. It symbolizes the importance of clear moral direction as we carry out our responsibilities in the public interest. The logo will be prominently displayed on the Ethics Resource Guide and on all materials to be included in the guide in the future. All employees will receive a copy of the guide in the Ethics Awareness Workshops. . . . From time to time, additional material will be distributed to all employees with the "Ethical Compass" logo. This logo will clearly mark the material as an update to their copy of the guide.

With Ethical Compass firmly in hand—the needle stuck straight up—I felt newly endowed with purpose and direction despite the bland ethical issues under discussion. Given the possibilities of narrative color inherent in the Barnard hearings, there was not a single mention of organized crime. Bags of meat. Joyriding in seized boats. Blue-jeans manufacturers offering sweetheart jobs to top Inspection officials.

Now in IRS ethics class, we read about naughty employees sneaking peeks at each other's computer files or dating each other. After our lunch break—not everyone came back after our lunch break—I couldn't resist giving Tony a teensy-weensy bit of a hard time. When the discussion turned to the subject of theft and destruction of government property, I stuck up my hand.

"Tony," I asked, "what about government documents? What if someone takes them home or throws them out? What if someone retires and cleans out their desk and takes everything home with them, including their files?"

"Well, Shelley." Tony didn't hesitate as he prepared to regurgitate the relevant rule from the manual (the one that nobody followed). "All IRS documents are government property." At least I had asked a real question. My fellow classmates were openly reading magazines, filing their nails, goofing and giggling uproariously as we wisecracked through a breezy sequence of role-playing games.

The top managers—who evidently needed in-depth ethical training much more than we—were treated to a far more comprehensive program of moral instruction. They endured a leisurely four-day schedule at Coolfont, the same luxury wilderness resort in West Virginia where, four years before, I and my fellow members of the HRT staff had repaired to prepare an ill-fated mission statement.

By 1992, HRT was history. But as investigative columnist Jack Anderson gleefully reported to his readers—just after tax filing deadline, on April 17, 1991—the IRS still patronized Coolfont with a vengeance. It had been willing to pay any price and bear any burden to ensure that its top managers were sufficiently steeped in our newly discovered Core Ethical Principles. The four-day junket conducted by the Josephson Institute—an organization exclusively devoted to this lucrative line of work—had morally rearmed the upper echelons of IRS management to the tune of $1,850 per employee.

More devastating, from the IRS's point of view, than Anderson's disclosure of the ethical junket were the disturbing results of a survey of top IRS management conducted by the Josephson Institute in preparation for teaching the top dogs new tricks. The survey revealed that *nearly half* of the IRS top managers admitted that *they would use their position to intimidate personal enemies. More than half* freely conceded that *they would look the other way if they discovered wrongdoing in the IRS.* A shockingly high number condoned lying to the press and to Congress *to protect the IRS.*

In July 1992 newly appointed IRS Commissioner Shirley Peterson (who came on board on February 13, 1992, after Fred Goldberg was kicked upstairs to assistant secretary for tax policy in the Treasury Department) appeared before Congressman Barnard's panel to proclaim proudly the emergence into the light of a new kinder, gentler IRS.

We have instituted an enormous ethics training effort. Just within the past year, all of our 13,000 managers have received training in ethics.

And, within the next year, about 106,000 employees—all the balance of our employees—will receive ethics training as well. Not only that, but the IRS has established an ethics action plan ... on a national basis, revised annually ... a long-term, comprehensive effort to address the systemic, organizational, and leadership issues that lie at the heart of an effective ethics program.

The IRS had established a strategic initiative called "Improving Awareness of Ethical, Integrity and Conduct Issues." It had commissioned an "Ethics Action Plan," which urged senior executives to "communicate expectations of ethical behavior to all employees." The one lesson unearthed by the welter of internal surveys conducted by the Josephson Institute and other outside consultants was that mid-level IRS employees felt that they were never told anything by their superiors, that they were kept in the dark about everything, as a matter of course and culture.

In response to these concerns, the IRS established an Office of Internal Communications, slated to fall under the supervision of newly appointed assistant commissioner for human resources and management, Dave Mader. Dave (hallway gossip would soon nickname him "Darth") Mader owed his brilliant rise in the IRS hierarchy to a close working relationship with our new commissioner, as well as to his own innate managerial talents.

A tall, thin, unsmiling, ungainly blond, "Darth" Mader hailed from Jersey City, New Jersey, and held a B.A. in political science from St. Mary's College in Emmitsburg, Maryland. After spending a year at the General Services Administration in New York—the agency in charge of maintaining and securing all federal office buildings—Mader joined the IRS in 1971, and did a few years in the New York District Office. He spent a year in Detroit and returned home to New Jersey before heeding the call to report to the national office in 1990. In the IRS context, Dave was not a tax man. He was a facilities and/or human resources guy from way back.

I had known Dave Mader before he became "Darth" Mader, when he was a relatively lowly deputy assistant commissioner for planning and research, before he was vaulted into assistant commissioner for human resources. Under Mader's hard-driving leadership, the new ethics program went from strength to strength, producing an impressive output of glossy brochures and magazines, one of which went by the enticing title *Practicing Ethics*. All 120,000 IRS employees received this biannual in-house publication. Our 13,000 so-called line managers received the swank *IRS Manager*, exclusively devoted to "subjects of ethics and integrity."

In its short life, the IRS ethics program had also compiled a thought-provoking list of "Core Ethical Principles," meant to go hand-in-hand with our Ethical Compasses as we navigated through the murky moral shoals of IRS "behavior scenarios." The ten "Core Ethical Principles" were:

1. Honesty
2. Integrity
3. Respect for others
4. Civic duty
5. Promise Keeping
6. Loyalty
7. Fairness
8. Pursuit of Excellence
9. Accountability
10. Caring and Concern for Others

The boys at the top sure had Ethical Principle #9 (Accountability) all taken care of. One of our "ethics publications" came complete with a signature line on its last page, which every employee was expected to sign, confirming that the booklet had been read, and its moral import assimilated. These signature pages were to be ripped off and turned in to management by a series of specified deadlines. It fell to the managers to make sure that all employees signed the signature page, tore it off, and returned it, thereby ensuring that no one could claim that the Core Ethical Principles had not been properly disseminated through the ranks.

Some individual IRS regional offices went a bit overboard. In January 1993 the IRS Western Region, on its own initiative (and expense), printed thousands of wallet-sized laminated "ethics cards" (IRS Publication #366) displaying the letters "GKC" at the top.

Baffled Western Region employees dubbed it the "GAK" card. Embossed on the face of the "GKC" were three cardinal moral principles.

> GKC Principle #1: All decisions must take into account and reflect a concern for the interest and well being of the stakeholders.

> GKC Principle #2: Ethical values and principles always take precedence over nonethical ones.

> GKC Principle #3: It is ethically proper to violate an ethical principle only when it is clearly necessary to advance another true ethical principle which, according to the decision maker's conscience, will produce the greatest balance of good in the long run.

Someone at the Western Region Office thoughtfully sent me a GKC card for my growing collection of IRS memorabilia. Since I couldn't figure out what GKC meant, I tracked down one lone IRS employee who claimed to know the meaning of "GKC."

"G" stood for the "Golden Rule," as in "Do unto others."

"K" stood for "Kantian," the translator said, as in "the eighteenth-century German philosopher Immanuel Kant, a founder of ethical principles." Personally, after hearing about the Jobean trials and tribulations suffered by Stan Welli and most of his fellow IRS whistle-blowers, I think the "K" should have stood for "Kafka."

"C" stood for "Consequentialism," which the IRS employee who translated the card for me described as "another philosophical view, different from Kant's, which says that if you can find a good enough loophole, use it."

Because I was more broadly enlightened about the deep inner meanings of "G" and "K" in this parallel moral universe, I begged my informant to explain the core concept, "Consequentialism." Could she apply it to a tax case? No, but she vividly recalled from her ethics class being instructed on the moral relativism of non-Jews breaking local laws to save Jews from Nazi death camps during the Holocaust. "Consequentialism" encouraged accounting for "larger consequences" when arriving at difficult moral decisions. But how pondering the principles involved in saving Jews from extermination could have helped an IRS agent see his way clear to turning in his boss for having an affair with his secretary sure beat me.

At his follow-up hearings of July 1992, an older, grayer, and wiser Doug Barnard waxed philosophical as he observed that "just initiating an [ethics] effort, or providing a training course on ethics to managers and employees, will not insure a positive change in the culture of those managers who in the past have been responsible for lapses in conduct or have observed such lapses and looked the other way."

To which ethics program executive Dave Mader cheerfully conceded, "It takes more than a couple of memos sent out to accomplish that goal. . . . We are going to change the culture by having our managers engage in meaningful conversations with our employees and that takes a lot of time and a lot of effort."

After Mader's pronouncement, Barnard introduced Stan Welli, who brought the committee up to date on his grievance case, still in the early stages of a tortuous path that remained unresolved even as Stan retired after thirty-four years of dedicated federal service in 1996. Then Barnard introduced Terry Dunford, a native of Buffalo, New York, and an IRS public affairs officer whose report of shabby treatment at the hands of the IRS shattered at a single blow all Shirley Peterson's and Dave Mader's remarks about having achieved a kinder, gentler IRS.

THE COOKIE CAPER

"Growing up," twenty-nine-year-old Terry Dunford began, "my parents taught me one of the best lessons I ever learned. That is, you always have to try to do what is right; and that what is right is not always popular and what is popular is not always right."

I believe that Terry Dunford gathered the courage to testify before Congress that day as a kind of posthumous tribute to his mother, who had passed away just two months before. Throughout her "lengthy illness," Dunford sadly related, he had not felt able to burden his parents with his difficulties at work, with a dispute with his boss.

His troubles began during the week of May 13, 1991, when his boss, District Director Donald Mitgang, decided to host a group of fellow district directors attending the North Atlantic Regional Conference in nearby Niagara Falls. Eager to show his friends and colleagues a good time, Mitgang had hired a "hospitality suite" in a Niagara Falls hotel where his guests and their families could spend time in the evening, eat a little, drink a little, maybe engage in some casual networking. Considerably less eager to raise eyebrows in high places by running up a hefty catering bill, the fatally frugal Mitgang "encouraged"—Dunford preferred "strongarmed"—four mid-level members of his training and resources management staff to go to a secretary's house during working hours to prepare "sandwiches and snacks" to be served—by them—at the hospitality suite in the evenings, after the conference sessions had concluded.

"Members of the Training and Resources Management Staff left daily at 11 o'clock to shop for beer, pop, and snacks to restock the hospitality suite," Dunford distinctly recalled. Digging his ethical hole even deeper, having made his volunteer bartenders, waiters, and waitresses an offer they couldn't refuse, Mitgang tried to compensate them for performing these menial extracurricular tasks by awarding them overtime pay. Unfortunately, Mitgang had failed to review the relevant IRS Rules of Conduct—not to forget federal labor law— which explicitly forbade the use of "volunteers" to entertain at agency shindigs, and further prohibited them from getting overtime pay for such unofficial work. Mitgang exacerbated matters by instructing Dunford to inform the "volunteers" that, as Dunford testified, "we made a mistake. We can't pay you."

By abruptly revoking the promised payments, Mitgang put himself in an even deeper pickle, because *not* paying employees for services rendered was just as illegal. Mitgang desperately tried to cope with his fast-lengthening string of ethical lapses by deciding to disguise the "overtime pay" as "management awards" ranging from $50 on up to $300.

What prompted Terry Dunford to blow the whistle was Mitgang's insistence—when the local newspapers, as they couldn't *not* have, got hold of this juicy story—that Dunford perform spin control with the press, hoping to cast the by-then locally infamous "Cookie Caper" in a more favorable light. As Dunford maintained, being obliged to "defend the IRS in the media accounts that followed" was simply too much for him to bear. It gave him moral heartburn.

After much soul-searching—and in keeping with IRS Rules of Conduct—Dunford apprised Mitgang of his intent to report the entire incident to Inspection in Washington. Certainly, the IRS could not be counted on to do the right thing on its own merely because a journalist uncovered yet another ethical lapse.

Predictably, according to Dunford's later testimony before Congress, Mitgang went ballistic. He threatened Dunford in gruesome detail with all the negative repercussions bound to befall him if he insisted on going "internally public." "In all cases such as this," Dunford told the astonished congressmen, "there has to be a fall guy. Well, you're looking at him."

This sound- and sight-bite was destined to air on any number of TV newscasts that night. That Dunford was himself a former TV newsman who'd finally gotten mad and hadn't been able to take it anymore made him an appealing figure to TV newscasters. Poor Shirley Peterson's proud prattlings about her "Ethics Action Plan" at the "new IRS" would have been lucky to make the 5 A.M. news.

Dunford's threat to report Mitgang to Inspection in Washington didn't go over well in Buffalo. Nor did it meet with any greater encouragement in Washington. In September 1991, after Dunford reported "his concerns" about the incident to Assistant Commissioner of Public Affairs Ellen Murphy, his own superior, her response (as Dunford testified) was "simple."

"If you don't like it, you can leave."

The all-too-common practice of showing whistle-blowers the door—and if they didn't eagerly sail right through it, forcing them out—had clearly not died at the IRS, despite countless dollars spent on luxurious ethical training seminars conducted at posh mountain resorts. Had anything *really* changed at the IRS since the revelations of 1989?

Dunford testified that he soon found—or was meant to find—a handwritten memorandum from Mitgang, reporting that Regional

Commissioner Connie Coleman had referred to Dunford as a "jerk." Coleman apparently also made reference in the same conversation to a remarkably similar comment ascribed to senior public affairs officer Ellen Murphy, who also called Dunford a "jerk." Jerk or not, at least a few things had changed around the IRS since Stan Welli's day. Instead of a "fucking scumbag"—Santella's phrase—Dunford was being referred to by the kinder, gentler epithet "jerk."

Jerk or no jerk, Dunford wasn't a patsy. Digging in his heels, he forced Teddy Kern's reluctant IRS Investigation Division to investigate the Cookie Caper. The Cookie Caper "investigation" did not result in any disciplinary action brought against Mitgang. In fact, he was offered a position in the IRS headquarters in Washington, D.C., just as the IRS had done with Joe Jech and Frank Santella. Mitgang opted to retire from the IRS, with full pension benefits intact. So much for accountability.

"A number of Special Agents I talked to," Dunford testified, "referred to it as a 'joke' and a 'sham.'" But before this internal "investigation" was complete, District Director Donald Mitgang bided his time, eventually finding a way to attack his employee who dared to step away from the IRS team. According to the text of an "Official Reprimand" administered by Mitgang to Dunford, in early 1992 Dunford was approached by the producer of a local TV program called *AM Buffalo* and asked to provide an in-house "tax expert" to answer commonly asked tax questions on the air.

Since Mitgang had not performed well on the air the filing season before, Dunford did not want to force Mitgang on them. He thought the IRS should be represented by someone who would invoke viewer confidence, in both style and technical knowledge. But District Director Mitgang, presumably eager to ingratiate himself with the local public, directed Dunford, by his own account, "*not* to pursue the interview any further if the District Director could not appear." After Dunford duly informed *AM Buffalo* of the moral and ethical quandary Mitgang had put him in, *AM Buffalo* agreed to let Mitgang on the air, but the only airtime available was the very next day. Now the question became whether Mitgang would be ready with such short notice. As it so happened, on the day in question, Mitgang was scheduled to be out of town.

This formed the basis of Terry Dunford's "Official Reprimand," a serious black mark on his record that followed him through all the rest of his days at the IRS—which were strictly numbered. According to Mitgang, Dunford had acted "in direct violation of Internal Revenue Service Rule of Conduct 25.2," which explicitly stated that all IRS employees are expected "to respond to the direction of their supervisors." For "failing to follow the orders of [his] supervisor . . . by securing the segment without checking first the District Director's availability," Dunford was not only officially reprimanded in writing, but cautioned that "any further violations of this nature or other misconduct may result in more severe disciplinary action, up to and including removal." As in getting fired.

For failing to follow up on Stan Welli's and George Ecola's and Ron Koperniak's allegations relating to Frank Santella's cavorting with reputed mob figures and accepting illegal gratuities, Joe Jech had been given an oral reprimand by his superior. For failing to check his boss's schedule and securing a TV interview for a day that his boss was available, whistle-blower Terry Dunford was threatened with removal.

By 1994 the situation worsened for Mitgang and improved for Dunford. While Mitgang was being prodded to accept the Washington assignment or take early retirement, Dunford had refused to resign from his job under intensifying pressure from Mitgang and his supporters at headquarters.

The *Buffalo News* lionized Dunford as an all too rare example of a guy who had the guts to stand up to the big bad bullies at the IRS. No matter how high they turned up the heat, good old Terry Dunford had just refused to budge from the kitchen. "If just by being there, I make them look in the mirror, and look at how they deal with their employees and the public, then I'm achieving something," Dunford proudly told the awestruck reporter writing the story.

But in the end, without any press or fanfare, Terry Dunford did leave the IRS. Precisely when Dunford got out of the hot kitchen is not ascertainable. Nor are the reasons for his resignation. When I tracked down Terry Dunford to ask him why he left, he refused to discuss it.

"I'm a full-time student now, studying for a master's degree," Terry told me, clearly eager to put his tormented IRS career behind him. When I asked if he had held down a job since his resignation, he said he had not. He refused to volunteer any details about his post-IRS life, except that he was a full-time student and that he had recently purchased his own home.

"Were you left an inheritance by a rich aunt?" I asked.

After a long pause, Terry said solemnly: "No."

"Did you win the lottery?"

"No."

"Have you recently received an inheritance from anyone in your family?"

"No."

Something just wasn't right. Here was a young man who'd recently resigned from a well-paying government job, had returned to school full-time, and had recently purchased a home. What was he living on?

"Is anyone supporting you?"

"No."

Over the years, I'd heard rumors—never confirmed, except by Stan Welli—that the IRS pays whistle-blowers large sums of money to buy their silence, to make them go away, to make them stop making trouble. These payments are typically dressed up as "grievance settlements" but they were hush money, pure and simple.

We know Stan Welli was offered $15,000 by Mike Murphy to settle his case, but only because Stan had been appalled and turned down the offer in disgust. If he hadn't, we never would have heard about it. That is the name of the game. But Stan Welli had been approaching retirement at the time, and really did not have as much to fear as twenty-nine-year-old Dunford, who had, as they say, a whole life ahead of him. Could Terry Dunford have been able to resist the IRS if it came calling with *your* checkbook in hand?

I'd heard rumors of payoffs to some whistle-blowers running as high as $300,000—more than enough to buy a nice house in practically any area of the country. Of course, if there are ex-whistle-blowers out there whose whistles have been silenced by payoffs, only your tax man knows for sure. And despite being steeped in the Core Ethical Principles, he isn't telling, I can assure you.

That would be confidential information kept from the public—in the IRS's public statements to protect the public—but in reality merely to protect the IRS.

DECLINE AND FALL

NOVEMBER 1992

A few months after Commissioner Shirley Peterson stood before Congress to introduce a kinder, gentler IRS, I spent an evening with an old friend from Nebraska, who'd come to Washington with her daughter to see the sights. What better way than by a Grayline tour?

"All a-b-o-a-rd!" the tour guide bellowed in time-honored whistle tones as we lurched, with a belch of black smoke, from the parking lot of Union Station, moving slowly past Capitol Hill. Our route took us past every must-see in the District, including the impressive Neoclassical Federal Triangle, the magnificent Department of Treasury building, and the shabbier IRS national office.

As we approached 1111 Constitution Avenue, the guide sprang into action. "Ladies and gentlemen," he cackled, "hide your heads! Duck everyone! We are approaching . . . the Boo Building!"

As I playfully ducked, our guide urged us to repeat: "B-o-o-o-! B-o-o-o!" The entire bus burst into a collective "Boo!" Gawking and gaping at IRS headquarters probably wasn't on anyone's itinerary of historic stops along the grand tour.

And why not? Other, prouder federal agencies had tours and museums and concession stands hawking thematically appropriate souvenirs. The Bureau of Engraving and Printing sells shredded bags and sheets of uncut currency. The Bureau of the Mint sells commemorative coins. The White House Historical Association does a brisk business in books and trinkets. The FBI has one of the most popular tour programs in the downtown district, though it doesn't, as yet, sell souvenirs.

If you'd stopped by IRS headquarters in the mid-sixties, you could have strolled into a public visitors' gallery and perused an intriguing collection of artifacts vividly portraying the controversial and complex evolution of the American tax system. The IRS visitors' gallery was the brainchild of IRS Commissioner Sheldon Cohen, appointed by President Lyndon Johnson, who wanted the public to know something about the tax system other than the sharpness and breadth of its bite.

The visitors' gallery survived until the early seventies, when some members of Congress started carping about the IRS's spending taxpayer's money on a museum to promote itself. Instead of defending its educational purpose—the center's primary sponsor having since retired—the IRS closed its tiny museum, hastily dismantling and distributing artifacts to other federal agencies under less congressional heat. A few choice pieces were "deaccessioned" to the Smithsonian across the street or fobbed off to the headquarters of the newly independent Bureau of Alcohol, Tobacco, and Firearms. By the time I joined the IRS, their little museum was nothing but a memory.

Of these lost artifacts, I exhumed two ancient stills, centerpieces of America's controversial first tax on whiskey. One of the two (allegedly from the private distillery at Mount Vernon) sat in storage in a Smithsonian sub-basement; the other was on display at the Oscar Getz Museum of Whiskey History in Bardstown, Kentucky. At headquarters, the only remaining relic was Chicago gangster Al Capone's gun, which the Criminal Investigation Division had purportedly snatched up and encased in glass in its hallway.

From time to time, I pushed colleagues to discuss the restoration of the museum. At one meeting, I was told, Commissioner Fred Goldberg wondered about selling promotional trinkets like "a ceramic mug with a bite chomped from it, with the slogan 'My mom and dad visited the IRS and all I got was this lousy cup.'"

The response to Goldberg's suggestion went unrecorded—or else the record has long since been destroyed. Inside the IRS, I never gained consensus on the museum's revival. While one vocal group took the position that ratcheting up the IRS's voluntary compliance rate by a minuscule fraction would benefit its reputation, others saw it as a diminution and trivialization of the sacred mission. Years before the Oklahoma City bombing, a small yet influential group of IRS insiders insisted that any widening of public access to the building would increase our vulnerability to terrorist attack.

To the enduring credit of Commissioner Shirley Peterson, she sincerely tried to reinvent the service as an agency more responsive not only to the citizenry—"customers"—but also to its own long-suffering rank-and-file.

Peterson first set up an 800 number and encouraged IRS employees to leave voice mail suggestions on how to improve performance and service. She actually listened to those messages herself, in her car to and from work. One day she was particularly struck by an employee's suggestion—not mine—that the IRS bring back its museum. Within days, I'd received word to begin drafting a proposal for the new museum right away.

We found the perfect space, off a foyer shortly to be constructed as part of a major project to reconfigure a new entrance to the Pennsylvania Avenue side of the building, using money from the General Services Agency to reconstruct a blunt, unfinished corner of the building then jutting obtrusively out into street. The space would be tight but comfortable. I met with the IRS in-house interior design staff to plan design and decor and talked to IRS retirees eager to staff the place. At long last, the IRS Historical Center verged on the light of day.

At the height of "Peterson Perestroika," newly appointed Assistant Commissioner for Human Resources Dave Mader invited me to his new office. I found "Darth" Mader standing stiffly beside a round table in the corner of the room, piled high with a thick stack of papers.

"Shelley, I've been thinking about your situation. I've been thinking"—Mader cleared his throat—"about the difficulty we've been having around here fitting your position into the organization."

For the last four years, I had chronically slid from department to department in what I called a "hockey puck problem." On the IRS organizational chart du jour, I fit into the FIMS (Facilities and Information Management Support) Division, headed by Jim Casimir, a soon-to-retire IRS lifer who seemed to enjoy stonewalling all of my proposals. In this newly dawned Era of Good Feelings at the IRS, I hoped that Mader was about to deliver me from the institutional ice rink.

"As you know," Dave Mader observed, "under Commissioner Peterson, we've established a new Office of Internal Communications."

How could I not know? Even the janitors knew about the all-new Office of Internal Communications and its plot to effect change in one of the most disturbing aspects of our private subculture: the fact that no one at the top told anyone anywhere else anything about anything. To showcase the new IRS, Dave Mader explained how the IRS had recruited candidates from the private sector. He added that the final choice for head of Internal Communications was Karen Hjelmervik, who boasted a stellar résumé as an internal communications specialist at Westinghouse. She would come on board any day to lead this crack unit. Dave Mader implied that joining up with this new staff would be my salvation.

Could I be any worse off under Karen Hjelmervik than the dread Jim Casimir? Would my role within the IRS finally make sense after five stop-and-go (mostly stop) years on the job? Maybe all this rhetoric about a new IRS wasn't total hooey. Maybe we were actually going to see real change in our lifetimes.

Not long after meeting with Mader, I stopped by a small reception for Orion Birdsall's replacement as deputy assistant commissioner for human resources—Mader's number two. Like so many other IRS senior executives, when Orion decided to retire, he moved quickly and seamlessly into private-sector tax consulting.

Orion's replacement, Tyrone Ayres, was a recent graduate of the IRS's Executive Development Program (known as "XD" to insiders)—the ultimate path to power inside the service. Aspirations to be selected for XD kept many midlevel IRS employees on the straight and narrow for years.

At his welcoming party, I introduced myself to Ty Ayres and explained what I did. Ayres was a handsome, affable African

American recruited for the top ranks of the IRS out of the Office of Personnel Management as the service attempted to achieve greater diversity in its ranks. Ayres was not a tax man and I held out hope that because he was new to the IRS bureaucracy he might be sympathetic to my plight. As I anticipated, Ayres was intrigued and demanded to know more about my job, the sort of projects I worked on, and how the IRS used its resident historian. Tempted to say, "Not much," I expounded upon my recent transfer to the all-new OIC and conveyed real eagerness about getting a new boss.

With no prompting, Ayres asked whether I spent most of my time combing through old IRS documents and records, culling them for information that might illuminate a variety of issues facing the IRS at the present time.

Not eager to delve into IRS record-keeping (and record-losing) policy and practices, I described how my hands were full soliciting and assembling papers for my own fast-growing private collection of IRS records and documents, which was of late bursting from my cubbyhole into the few places allotted for overflow.

Ty Ayres asked to see the collection. And so, on November 5, 1992, I gave him a Cook's tour of my three central storage facilities, starting with my own tiny office, to Room 5120 on the fifth floor (containing the vault of Special Services Staff and Watergate records), and the damp filthy room in the basement—not far from the mercury spill—where I kept miscellaneous files from employees. Last came the grandly named Commissioner's File Room in the basement, which I first entered three years before when outgoing Commissioner Larry Gibbs asked me to peruse his official files one last time. This dumpy space conveyed the sorry state of IRS record-keeping and archival practices in the latter half of the twentieth century.

Larry Gibbs, commissioner when I was hired, asked me to salvage whatever contents could be spared the inevitable purge. Even though some IRS quarters actively discouraged climbing above rank—no one beneath the august rank of assistant commissioner should ever have face-to-face dealing with the commissioner himself—I'd made an effort to cultivate Gibbs. After all, at the Defense Department, the division historian enjoyed free and total access to the commanding officer.

Larry Gibbs was by far the happiest tax commissioner I ever knew. Always cheerful, always ready to flash a winning smile in the hallway, he was the only IRS commissioner confident enough to pose informally for his official photo, standing jovially beside his chair, instead of seriously frozen before the camera.

When I heard that Larry Gibbs was out and Fred Goldberg in, I called Records Management to check on their plans for conducting a full inventory of the outgoing commissioner's papers and records.

I was told there were no such plans, by a staff member apparently confused about why I would ask the question. Because it's the law. "Because, if you weren't planning to, I was thinking of doing the inventory myself," I replied.

Quite clearly, the folks in Records Management—all of whom, in my opinion, lacked adequate professional training for the job—were evidently unaware that, in most federal agencies, Records Management immediately starts sorting through an official's files as soon as that person is formally slated for replacement.

"Go right ahead, Shelley, take what you need," Gibbs invited as I strolled into his huge, plushly appointed office. "I've gone through and pulled all my personal files. Everything else is fair game."

An outfit known as the Executive Secretariat exerted total control over the commissioner's files, which, as I soon learned, maintained what were known as reading files—duplicate copies of original memoranda, correspondence, and the like—in a basement storage room. Though it was grandly and officially denominated the Commissioner's Filing Room, the room itself was concealed behind an unmarked steel door off a dark, nondescript hallway, inconspicuously labeled Room G–130.

There I found boxes of what looked like office supplies scattered higgledy-piggledy among the outgoing commissioner's correspondence, filed in chronological order in dozens of three-ring binders, occupying row after row of large lateral filing cabinets. Haphazardly shoved up against the walls sat dozens more boxes, some old and battered, some relatively intact, some carefully covered with plastic sheeting. Not a good sign.

The secretary nominally in charge of this splendid facility told me, "These are mainly old records from former commissioners. Mostly a lot of old stuff. Someone must have thrown these plastic sheets over them so they'd stay dry. . . . The room has leaky pipes and a history of flooding." She concluded this offhand remark with what I'd come to call the "IRS Shrug," a real Alfred E. Neuman shoulder-bender, indifferently conveying "What me worry?" Indeed, why should she care? Had she been encouraged or been given any incentive to care? It was my job to care, and Records Management's job to do something about it. Here was a clear dereliction of duty. In the army, we'd all have been court-martialed.

I found a mixed bag of documents: minutes of staff meetings; commissioner's calendars, reports, and studies; information relating to the IRS leak of President Nixon's tax returns to the press; files on some of the more controversial IRS criminal investigations, including Operation Leprechaun, described earlier in this book.

The secretary might have been unimpressed, but I knew that I'd just struck paydirt. I conducted a brief preliminary inventory of the files and sorted out some of the more valuable records for protection from imminent destruction.

Three years later, the Commissioner's File Room remained essentially unchanged for Ty Ayres's tour of my holdings. The pipes still leaked. The boxes remained shrouded with plastic. But it was Ayres who noticed the addition to the room since my last visit. Up in a high corner, a bird had built a nest. How nice, I thought. Now we'll have bird droppings as well as water to worry about. Ayres, to his credit, expressed shock at both the state of the documents and the bird's nest.

"Something has *got* to be done about this," he exclaimed. Appalled by the decades-old disaster before him, he repeated that he couldn't believe a major federal agency like the IRS maintained—or failed to maintain—its records under such disgraceful conditions.

"You know," Ty Ayres ruminated, "I think this could qualify as a material weakness," a government term used to describe managerial and financial issues that might inhibit the ability of a federal agency to properly accomplish its mission or perform its most basic function. For example, the Filing Season from Hell had exposed a number of material weaknesses suffered by the IRS, including faulty implementation of the most up-to-date technical resources needed to solve the problem of automating tax return processing. The IRS was required annually to provide separate reports on its progress—or lack of it—in resolving a long list of material weaknesses identified by a number of federal oversight agencies, including the General Accounting Office.

Immediately upon returning to his office, Ty Ayres asked me to conduct a full-fledged study of IRS record-keeping practices, commencing immediately, analyzing the problem from a technical, historical, legal, and archival standpoint.

I explained that Records Management and I had agreed to disagree on our interpretations of laws relating to maintaining and preserving internal records. I warned him that any effort on my part to conduct a serious study of the records problem would result in resistance from those who were supposed to be doing this job in the first place.

"In my opinion," I elaborated, "the IRS has abdicated its responsibility to adhere to the requirements of the Federal Records Act."

His eyes widened. By allowing records to be preserved in such a substandard fashion, or even worse, discarded or destroyed willy-nilly according to the individual whims of department heads or secretaries, the service was in direct violation of federal law. In other words, this was of greater gravity than a material weakness. It was illegal.

"But why," Ayres said, gulping, "has this been allowed to continue for so long?" Like most other senior IRS executives, he'd simply never given the matter a moment's thought.

"It's considered more important," I replied, "for the IRS to maintain control over its internal records than to let them fall under the control of any outside agency or entity. It is more important for the IRS to periodically and routinely clean out and destroy its own files than to permit the possibility that outsiders might one day get their hands on them."

Ty Ayres suggested that I write up a brief memo explaining that he had ordered me to prepare a study of IRS record keeping and that I was to prepare the study on my own, without interference from Records Management. Within an hour, I had the memo on Ayres's desk.

*   *   *

I was making real progress on my study when Jim Casimir, head of FIMS and still technically my boss—my transfer to Internal Communications having not yet taken effect—called me into his office.

"Why can't you all just work together?" Casimir referred to the friendly folks at Records Management. Of course, he knew that Ayres expected an impartial critique of current record-keeping policies. Nonetheless, my reluctance to "cooperate" would hand Casimir the perfect opening to brand me noncooperative, not a team player, and—the new term currently being bandied about—a "lone ranger."

And so I dropped Ty Ayres's memo on his desk. He shrugged and muttered, "Have it your way." Somehow, I couldn't imagine that I would.

Not long after President Bill Clinton's election in November 1992, Deputy Commissioner Mike Dolan (Dave Mader's boss) asked me to prepare a series of brief historical summaries of major IRS initiatives to present to the members of the Clinton IRS Transition Team, composed of prominent people in the field of taxation, mainly tax law professors and big-league tax attorneys. The second part of my assignment was to observe the transition meetings in action, and the last part was to write an informal report on the proceedings for debriefing Dolan and his cohorts at the top of the IRS pyramid.

Though the meetings were more packaging than substance, I took the assignment itself as a sign of Dolan's support for my work. But, when the Clinton team concluded its business three days before Christmas break, Dolan didn't invite me to the massive meeting of IRS executives, expressly to unveil, debate, and discuss a major reorganization plan in the works for months, before announcing its various initiatives officially to the public.

Thinking that Dolan had just overlooked the importance of this final meeting to my efforts to record emerging historical events, I called his office to ask about attending it. I also focused on finishing my records study before the executive meeting (slated for early in the new year), so that a few key administrators could consider my proposals in the context of the greater reorganization. One of my major propositions was the consolidation of the historical function with a record-keeping/archival function. Dolan never got back to me, but word was sent that the meeting was closed to all nonexecutives, myself included.

INTERNAL MISCOMMUNICATIONS

My new manager, Karen Hjelmervik, head of our new OIC—Office of Internal Communications—did attend the executive rendezvous in Martinsburg, West Virginia. She shared with us all the marvelous new changes ahead for the new IRS during a routine staff meeting in March at the Office of Internal Communications, located about a mile from the Federal Triangle in a new office tower familiarly known as the CNN building. I had resisted moving my office to this organizational Siberia because it lacked storage room for my documents and was located so far from the center of IRS operations.

Hjelmervik reported that the proposed reorganization would eliminate unnecessary middle-management layers to enhance accountability and close a number of redundant field offices. Since I'd been around the IRS block a few times, I was rather skeptical about these brave new IRS management initiatives, no matter how splendidly conceived and persuasively presented.

After the staff meeting, Hjelmervik called me aside to discuss a few issues "relating to the role of the historical function and its fit on the OIC staff." Her tone sounded ominous.

It was quite different from that of our first meeting in January. Upon her arrival after the new year, Hjelmervik had met with each member of her team individually, like the good veteran of Westinghouse that she was. Her credentials in internal communications were as impressive as her appearance. At fifty, this short slender blond was in phenomenal shape, with a perky personality to boot.

To prepare for this introductory interview, I assembled what I hoped was a persuasive package of proposals outlining my various initiatives: a kit on the proposed historical center, a copy of Assistant Commissioner of Human Resources Bob Johnson's memo in support of my proposed consolidation of the history/archival function with the records management function, and a précis of the nearly completed study of IRS records management, past, present, and future.

At our first talk, Hjelmervik gushed about how excited she was to have a qualified employee like me on board to record the ongoing transformation of an American institution. She called my proposed historical center a great idea. As for the proposed consolidation of records management, history, and archives, she admitted her unfamiliarity with the issue to debate it one way or another. Regarding the records management study, she nodded in agreement with its overall goal. A more specific response would come when she'd read the study itself.

Now, in March, Hjelmervik asked me for my reaction to her effulgent summary of the executive meeting to which I'd not been invited. I communicated that, as official historian, I would have vastly preferred to observe and chronicle the meeting firsthand rather than rely on her commentary. Historians don't like hearsay when we can do our own reporting.

Her smile froze. She snapped, "You realize that you upset a lot of people around here by breaking the chain of command by soliciting Mike Dolan for an invitation to the meeting . . . that you've taken a lot of personal risk by insisting on operating as a lone ranger."

In IRS vernacular, the words "lone ranger," when combined with the phrases "breaking the chain of command," "refusing to cooperate," and "not playing as a team member" were euphemisms for treason. Just a few weeks before, I was in. Now, I was out. The one possible reason for her sudden shift in attitude toward me was that I was publishing my potentially controversial records study any day now. I couldn't help surmising that those likely to be most adversely affected by the study had engaged in a preemptive strike.

"Don't you realize that you've developed a reputation around here for caring only about yourself?" Hjelmervik demanded. "That you're too dedicated to pursuing your individual role as an historian to see the need to meet the greater needs of the IRS?"

In the midst of this commanding display of internal communication skills, Karen Hjelmervik had unwittingly hit upon one of the great dilemmas facing all government historians. A historian's greatest professional responsibility is to the truth; a bureaucrat's greatest commitment, in the eyes of most bureaucrats, is to the organization.

At the Defense Department, though I'd never experienced the conflict personally, I was well aware of the pain and suffering and conflict experienced by the compilers, for instance, of the Pentagon Papers—comprising the secret history of the Vietnam War. While the generals and admirals kept telling the politicians that the war could be won, and was in fact *being* won, the historians and analysts were forced to forego the rhetoric and lay down the facts, as they saw fit, in black and white. Daniel Ellsberg and his colleagues had faced up to the truth, and been pilloried for it. The admirals and generals and information specialists at the Pentagon had only been acting according to their values and ethics by glossing and papering over the facts to achieve their version of a higher truth: a fiction that if we claimed we were winning, we might actually win.

I zoned back into the conversation just as Hjelmervik began laying down the law under which I might be permitted to rejoin the OIC fold. For starters, I was to set aside my records management study. It was bound to make too many waves.

"Certain people," she said, "don't think that you should be messing around with the records issue at all. They don't believe that it's any of your business. So you're going to have to put that one on the shelf, and not release it, to free up your time and energy to tackle some more pressing needs."

"Without records," I asserted, "there is no history."

"Well," she conceded, "just wrap that one up as quickly as possible so we can move you onto more important things. As for your proposed historical center, not only will there be no museum, Shelley, but there will be no discussion about it."

That was it. I was dismissed.

As a footnote to Karen Hjelmervik's eruption at me, I found myself in a similar soup to that which nearly drowned Stan Welli. After Karen lowered my performance appraisal, citing my lack of willingness to be a team player and insistence on maintaining my "lone ranger" status, I filed a grievance against her, citing retaliation. While the IRS didn't offer me a cash settlement, they quickly agreed to move me out of her reach. I found myself ensconced in another new office, the assistant commissioner for strategic planning and communications, with yet another new boss.

THE IDES OF MARCH 1993

"IRS Records Keeping Practices: A Preliminary Overview" painted a depressing picture of the current ability of the IRS to preserve its own past. "The data presented in this report," I concluded in my executive summary, "confirm that there has been a breakdown in records keeping practices in the IRS National Office. Critical records related to the management, policies, procedures, and related areas have been lost. Such records will continue to be lost unless action is taken in the near future to revitalize IRS records keeping practices."

Deliberately dry in narrative terms, it was a bombshell in terms of bureaucracy. The evidence of outright neglect was there for any IRS employee—indeed, any American citizen—to see, in the yards of empty steel shelving at the National Archives where the IRS records should have been. "The last accession of permanent IRS records into the National Archives occurred 22 years ago, in 1971," I wrote, "when the National Office sent six volumes of tax assessment lists from the years 1909–1917 to the Archives." By setting the relevant dates 1909–1917 in boldface type, I hoped to clarify that this dereliction of duty was hardly of recent origin. "Virtually no permanent records of the activities, policies, and procedures of the IRS have entered into the National Archives since the 1920s," I concluded. The IRS had been stinting the Archives of its rightful role in the cycle of IRS records for seventy years. Finally, I cited the relevant statute (USC Chapter 101):

> Whoever wilfully and unlawfully conceals, removes, mutilates, obliterates, or destroys, or attempts to do so, or with intent to do so takes and carries away any record, proceeding, map, book, paper, document or other thing ... shall be fined not less than $2000 or imprisoned not more than three years, or both. The same remedies apply to those who have custody of such materials and also holds that such individual be imprisoned for not more than three years, forfeit office, and be disqualified from holding any office under the United States.

My modestly illustrated study (with my own photographs of dingy sub-basement storage areas) landed on the solid wood desks of those top IRS officials whom I believed might pay it some heed. My most important readers were Dave Mader and Ty Ayres, either of whom had the power to right these wrongs.

The official response, such as it was, to my effort was little more than a roaring silence, then a yawn. From Dave Mader, I heard nothing. From Mike Dolan, nothing. Ty Ayres, who had commissioned the study, politely acknowledged my hard work and promised to read it as soon as he could, but beyond that, nothing. Nothing official. When no one was looking, one division head in the Information Systems group pulled me aside to express shock and regret at my revelations.

I felt like Ray Keenan, the former director of the Memphis Computer Center, who desperately tried to persuade the systems people in Washington that the new tax return processing system was badly broken and wasn't fixable any time soon. They hadn't listened, and their failure to listen had come back to haunt them.

My old friend Don Curtis sat in his deep men's club armchair in his office, riffling the pages of one of the first copies hot off the presses, whistling from time to time as his eyes lit on a particularly hard-hitting passage. I saw one eyebrow cock practically up to his hairline. Don carefully laid the report on his brochure-laden coffee table, handling it gingerly, as if afraid the virus contained between its covers might be contagious.

"Shelley, you've really gone and done it now," he lamented. "This time," he said, "you have gone too far. Don't you realize that you've just stepped into the biggest minefield the IRS has? This is far, far bigger than the computer caper, I can assure you. And I can assure you of one thing, this one is going to explode in your face."

I had hoped for something more supportive, more encouraging, more along the lines of: "You may be risking your neck, Shelley, but it's worth it for the greater good of the country." Instead he was trying to protect me or at least to warn me of the impending dangers.

At long last, my study received its due from one official quarter, couched in the form of a rebuttal prepared by Ray O'Brien, a former member of the Records Management office, who had since attached himself to the IRS Disclosure office in some indeterminate capacity.

O'Brien had worked in Records Management for years, and considered himself the reigning expert on the issue. The memo, officially signed by Jim Casimir as the head of the FIMS, was written with great authority. One had to be well versed in the nuances of the issue—in other words, you had to be one of a handful of people trained in the area—to grasp the subtle deviations in logic laced through it like the watermarks in a dollar bill.

The central conclusion of the FIMS response was that my recommendations "offered little opportunity for the improvement of the Service's current records management practices" and "indicate[d] a lack of understanding of the components of records management and their relationship to archives administration."

In my response to their response, I tried to point out that "the current restrictions on access should not be interpreted as a license to destroy all records. Just as national security records, FBI case files, and CIA records are protected under various statutes, IRS records *should be protected, not destroyed* if they contain historical or legal value, to the extent provided by law." No matter how hard I tried, the IRS never picked up on the fact that lack of authority to disclose information was *not* tantamount to authorization to destroy documents.

APRIL 1994

Five days after the death by massive stroke of former President Richard M. Nixon—whose tumultuous presidency probably contributed more to the current sorry state of IRS affairs than the tenure of any other twentieth-century president—Tom Baker, an old friend who also happened to be an IRS attorney, gave me a call. I could tell by the urgent tone of his voice that he was not calling up for a friendly chat. Tom was with the IRS's Office of General Legal Services, whose job was to handle nontax legal issues relating to personnel, labor relations, and even, as it so happens, records management.

"Have you heard," Tom asked, "about the plan to shred Nixon's and Agnew's tax returns?"

I'd known Tom Baker for going on fifteen years by that time, having first run into him in a bar on the road between Mount Vernon and Washington into which a group of fellow bike riders and I had ducked to take shelter from a summer storm. That was during the summer of 1979, my first summer in Washington, when I was an intern working for the Air Force, and Tom Baker was a young lawyer working for the Department of the Treasury.

Over the years, we'd kept in touch sporadically, but our contact had fallen off as our lives drifted further and further apart. I happened to come across his name while perusing the IRS phone book on one of my first days on the job. We'd revived a casual friendship, and every once in a while we would meet for lunch to catch up on each other's increasingly disparate lives.

"Maybe I shouldn't even be telling you this," he murmured, but when he realized that I hadn't heard about the shredding, news that intimately related to my job, Tom was nearly as disturbed as I was. His motivation in making the call, I believe, was to intervene to save President Nixon's and Vice President Agnew's tax returns from the shredder. But why would anyone want to go to the trouble of destroying Nixon's and Agnew's tax returns?

How did Tom know about the scheduled shredding? The Records Management office had sent his office a peculiar memo oddly coincident with the President's death. The memo restated the IRS's standard policy for destroying individual tax returns after six years and nine months. A line at the bottom of the two-paragraph memo asked General Legal Services to sign off on the dotted line if it concurred with the memo's contents. The memo was strange, Baker elucidated, not so much for what it said but for the fact that it was sent at all.

Now why, Tom Baker wondered to me, would Records Management be bothering to send him a memo asking if his office agreed with something so utterly routine as the retention policy for individual tax returns? He didn't see any reason for sending the memo. Unless there was some hidden agenda.

Tom called Records Management and spoke to a member of the records staff. Tom recounted to me that the staffer point-blank confided in him that the true purpose of the memo was to obtain authorization for shredding Nixon's and Agnew's tax returns.

To this day, I have no idea who hatched this bizarre plan or why. What mattered more was what to do about it. While Internal Revenue Code Section 6103 protects the privacy of all tax returns, including presidential ones, it didn't specify that some tax returns were more interesting or historical than others. Since presidential tax returns were possibly the most telling, the IRS had separated them from all others. According to Archives policy, such a separation constitutes the creation of a distinct group of records. Thus, the destruction policy didn't apply to them, as far as I could tell.

Of course, Nixon's tax returns possessed enormous historic significance because the IRS had conducted a controversial audit of them while he was in office. Vice President Spiro Agnew resigned from office after pleading no contest to charges of tax fraud. As to the historic significance of both men's returns, there was simply no question. But why shred them now, so soon—just a matter of days—after President Nixon's death?

Could this move possibly be one of retaliation for whistle-blowing (in the form of my records management study)? Since I'd been the last to examine these presidential returns at Mike Killfoil's request, was the Records Management department trying somehow to frame me by destroying them? The IRS breeds such paranoia.

SEARCH AND DESTROY

I barely had time to call Tom Baker for an update on the impending Nixon-Agnew shred job before receiving an equally strange phone call the next day from Tony, my old friend and ethics instructor from Records Management. His call came in quite late in the day, after five-thirty, as if he wanted my voice mail, not me.

"We were just wondering," he began, "if you might be interested in acquiring a few old documents from the fifties that we recently came across while conducting an inventory."

An inventory of what? I thought that I knew where most of the skeletons were buried as far as IRS records were concerned.

"Oh," Tony faltered, "it doesn't really matter where they came from. We just thought we'd do you a favor by letting you have them. We've been conducting an inventory of the Commissioner's File Room . . . and we just came across a whole bunch of old stuff."

"Why didn't you ask me to help with the inventory?" I wondered.

"We didn't have your phone number."

"But Tony! You just called me!"

Silence. Tony got off the phone in a hurry, leaving me with my increasingly ominous thoughts. The first name that popped into my mind was Assistant to the Deputy Commissioner John Stocker, the man who had replaced Mike Killfoil, and Mike Dolan's assistant. I'd worked fairly closely with John on one of my small booklet histories when he had been deputy director of the Detroit Computing Center, and I considered him a decent person. John, I told myself in mounting desperation, should be able to straighten out this whole bizarre situation, if anyone could.

The next morning, I called John Stocker's office. His secretary told me that he'd be in meetings all day, but that his executive assistant, Peggy Williams, could handle my questions in his absence. I stressed to the secretary that it was absolutely critical for me to reach Mr. Stocker immediately—I wish I could have used the phrase "national emergency." Of course, in a sense, it was. But the best she could do was pass me off to Peggy Williams.

"I'm extremely concerned about this so-called inventory," I told a stern-faced Peggy Williams, who looked more like a matronly librarian than an IRS executive assistant. "I'm particularly concerned about the fact that I wasn't consulted before they began."

I asked to see the inventory that Tony said his office had prepared and presented to John Stocker. After some obvious internal debate, she reluctantly handed me a copy. Practically whipping it off her desk and dashing down the hall, I read it on the run on the way back to my office. Page after page listed the boxes of documents in the basement room. Next to nearly every entry was typed the ominous phrase: "destroy immediately."

How could they do this, I wondered, to one of the few remaining collections, however small, of documents recording the twentieth-century history of the IRS? And why? By the time I finished marking up my copy of the inventory it was covered with yellow high-lighter marks and urgent scribbles. I called Don Curtis for his reaction to these developments. He told me to come to his office immediately and show him the inventory.

"You've got to save these records," he urged me. "There's no one but you who can do this. If you don't put a stop to the destruction, you'll have to live with yourself for the rest of your life for not taking the proper action when you had the chance."

The next morning, I insisted on meeting with John Stocker in person. He still wasn't available. In lieu of a face-to-face confrontation, I dashed off a strongly worded memo to Stocker, putting him on notice: If he allowed Records Management to destroy this inventory, then he would be guilty of aiding and abetting a federal crime.

"We are in *grave danger* of destroying valuable records without appropriate review or authority," I wrote. "Such action may be illegal in some cases; in others, it would simply be inappropriate without sufficient evaluation."

I was most concerned that Records Management be prevented at all costs from following through on its self-assigned mission to destroy immediately the greater part of this literally priceless collection of documents. In the strongest possible terms, I urged John Stocker to "not concur with this document as prepared. It is my understanding that the National Archives has not been notified of this inventory, and has not agreed with the proposed dispositions."

I went on to note that among the documents Records Management had slated for immediate destruction were board of director's minutes, taxpayer letters to the commissioner, and documents related to Operation Leprechaun and other covert initiatives that had been described to me as red-hot. What, in short, was the purpose of staging this slash-and-burn so-called inventory at this time?

Knowing full well that in so doing, I was probably sealing my fate at the agency, I carried the memo to Stocker's office and left it with Peggy Williams. "Please, Peggy, don't let John sign off on the inventory without reading this first. If you do, you, too, will be breaking the law." Peggy just stared at me.

Desperate to stop the destruction at any cost—even that of my career—I dug out my copy of the Federal Records Act and literally read her the riot act.

"The law says, and I quote: 'Federal employees must notify the National Archives if removal or destruction [of documents] occurs or threatens to occur.' There it is, in black and white," I assured her, practically shoving the passage in her face.

Then I called the National Archives. I went outside the agency. Of course, internal Rules of Conduct expressly instructed me to do so or face the consequences; but that reason wouldn't stand in any kangaroo court before which the IRS would see fit to haul me.

James W. Moore, the assistant archivist in the National Archives and Records Administration, immediately faxed an urgent letter to John Stocker's office advising him to take no precipitate action—or to allow anyone under his command to do so—until the Archives was given a chance to review the documents in question to judge their historical value. As Moore wrote:

> The IRS's mission and functions are central to the effective operation of the federal government. Yet the paucity of IRS records among our holdings prevents the proper documentation of that mission. No twentieth-century Commissioner's records have been accessioned or scheduled for transfer to the National Archives. As this body of records may help to fill this void, we ask that no action be taken to destroy any of these files until a formal appraisal is made as to their historic significance.

My days as official IRS historian were numbered. But I felt a vast sense of relief wash over me as the National Archives lurched into action. I had done my job. To paraphrase whistle-blower Terry Dunford, I had done the right thing that wasn't popular, and not done the popular thing that wasn't right.

My old friend John Stocker never even bothered to respond to my memo. Instead, my new supervisor, a nice, mild-mannered man named Frank Spiegelberg, summoned me to his office. He began, "I've been told to give you an oral reprimand for going outside the agency."

Ridiculous. I had broken no official rule of conduct by calling the Archives. From Frank's pained expression, I could tell that he considered this order equally absurd. But what could he do? Frank told me that IRS management had been far more outraged by my treacherous action in calling the National Archives than by Records Management's decision to destroy half the documents remaining in the Commissioner's File Room.

To his credit, Frank had tried to defend me by pointing out that I had only done what I thought was right. But he was directed to forbid my having "any future contact with the National Archives." I was not, on pain of further disciplinary action, to operate outside the agency.

Frank said, "I am to tell you that you are supposed to let Records Management handle all records issues."

"You've told me." I replied.

Frank also claimed that Dave (Darth) Mader, my former advocate, had branded me a problem employee, and that another IRS executive didn't believe that I "understood the requirements for protecting taxpayer information" even though I had been granted a top secret clearance at the IRS. My disclosures, such as they were, had nothing even remotely to do with taxpayer information, which would have been protected by IRC 6103. I wasn't even disclosing any IRS internal documents. I was exposing IRS internal actions.

At that point, I took the additional precaution of placing a confidential call to IRS Internal Security, the office charged with investigating employee misconduct, to report the illegal attempt to destroy government records. On May 26 I met with Steve Raisch, a supervisory investigator with IRS Internal Security, to whom I dutifully reported in copious detail the disturbing events of the previous two months, starting with the search-and-destroy mission directed against the presidential tax returns and the misguided inventory—another search-and-destroy mission in disguise—of the Commissioner's File Room.

I assumed, in the last vestiges of my original innocence, that Special Agent Steve Raisch would take my complaint seriously, and possibly even do something about it. To that end, I gave him a copy of my memo to Stocker, told him about being labeled a problem employee by Dave Mader, and ran through the rigmarole concerning the destruction of documents.

With his hands folded across his chest, Steve Raisch listened quietly. When I was finished he threw me the old IRS shrug. "Well Shelley, I'm sorry but there's nothing I can do," he explained, "because you mentioned IRS executives. Whenever there's a complaint about an IRS executive, it has to be handled by the Department of the Treasury's Inspector General's office."

An unanticipated twist.

"Call the Inspector General's hotline," Raisch recommended and calmly scribbled the number for me. After several deep breaths, I made the call. I repeated what I had told Raisch, then left a few hours later for a trip home to Nebraska. It was my brother's fortieth birthday. I couldn't think of anywhere I'd rather be than in the heartland, where people would have a hard time grasping the complexities of this particular moral dilemma.

On June 1, back in my office, I promptly photocopied an article by a Georgetown University law professor making a clear case for records preservation in the federal government, to which I attached a *Far Side* cartoon captioned: "Indians shmindians! Mexicans shmexicans! Genghis shmengis! Neanderthals shmeanderthals!" The bottom line read "History shmistory." Under that, I whimsically added: "IRS ShmIRS!" Then I personally dropped off copies of my workmanship at Dave Mader's and John Stocker's offices. And waited for the shit to hit the fan.

It hit quickly. Splattered even. Frank Spiegelberg was immediately blasted for not controlling his problem employee and was ordered to summon me to his office again. This time, he commanded me to stop sending cartoons around the IRS. Their recipients didn't appreciate them, and they confirmed my colleagues' sneaking suspicion that I was going off the deep end.

12

THE END OF HISTORY

FOIA

Amid the amazing amount of bureaucratic junk mail that landed on my desk each day, I found a letter from a history professor at Franklin and Marshall College, a small liberal arts school in Lancaster, Pennsylvania. The IRS Disclosure office, run by my old pal Earl Klema, had forwarded it to me. Professor John Andrew was looking for any information pertaining to an IRS entity called "The Ideological Organizations Audit Project."

It sounded familiar, like something Paul Wright of the Special Services Staff might have dreamed up, though I didn't recall the name specifically. To save time, I asked the Freedom of Information office for permission to call Professor Andrew to clarify his request. No problem.

The group that Professor Andrew was studying had been investigating right-wing as opposed to left-wing ideologues. In his research on the origins of a right-wing group called Young Americans for Freedom, Andrew had stumbled across a few references to IRS efforts to target tax-exempt organizations for scrutiny in the early sixties, during the Kennedy presidency. So this had not been a Nixon initiative coming from the right, but a Democratic initiative coming from the left. Andrew was curious about whether the YAF might have been targeted by the IRS.

I told him that I was not optimistic about finding much, given the paucity of records, but I decided to take a quick peek at the files in the fifth-floor vault, the one hidden behind the Wizard of Oz curtain.

I pulled a pile of administrative files from the shelf and found a number of documents from the sixties and tracked down a few references to the "Ideological Organizations Audit Project." I read through the pages—some of them were beginning to fade, but most were in pretty good shape, seemingly untouched by human hands in three decades. I gathered the small pile of documents and delivered them to Hal Williams, my contact in the Disclosure office.

I asked Hal whether he could have someone copy these documents and return the originals to me as quickly as possible. Hal bluntly explained that there was no one there to do that at the moment. I glanced at the secretary filing her nails off to one side, and then at the other secretary taking care of a baby. Then I reconsidered. I didn't want these precious documents left in the hands of a nail-filing secretary who had no idea what she was dealing with.

I copied the documents and left them with Hal and forgot all about it. Some six months later, Professor Andrew called again; did I know anything about the status of his FOIA document request? I called Hal.

"We're looking into releasing the documents," he said. "We've also decided to let a couple of our other offices take a look at them, too. . . ."

That, of course, was a time-honored Disclosure office delaying tactic, usually good for a few months, maybe up to a year. I informed Professor Andrew and promised to check back with Disclosure every few months for an update.

At around the same time, I got a letter from the Treasury Inspector General's office, essentially passing the buck on my official complaint about the records destruction back to the IRS Office of Internal Security, where I had gone in the first place. The letter implied that Treasury IG had made the referral to the IRS some time before. Assuming that Internal Security would now be overseeing the investigation, I took the letter to Steve Raisch.

Raisch stood in the hall in front of his office, staring at the piece of paper for a long time. I broke the silence: "Is there a problem?"

"Well, this is all news to me," he said. Raisch promised to look into it and get back to me. He never got back to me. I called him a few times before year's end, and his response was always the same: We'll get back to you on that. I was feeling pretty disheartened. My complaint had become a ping-pong ball batted between the IRS and Treasury Department's internal police functions. As long as they kept the ball moving, no one would ever have to deal with it.

JANUARY 8, 1995

It was a nice, clear, crisp winter Sunday morning in northern Virginia. I was sitting in Dulles International Airport waiting for a friend's plane to take off, flipping through the morning's *Washington Post*. My eye landed on a tiny article in the Metro section, "TWO KILLED IN PRINCE WILLIAM COUNTY ACCIDENT."

I wouldn't have read further, had the accident not occurred in Prince William County, Virginia, where I'd moved six months earlier. My body stiffened: "Donald Curtis, 61, and his wife, Christine, 61, were killed . . ."

I took a deep breath. I felt as though someone had kicked me good and hard in the gut. I shook my head. Don Curtis was my pal, my confidant, my mentor at the IRS. Curtis was a common name. There were lots of people named Curtis and lots of people named Don. It couldn't be *my* Don Curtis. But how many Don Curtises lived in Prince William County? My Don Curtis did.

As soon as I got home I called the Prince William County Police Department and found myself on the line with the trooper who had handled the accident.

"Was this the Don Curtis who worked for the IRS?"

"Are you related to him?" the officer asked.

"A good friend."

After confirming my worst fears, he briefly outlined the accident to me, explaining that Don and his wife had both been killed instantly as a car coming toward them strayed into their lane. The weather had been clear and neither car was speeding. Don was the type of guy who drove other drivers nuts by obeying the speed limit.

Don once called me the "conscience" of the IRS. I'd always considered him its soul. Without him, there was nobody else in the IRS who cared as deeply as I did about preserving the past. As I sat through Don's funeral, I pledged to complete my mission—as I defined it—alone despite any risk to my career. Don would have wanted me to do that. Even though the IRS had stonewalled and demoralized me for almost a year now, I decided to continue fighting from the inside for a while longer. After all, if I went public with my allegations, at this point the IRS would simply announce that an investigation was under way and make no further comment. There was no investigation in progress, but such an announcement would appease the press and effectively dilute my charges.

On January 23, 1995, with renewed courage, I marched up to Steve Raisch's office again, intending to remain until he told me what was really going on with his "investigation." Weary of my persistence, Raisch had developed the off-putting habit of folding his arms across his chest, leaning back in his chair, propping his feet on his desktop, and taking a deep breath before saying, "Well, yesssss, Shelley, I do realize that, but you have to realize . . . "

For the umpteenth time, I demanded to know why he wasn't properly investigating my complaint, a clear case of breaking the law. This time, Raisch tried a new move: He passed the buck, big-time. "Your case," he declared, "has been placed in the hands of the IRS Ethics office."

The Ethics office was Dave Mader's department. "Darth" Mader, my former guardian angel, had branded me a problem employee and taken a position on the issue—he wouldn't touch it. Raisch effectively handed the investigation over to the target of the investigation. Smooth move.

Tired of my haunting his office, Raisch relented enough to pledge that he would open a "limited investigation" of my complaint and that he would send an investigator to interview me any day now. At least he finally acknowledged that there was something worth investigating, and so I considered that a victory of sorts. Of course it was also an easy way to get rid of me.

On January 24, 1995, a young black woman who wore her hair in a severe Egyptian cut and seemed extremely nervous timidly ducked her head into my tiny office cubicle and handed me her business card: Karen Parker, an investigator with IRS Internal Security.

I spent more than an hour with Karen Parker detailing every aspect of my complaint: the secret effort to shred presidential tax returns; the blatant attempt of the Records Management department to destroy federal records; the refusal of Dave Mader's self-styled Ethics office to respond to my allegations in any substantive fashion other than to label me a problem employee. I emphasized Mader's tremendous power in the organization based on his close working relationship with our commissioner, Margaret Richardson. (I didn't tell Parker that insiders frequently referred to Richardson as "the Commissionatrix.") Among a pile of documentation I handed her was a copy of my 1993 records mismanagement study and an Archives brochure clearly explaining the Federal Records Act.

As I spoke, Parker scribbled furiously, taking copious notes. After I finished, she asked me the same question that the Treasury IG had asked: Did I wish to remain anonymous? I laughed. Everyone knew this was "the historian's issue." Sure, I worried about retaliation from Dave Mader and those in his chain of command; and Parker agreed with me that she saw this as a valid concern based on what I had told her.

"I'm sure," she said, "that you'll be hearing about my investigation as we begin our preliminary round of interviews. Give me a call right away if you have any problems with anyone relating to the investigation, or if anyone gives you a hard time."

On her way out the door, Parker asked what my goal was for pressing the pursuit of the investigation. "Do you think," she asked, "that the Records Management staff should be brought up on charges of violating the Federal Records Act?"

I paused, impressed with the apparent seriousness with which Karen Parker was taking my allegations. After a moment's thought, I told Parker, "I don't think that would accomplish anything at all. I think what the IRS needs to do is hire a professionally trained records management staff, place it higher in the organizational structure, and establish a strong training program to get IRS employees thinking about the need to preserve records."

As instructed, I waited. I waited with both anticipation and trepidation for signs of some investigation under way. Every time I visited my supervisor, Frank Spiegelberg, I hoped for some hint that Karen Parker had interviewed him, since I had suggested that she start with his take on the situation. As February turned into March, I waited. Frank gave no indication that anyone had talked with him about my charges. What was Parker doing?

Every once in a while, I'd run into her at the IRS gym. Since she never approached me, I decided to approach her and ask politely how her investigation was going.

She smiled sweetly. "Well, I've been a little busy. I've been in training and I'm just getting started setting up my first round of preliminary interviews. You know how crazy things get around here. . . . "

Not knowing what else to do, I waited. And waited some more. Spring turned to summer. In June John Stocker called—a surprise, because he had neither responded to my warning memo on the Records Management purge nor contacted me since.

"I've left Washington," he stated, "to become district director in Tennessee."

"My heartfelt congratulations."

In IRS terms, that was a promotion. Stocker's tone couldn't have been warmer and friendlier. "I need some help, Shelley," he finally said. He was writing a research paper for a master's degree program, and his chosen subject was the history of the income tax in America.

"I haven't had much luck tracking down many books about the IRS in my local library, or my bookstore," he went on, "so I was sort of wondering if you might be able to help me out with some research materials."

The guy who wouldn't help me stop the destruction of records, who refused to help stop the whole escapade, forcing me to go to the Archives to save the records, getting myself reprimanded in the process, was calling me for assistance on researching the history of the income tax.

"John, don't you see even the slightest connection between your not being able to find much information about the IRS in your library or your local bookstore and the IRS's incessant compulsion to destroy its own records?"

There was a long pause at the other end. Evidently Stocker wouldn't or couldn't see the connection.

"Shelley," he begged, "come on now, that's ancient history."

"You're telling me!"

"Will you help me?"

I took a deep breath. Educating the ignorant was my responsibility. I agreed to send him the information needed.

"Shelley," he said, "believe me, I did everything I could."

I almost choked as I hung up the phone.

On the morning of August 4, 1995, I saw Karen Parker signing someone into the building. Not having seen her for several months, I walked over and asked about her progress since our first meeting six months ago. At last, Parker had news for me.

"There have been developments."

Since her reference was so vague, I asked for clarification.

"You mean related to my complaint?"

"Oh yes, definitely related. But I won't be able to discuss it with you until next Thursday. I'll call you on Thursday," she promised. "We'll need to meet in person."

The following Monday morning, Professor John Andrew called from Franklin and Marshall College in Lancaster, Pennsylvania. I hadn't heard from him for months. I expected him to share joyful news of finally receiving the documents on the Ideological Organizations Audit Project that I had pulled for him well over two years ago. Instead, in a strangely strained voice, he began: "Shelley, something peculiar is going on. I was wondering whether you might be able to fill me in on the details."

I couldn't imagine what he was talking about.

"A woman named Karen Parker called me today," he replied. "She said she was with IRS Internal Security. Do you know her?"

"As a matter of fact I do," I replied. Why would Karen Parker, of all people, be interested in speaking to Professor John Andrew?

"She wants to pay me a visit," Professor Andrew continued. "Here. In my office. As soon as possible. Something to do with my Freedom of Information request."

He sounded worried. So was I. Why was Karen Parker interested in those documents plucked from the fifth-floor vault room and forwarded to the Disclosure office for review? In terms of Professor Andrew's FOIA request, I had followed every rule in the book. Besides, those documents had nothing to do with the investigation Parker was supposedly conducting on my behalf. The only connection was me, the problem employee. My stomach churned.

"I agreed to meet with Ms. Parker on Wednesday, August ninth," Andrew said. "I'll let you know how it goes."

Of course. Karen Parker couldn't speak to me until Thursday because she was traveling to Pennsylvania to interview Professor Andrew in person on Wednesday. I'd quit smoking, but I rushed right out and picked up a pack of butts. I smoked five in a row. Though I felt physically sick, the nicotine rush calmed me down.

All day Wednesday, I couldn't focus. I bought another pack of cigarettes. I waited for Professor Andrew to call. I smoked and sat, and smoked and sat. He had said the meeting was scheduled "around lunchtime." Around two that afternoon, he called. When I picked up the phone, he was chuckling to himself.

"Well, your Karen Parker was prompt, you can say that for her," Andrew began, as if getting quite a kick out of the whole thing. "She brought another agent with her, by the way."

"Really?" I said. "Who?"

"His name was Steve Raisch."

Raisch? Raisch *and* Parker with Andrew?

"The entire visit was just so bizarre," Andrew went on. "They were real Keystone Cops. . . . For one thing, Raisch did all the talking. Karen Parker just sat there taking notes, saying nary a word. She seemed pretty inexperienced."

"And?"

"Well, I just thought that was odd since she set up the meeting," Andrew continued. "But Raisch started in by informing me that I was not a target of the investigation. I thought that was rich. I mean, why bother coming all the way to Pennsylvania in person, with two people, to talk to me if I wasn't even being investigated!" Andrew laughed. He continued, "Of course, I knew that Internal Security doesn't investigate taxpayers. Then Steve Raisch announced, 'We are investigating the IRS historian!'"

The IRS had turned again on the whistle-blower. Though I was never confident in Steve Raisch's ability to grasp the substance of my complaint, I was shocked that he was so willing to kill the messenger. And, by then, the only man on the planet who might have sympathized with my plight, Congressman Doug Barnard, had retired.

Professor Andrew wasn't quite finished. "The entire visit lasted no more than half an hour. Most of their questions were clearly designed to get me to tell them how I'd come across the Ideological Organizations Audit Project in the first place. Obviously, they were hoping to get me to tell them that you had been feeding me information on specific documents to ask for in my FOIA request."

So that was the point of this exercise. It appeared that the IRS thought that if they could prove that I had helped Professor Andrew word his FOIA request precisely enough to request certain documents, that I must have been guilty of disclosing taxpayer information. They were wielding their most lethal weapon, Internal Revenue Code Section 6103.

"They didn't seem very aware of how to conduct research," Andrew ruefully declared. "I pulled out my trusty copies of the congressional investigation of the IRS back in the seventies, and pointed to the exact footnote specifying the documents I'd listed on my request. I showed them where the Ideological Organizations Audit Project was discussed in the public record. They seemed absolutely flabbergasted that all this had been discussed in public. It's as if they don't believe that the Congress has any business even discussing the IRS! It was incredible, and if you don't mind me saying so, pretty stupid. They didn't even know what information was available about the IRS in the public record."

At least I knew what I was up against: standard retaliation, trumped-up charges. By assigning Raisch and Parker to the investigation of me, the IRS laid the groundwork for a major grievance against it, because retaliation was so blatant a motive.

When Karen Parker didn't call me by noon on Thursday as promised, I called her. She wasn't in. I left a message on her voice mail to call me but never heard back. I tried again on Friday and left another voice mail message. She never called back. We never spoke again.

I had seen the relentless power of IRS internal security turn against the likes of the Chicago Three and others. It looked like my head was next up on the chopping block. I had no choice but to leave before the IRS tarnished my image and blackened my name, trying trumped-up charge after trumped-up charge. I would miss my steady salary, especially with my new mortgage, but I wouldn't miss the "new IRS," which didn't seem any better than the old one.

On September 8 Frank Spiegelberg called me into his office to discuss the historian's position in yet another IRS reorganization.

"I'm resigning," I said, "effective January 1, 1996"—the date by which I had calculated that I would be able to pay off my outstanding debts, and at least face the cold, cruel world free and clear. I must say, I went out on as bizarre a note as I went in. In my last month on the job, George Munoz, assistant secretary of the Treasury, asked me to prepare a presentation on my efforts to develop a comprehensive historical program at the IRS—an ideal opportunity to blast Dave Mader, John Stocker, Steve Raisch, Karen Hjelmervik, and all those other creeps from the IRS and the Treasury Department, which has overall jurisdiction over the IRS. But I didn't. After all, the Treasury Department should have an in-house historian. I didn't want to burn all my bridges.

Just weeks before my scheduled departure from the IRS, I spent an hour describing the history of the tax collector and my seven-year-old historical program to the assistant secretary of the Treasury and his staff. I handed out copies of all my handsomely bound and printed IRS publications, including my two personal favorites, the history of the Whiskey Rebellion and the pocket history of the Memphis Service Center. Those had been the most fun, and most enlightening, of all my work. I also distributed bound transcripts of the oral histories that I had conducted with several former commissioners.

George Munoz seemed impressed by my presentation. A few weeks later, just days before my last day in office, Munoz sent a letter of appreciation to Commissioner Margaret Richardson's office, specifically requesting that the commissioner send him a response to the following question: "What is your office planning to do to strengthen the IRS historical program?" Obviously, no one had told the assistant secretary of the Treasury that the IRS historian was under investigation for one of the most heinous crimes against the tax system, guilty or not.

I received a courtesy copy of Munoz's letter, though for obvious reasons, I received no courtesy copy of Commissioner Richardson's reply. Had she acknowledged to her boss that she and her minions were abolishing the position entirely, that I, too, would go down in unrecorded IRS history as the first and last official IRS historian?

For what seemed like the first time in months, I laughed. I finally absorbed why Professor Andrew had chuckled after Parker and Raisch left his office. The organization, in nearly all its dealings within its walls and with the public, behaved so peculiarly that you just had to laugh. And so I did. And so did all my friends. What poor son of a bitch had been assigned by our dear old Commissionatrix to respond to Munoz's letter, I wondered?

That poor soul, believe it or not, turned out to be me. The original letter landed on my desk with a request for me to write a response. At the IRS, the truth is often stranger than fiction. And so my last official task as the IRS historian was to explain why the IRS was eliminating my position, for now and in perpetuity. I had been expunged, and all my works with it.

Try as I might, I couldn't do it. And I wouldn't do it. I felt too sad and bad about it. Seven years is a long time. Seven years is a long time to be frustrated and stymied and thwarted at every turn. Instead of sending out some claptrap under the commissioner's signature, I sent George Munoz a frank letter explaining in my own words the unfortunate demise of my position. I left the commissioner hanging to compose her own response.

On November 21, 1995, I sallied forth to Steve Raisch's office with a copy of George Munoz's letter singing the praises of my recent presentation and asking about beefing up—not obliterating—the IRS history program. Without bothering to glance at it, or at me, Steve Raisch put the letter aside, en route to the nearest circular file.

"It doesn't matter anymore," Raisch said. "Your case is closed. The file is closed. And as far as I know, the investigation of your complaint is closed."

That was news to me. Everything was closed. They'd done their job perfectly: They'd hounded me out of the service. I had one last question with which to pester Raisch.

"Don't you tell your employees when a case is closed?" I asked.

Folding his arms even tighter across his chest, Raisch drawled, "If you'd like more information, you'll have to file a FOIA request. Sorry, but I can't do anything more for you."

"I don't believe the investigation into my complaint is complete," I said coldly, "because I've had no indication that it had ever begun."

Steve Raisch waved his hand in the air and asked condescendingly, "Wasn't it just some sort of disagreement over records destruction schedules?"

"That's Records *Control* Schedules, if you really want to know, which you obviously don't," I snapped.

"Whatever. It doesn't matter anymore, does it?" He was still smiling, before admitting that that last little Freudian slip—"destruction" instead of "control"—"reflected twenty years of bias on my part."

I desperately wished I had slipped a tape recorder into my pocket, because here was the special agent assigned by the IRS to my complaint admitting that he had "a twenty-year bias" in favor of destroying records!

In lieu of a tape recorder, I had my memory. Rushing from his office, I dashed down the two flights of stairs to my office to record our last conversation on my office computer. I wanted to make absolutely sure that, for the record, I had it down accurately. I didn't want to forget the exact words Raisch had used, still shocked at his outrageous admission of blatant bias.

For good measure, I pounded out a Freedom of Information request and sent it off by certified mail to our Disclosure office, asking for all records related to the IRS investigation of my complaint as well as to their investigation of me. At least, after seven years at the IRS, I knew enough not to hold my breath.

I turned my attention to composing my resignation letter to the commissioner, clearly explaining that I was resigning in protest against the IRS's refusal to investigate my serious allegations of wrongdoing and its trumped-up investigation of me. On my official Department of the Treasury, Internal Revenue Service stationery, I wrote:

The purpose of this letter is to inform you of my official resignation from the position of IRS Historian, effective December 29, 1995. I am resigning with tremendous sadness and in protest over the IRS's unwillingness to address concerns I have brought forward over the past five years regarding our records keeping policies.

After describing in detail my original records management study, and the subsequent attempts to destroy records that I believed were prompted by the threat of reform posed by my study—if its proposals were accepted and implemented—I detailed my contacts with NARA "as required by the Federal Records Act," and the reprimand I had been given in response. After lodging a complaint, first with the IRS internal investigation authorities, and second with the Treasury Inspector General, there was no evidence whatsoever that my complaint was ever seriously investigated. "But," I added, "the same Internal Security investigators investigated me!

"It was this final instance of retaliation," I wrote, "that made me realize that I had exhausted all available internal channels to resolve this issue. . . . Without solid policies and programs in place to ensure that vital documentation is not destroyed, there can be no history."

FEBRUARY 28, 1996

It was well after one in the morning by the time I drove home from Dulles Airport, after flying back from a short trip to Atlanta. Exhausted as I was, I glanced at the mail sitting on the kitchen counter. Prominently displayed at the top of the pile was a large yellow envelope, displaying the return address "Internal Revenue Service" and marked with the legend: "Official Business Only." Handwritten below the IRS label were the letters: "I:IS:P:D."

The first "I" stood for "Inspection," the "IS" for "Internal Security." I didn't know what the "P" stood for, but the "D" I knew stood for "Disclosure." Before I even opened it, I knew that this was the official response to my FOIA request of November 21, 1995, which I'd sent off only moments after leaving Steve Raisch's office for the very last time.

The letter enclosed had been signed by Keith Alan Kuhn, deputy director, Office of Policy and Oversight, whatever that was—no doubt some new item on the ever-shifting IRS organizational chart. The first page was all letters and numbers that didn't mean anything to me:

"Enclosed are copies of ROI # 8–0295–0003 and MIF #0–1293–9923 in their entirety [please note we will address the disposition of MIF # 0–1293–9023 (after we have completed our search) when we respond to your February 5, 1996 FOIA request.] ... " Okay, I thought to myself, get to the point. I found the point at the top of page two. The first line nearly knocked me off my chair. "All notes associated with the requested files were destroyed in accordance with Inspections Procedures regarding the retention of notes." So they destroyed the notes. According to "Inspections Procedures."

ROI stood for "Report of Investigation," and mine stated that the investigation of my complaint had been conducted between January 24 and August 3, 1995. That was six months. As far as I knew, there had been no investigation. On January 24, Karen Parker had interviewed me in my office.

As released to me under my FOIA request, Parker's report on that initial session read, in part: "[The historian] became aware that the Records Management Office had conducted an inventory of the records and their proposed action was to destroy eligible records by appropriate methods."

That was, of course, absurd. "Their proposed action was to destroy eligible records by appropriate methods" would hardly have been a transcript of my complaint—these were obviously *not* appropriate methods. This had evidently been altered after the fact; presumably that was why the notes had been destroyed, because they would have contradicted her distorted "summary."

There was more. "She [the historian] felt her expertise in evaluating the historical value of these records could have been used by Records Management staff. She believed that it was an intentional act not to have her involved in the inventory of records."

This phrasing made it look as if I were upset about not being invited to a destruction session. There was no mention of the legal and ethical issues involved. No mention of the fact that the proposed destruction, if it had been allowed to go forward, would have erased from the record one of the last remaining collections of IRS documents anywhere; that the IRS would have been in direct violation of a federal law.

There was no indication in Parker's record of any investigatory activities at all until August 3, 1995. It appeared clear to me that, as I had suspected, Karen Parker never conducted a single interview after our January meeting. The whole thing had been a sham. On August 3, 1995, Steve Raisch and Karen Parker had consulted with Charles Fowler, deputy assistant chief inspector of the IRS, to "close out" the investigation. On that same day, yet another chief inspector (Doug Crouch) had consulted with Deputy Commissioner Mike Dolan about my allegations. Dolan told him that "they"—presumably meaning the IRS brass—"were all aware of [the historian's] differences of opinion on the destruction of certain IRS records. The records have not been destroyed. Therefore, there is no basis for further investigation." There it was. The unbridled power of the IRS directed at me. The senior employee of the entire tax agency had dismissed my complaint on the basis that my intervention—which got me reprimanded and investigated—had been successful. Time to put a halter on that horse.

Three days later, Raisch and Parker were off on a different assignment, to see Professor Andrew. The documents relating to this meeting were extensively blacked out, with the deletions justified by FOIA Subsection (b)(7), which "prohibits the release of information which could reasonably be expected to constitute unwarranted invasion of a third party or third parties' personal privacy."

Would that have been Professor Andrew's privacy, or mine? The document did reveal that one Diane Grant and James McGovern, the assistant commissioner for employee plans and exempt organizations, had each lodged allegations against me with Internal Security. Their complaints presumably inspired the investigation. Funny, though. I had never laid eyes on either of these people.

All but two sentences of Raisch's and Parker's report on their taxpayer-funded road trip to the lovely Amish countryside of Pennsylvania had been blacked out. The two sentences simply confirmed that contrary to their aroused suspicions, I had not "provided any file names . . . [I] had only assisted with the titles of individuals and made sure they were correct in [Andrew's] draft."

In other words, they had been sent off on a fishing expedition and come back empty-handed. At least I knew they'd tried to besmirch me and failed.

Free at last, I could finally write my secret history of the IRS, the one I never would have been able to write from inside. My real motivation in writing this book is to prove that the IRS—even though it might be able to destroy all its documents and even itself—in all its unbridled power, cannot destroy its own history.

Consider what you have just read one long whistle-blow, summoning up the tough truth from where it lay buried, in vaults filled with paper and typewritten words cached throughout that vast building, in obscure nooks and crannies where anonymous people carefully secreted it, away from prying eyes and hands, so that one day someone who cherished its value would find it and free it. Blow, whistle, blow!

NOTE ON SOURCES

One of the primary premises of this book is that the IRS has system-atically discarded most of its records through the twentieth century. A quick visit to the National Archives and Records Administration in College Park, Maryland, will confirm this reality. On the shelves which by law should hold the records of one of our most important and powerful federal agencies is empty space. Records that should be there are not. You can visit the Archives and view materials from virtually every other agency of our government, but ask for IRS records and you will find very little.

The paucity of official records from the IRS is a national tragedy. Beyond that, this lack of documentation makes it very difficult to research and write about the agency that is ever-present in our lives as American citizens. Much of what I have written is based on my personal experiences inside the IRS, on notes I wrote as I lived through the events detailed in this book, and from my memory banks.

For the chapters which discuss specific IRS initiatives or events, I used whatever sources were available. Following, by category of records, is an abbreviated listing of some of the available materials I used to prepare this book. Just perusing the titles of various sources gives the impression that the IRS is an agency in need of greater oversight, control, and reform.

I encourage all Americans to learn more about the activities of our tax collector by reading some of these materials or by requesting specific materials from the IRS through the Freedom of Information Act. It is our right as Americans to demand that the IRS retain and reveal documentation of what it does.

BOOKS ABOUT THE IRS

Adams, Charles W. *For Good and Evil: The Impact of Taxes on the Course of Civilization.* New York: Madison Books, 1993.

Berman, Jerry J., and Mortin H. Halperin, editors. *The Abuses of the Intelligence Agencies.* Washington, D.C.: Center for National Security Studies, 1975.

Block, Alan A. *Masters of Paradise: Organized Crime and the IRS in the Bahamas.* New Brunswick, N.J.: Transaction, 1991.

Bovard, James. *Lost Rights: The Destruction of American Liberty.* New York: St. Martin's Press, 1994.

Brown, Thomas H. *George Sewell Boutwell: Human Rights Advocate.* Groton, Mass.: Groton Historical Society, 1989.

Burnham, David. *A Law Unto Itself: Power, Politics, and the IRS.* New York: Random House, 1989.

Dean, John. *Blind Ambition: The White House Years.* New York: Simon and Schuster, 1976.

Farbenblum, Marcus. *The IRS and the Freedom of Information Act and Privacy Act of 1974: The Disclosure Policies of the IRS and How to Obtain Documents from Them.* Jefferson, N.C.: McFarland, 1991.

Gross, Martin L. *The Tax Racket: Government Extortion from A to Z.* New York: Ballantine Books, 1995.

Irey, Elmer L., as told to William J. Slocum. *The Tax Dodgers: The Inside Story of the T-Men's War with America's Political and Underworld Hoodlums.* New York: Greenberg Press, 1948.

Kaplan, Martin, and Naomi Weiss. *What the IRS Doesn't Want You to Know: A CPA Reveals the Tricks of the Trade.* New York: Villard Books, 1994.

Kobler, John. *Capone: The Life and World of Al Capone.* New York: Putnam, 1971.

Litchfield, Carter. *History of Oleomargarine Tax Stamps and Licenses in the United States.* Kemblesville, Penn.: Olearius Editions, 1988.

Messick, Hank. *Secret File.* New York: Putnam, 1969.

Miller, Wilbur R. *Revenuers and Moonshiners: Enforcing Federal Liquor Law in the Mountain South, 1865–1900.* Chapel Hill: University of North Carolina Press, 1991.

Slaughter, Thomas P. *The Whiskey Rebellion: Frontier Epilogue to the American Revolution.* New York: Oxford University Press, 1986.

Spiering, Frank. *The Man Who Got Capone.* New York: Bobbs-Merrill, 1976.

Stanley, Robert. *Dimensions of Law in the Service of Order: Origin of the Federal Income Tax, 1861–1913.* New York: Oxford University Press, 1993.

Strober, Gerald S., and Deborah H. Strober. *Nixon: An Oral History of His Presidency.* New York: HarperCollins, 1994.

Wilson, Frank, and Beth Day. *Special Agent: A Quarter Century with the Treasury Department and the Secret Service.* New York: Holt, Rinehart & Winston, 1965.

ARTICLES ABOUT THE IRS

"All the President's Taxes (And Yours, Too)." *Kiplinger's Personal Finance,* February 1993.

Arnold, Mark R. "Congress Says Yes to Privacy, No to Secrecy." *National Observer,* November 25, 1974.

Behar, Richard. "Delinquent Taxmen." *Time,* May 29, 1989.

———. "Don't Whistle While You Work." *Time,* July 16, 1990.

Boroughs, Don L., and Douglas Stanglin. "A Messy Business: Can the IRS Clean Up Its Act and Pacify the Nation's Angry Taxpayers?" *U.S. News & World Report,* April 8, 1996.

Bovard, James. "The IRS vs. You." *The American Spectator,* November 1995.

Chambliss, Lauren. "The IRS: The Gang That Can't Shoot Straight." *Financial World,* March 21, 1989.

Chineson, Joel. "IRS Exhibit Another Taxing Experience." *Legal Times,* April 11, 1988.

Coyle, Joseph S. "The IRS Mess." *Money,* April 1990.

Danca, Richard A. "IRS Bounces CHEXS: Too Expensive, Off Target." *Federal Computer Week,* March 30, 1992.

Gleckman, Howard, and Richard S. Dunham. "Tax Reform's Split Personality." December 5, 1994.

Goldstein, Mark L. "The Taxed Tax Agency." *Government Executive,* December 1990.

Goodgame, Dan. "How to Simplify the Crazy Tax Code." *Time,* April 20, 1992.

Gordon, John Steele. "American Taxation." *American Heritage,* May–June 1996.

Greene, Daniel St. Albin. "Look Who Made the IRS 'Watch List,' Sort Of." *National Observer,* October 14, 1975.

Hock, Sandy, and Robert W. Scott. "IRS Stirs Uproar on Filing Options." *Accounting Today,* June 20, 1994.

Hughes, Ken. "IRS Managers Admit Wielding Power on Friends, Foes." *Federal Times,* April 1, 1991.

Jackson, David. "The S&L Fiasco's Invisible Man." *Chicago Magazine,* August 1990.

Kahan, Stuart. "The Electronic Filing Debacle." *The Practical Accountant,* June 1995.

"Keeping a Little List at the IRS." *Time,* August 13, 1973.

Kinsley, Michael. "My Failed Jobs Program." *Time,* April 4, 1994.

Kyvig, David E. "Can the Constitution Be Amended? The Battle Over the Income Tax, 1895–1913." *Prologue,* Fall 1988.

Lalli, Frank. "Horribly Out of Control." Editor's Notes. *Money,* June 1990.

MacDonald, Elizabeth. "Court Musicians." *Worth,* March 1996.

————. "How the IRS Targets You." *Money,* August 1994.

Minahan, Tim. "IRS Asks $1 Billion for TSM, But GAO Says It's a Bad Risk." *Government Computer News,* March 6, 1995.

Ness, Gerri M. "The Future of Electronic Filing." *Tax Practitioners Journal,* Winter 1994–95.

"Notes from Underground." *Time,* June 17, 1991.

Samuelson, Robert J. "We Are Not a Nation of Tax Cheats." *Newsweek,* April 11, 1994.

Schrag, Philip G. "Working Papers as Federal Records: The Need for New Legislation to Preserve the History of National Policy." *Administrative Law Review,* Spring 1994.

"Shake Up in the Tax Bureau." *U.S. News & World Report,* December 14, 1951.

Tritch, Teresa. "The $150 Billion Tax Cheats." *Money,* March 1995.

Tritch, Teresa and Mary L. Sprouse. "*Money* Audits the Clintons." *Money,* April 1994.

"The United States Tax System Just Ain't Fair." *Fortune,* November 11, 1995.

"What If We Abolished the Income Tax?" *Parade,* January 1995.

"There Is a Serious Morale Problem Among Senior Executives. . . . An Interview with William E. Williams." *Management,* Spring 1981.

Varon, Elana. "NRC Review Says IRS Operations Reengineering to Delay TSM." *Federal Computer Week,* August 23, 1993.

"Why April 15 Is Getting Worse and Worse." *Forbes,* March 18, 1991.

Zeidner, Rita. "The Revenuers Reform." *Government Executive,* June 1994.

TAX NOTES ARTICLES

Tax Notes is the publication of Tax Analysts, a private organization located in Fairfax, Virginia, dedicated to tracking developments in the world of United States tax policy and administration.

Donmoyer, Ryan J. "Does the IRS Need a Set Term for Commissioners?" *Tax Notes,* April 24, 1995.

————. "Executive Brain Drain Leaves IRS Searching for Leadership." *Tax Notes,* August 21, 1995.

————. "IRS Announces Consolidation of Regional and District Offices." *Tax Notes,* May 4, 1995.

————. "IRS Anti-Fraud Efforts Continue to Draw Fire." *Tax Notes,* March 6, 1995.

————. "TSM Comes Under Microscope As Congress Considers IRS Budget Hike." *Tax Notes,* February 17, 1995.

Godfrey, John. "IRS Presents Modernization Plan." *Tax Notes,* June 17, 1991.

————. "Service Gets Mixed Review In Ethics/Whistleblower Survey." *Tax Notes,* July 29, 1991.

Guttman, George. "Electronic Filing of Returns." *Tax Notes,* March 7, 1994.

———. "Electronic Filing: Who Pays, Who Benefits." *Tax Notes,* March 20, 1995.

———. "Records Management Program Panned by National Archives." *Tax Notes,* January 1, 1996.

———. "Threat of Refund Fraud Reduced, But IRS Remains Vulnerable." *Tax Notes,* February 19, 1996.

Stratton, Sheryl. "A History of the IRS? Don't Count on It." *Tax Notes,* January 29, 1996.

———. "'Black Hole' of IRS Records Forces Historian to Resign." *Tax Notes,* January 24, 1996.

Tannenbaum, Ira L. "Special Report: Income Tax Treatment of Donation of Nixon Pre-Presidential Papers." *Tax Notes,* July 30, 1973.

Xu, Fang. "Chinese Scholar Urges IRS to Face, Not Erase, Its Past." *Tax Notes,* February 12, 1996.

Zeidner, Rita L. "TSM: How the Service Plans to Move into the 21st Century." *Tax Notes,* June 6, 1994.

GENERAL ACCOUNTING OFFICE (GAO) REPORTS AND TESTIMONY

"An Analysis of IRS' Proposed Tax Administration System: Lessons for the Future." GGD–78–43, March 1, 1978.

"Computer Technology at the IRS: Present and Planned." GGD–83–103, September 1, 1983.

"Examples of Waste and Inefficiency in IRS." GGD–93–100FS, April 1993.

"Federal Records: Document Removal by Agency Heads Needs Independent Oversight." GGD–91–117, August 1991.

"Financial Managment: IRS' Self-Assessment of its Internal Control and Accounting Systems Is Inadequate." AIMD–94–2, October 1994.

"Government Management: Status of Progress in Correcting Selected High Risk Areas." Testimony, February 3, 1993.

"Information on IRS' Philadelphia Service Center." GGD–86–25FS, November 1985.

"Information on IRS' Service Centers in Austin TX and Fresno CA." GGD–85–89, September 30, 1985.

"Information on IRS' Taxpayer Compliance Measurement Program." GGD–96–21, October 1995.

"IRS Can Better Plan For and Control Its ADP Resources." GGD–79–48, June 18, 1979.

"IRS Can Strengthen Its Efforts to See That Taxpayers Are Treated Properly." GGD–95–14, October 1994.

"IRS Employee Views on Integrity and Willingness to Report Misconduct." GGD–91–112FS, July 1991.

"IRS Progress on Integrity and Ethics Issues." Testimony, July 22, 1992.

"Managing IRS: IRS Needs to Continue Improving Operations and Service." Testimony of Lynda D. Willis, July 1996.

"A Proposed Automated Tax Administration System for IRS—An Evaluation of Costs and Benefits." LCD–76–114, November 23, 1976.

"Replacement of Service Center Computers Provides Lessons for the Future." GGD–87–109, September 1987.

"Safeguarding Taxpayer Information—An Evaluation of the Proposed Computerized Tax Administration System." LCD–76–115, January 17, 1977.

"Status of TSM, Tax Delinquencies, and the Tax Gap." Testimony, February 3, 1993.

"TSM: Actions Underway But IRS Has Not Yet Corrected Management and Technical Weaknesses." AIMD–96–106, June 1996.

"TSM: Concerns Over Security and Privacy Elements of the System's Architecture." IMTEC–92–63, September 1992.

"TSM: IRS' Use of Consultants to Do the TMAC Price/Technical Tradeoff Analysis." IMTEC–93–4BR, October 1992.

LEGISLATIVE BRANCH DOCUMENTS

"Examination of President Nixon's Tax Returns for 1969 Through 1972." Joint Committee on Internal Revenue Taxation, Report No. 93–768, 93rd Congress, 2nd Session, April 3, 1974.

"Intelligence Activities and the Rights of Americans." Books II and

III. Final Report of the Select Committee to Study Government Operations with Respect to Intelligence Activities. United States Senate, 94th Congress, 2d Session, April 26, 1976.

"Internal Revenue Investigation." Subcommittee on Administration of Internal Revenue Laws, House of Representatives Ways and Means Committee, 82d Congress, 2d Session, January 3, 1953.

"Investigation of the Special Services Staff of the IRS." Committee Print of the Joint Committee on Internal Revenue Taxation. 94th Congress, 1st Session, 1975.

"IRS Senior Employee Misconduct Problems." Hearings Before the Commerce, Consumer, and Monetary Affairs Subcommittee of the House of Representatives Committee on Government Operations, 101st Congress, 1st Session, July 25–27, 1989.

"Misconduct by Senior Managers in the IRS." Report of the Committee on Government Operations, House of Representatives, 101st Congress, 2d Session, October 4, 1990.

"Operation Leprechaun." Hearings Before the Subcommittee on Oversight, House of Representatives Ways and Means Committee, 94th Congress, 1st Session, December 2, 1975.

"Oversight of the Federal Tax System," Committee Print of the House of Representatives Ways and Means Committee, 101st Congress, 2nd Session, June 4, 1990.

"Progress Report on the Government's Response to Misconduct by IRS Senior Level Officials." Hearings Before the Commerce, Consumer, and Monetary Affairs Subcommittee of the House of Representatives Committee on Government Operations, 102nd Congress, 2d Session, July 22, 1992.

"Reorganization Plan Number 1 of 1952, Providing for Reorganization in the Bureau of Internal Revenue." Report No. 1259, 82d Congress, 2d Session, March 10, 1952.

"Role of the IRS in Law Enforcement Activities." Hearings Before the Subcommittee on Administration of the Internal Revenue Code, United States Senate Committee on Finance, 94th Congress, 1st and 2nd Sessions, December 1–3, 1975, and January 22, 1976.

Statement of Senator Lloyd Bentsen Before the Subcommittee on Administration of the Internal Revenue Code, United States Senate Committee on Finance, April 26, 1975.

"Tax Deduction for Gift of Papers." Book X, Hearings Before the Committee on the Judiciary, House of Representatives, 93d Congress, 2d Session, May–June 1974.

INTERNAL REVENUE SERVICE DOCUMENTS

Annual Reports of the Commissioner of Internal Revenue, 1864–1993.

"Chief Financial Officer Annual Report." Fiscal Year 1994.

"Guide to the IRS for Congressional Staff." Publication 1273, (Rev. 1–95).

"Information Systems News." Vol. XII, Issue 4, February 1995.

"IRS Business Master Plan, 1995–2001." Document No. 9255, January 31, 1995.

"IRS Strategic Business Plan Thru FY 1996." Document 7382, August 1990.

"IRS Strategic Business Plan, FY 1994 and Beyond." Document No. 7382, September 1993.

"IRS Transitions: Helping IRS Employees Effectively Manage Change." Newsletter, 1993–1995.

"A Plan for Reinventing the IRS." Publication 1740, November 1993.

Testimony of various IRS officials, including Donald Alexander, Michael P. Dolan, Fred Goldberg, Shirley Peterson, Henry Philcox, Margaret Milner Richardson, Larry Westfall, before House of Representatives and Senate Committees, 1970s through 1996.

OTHER DOCUMENTS

"Compliance Costs of Alternative Tax Systems II." Special Brief of the Tax Foundation, by Arthur P. Hall, March 1996.

"Computer Systems of the IRS: Past, Present and ... Future?" Senior Honors Thesis by Kecia McDonald, University of California, Santa Barbara, June 1993.

"The First 75: The Internal Revenue Code from Wilson to Reagan." Pamphlet published by Commerce Clearing House, Inc., 1988.

"Growth of the Federal Government Tax 'Industry' Parallels Growth of Federal Tax Code." Special Report of the Tax Foundation, #39, September 1994.

"The Internal Revenue Code: Then and Now." Pamphlet published by Commerce Clearing House, Inc., 1990.

Merit Systems Protection Board. Documents and trial transcripts related to the case of Stanley D. Welli versus Frank Santella and Joseph Jech, 1991–1996.

"Records Management and the Law." Pamphlet published by the National Archives and Records Administration.

Walter D. Teague III v. *Donald C. Alexander, et al.,* Civil Action in the United States District Court, Washington, D.C., No. 75–0416, 1975.

NEWSPAPERS

Articles from the following newspapers, spanning the years between 1970 and the present were used to track IRS developments as well as the depth of reporting on the tax agency.

Anchorage Times
Baltimore Sun
Boston Globe
Buffalo News
Chicago Sun-Times
Chicago Tribune
Cincinnati Enquirer
Dallas Times-Herald
Los Angeles Times
Las Vegas Sun
Miami News
Milwaukee Journal
New York Daily News
New York Newsday
New York Times
Philadelphia Inquirer
Providence Journal-Bulletin

Seattle Post-Intelligencer
USA Today
Wall Street Journal
Washington Post
Washington Star
Washington Times

Index

275

Index

Index